The Conceptual Basis of Language

P
37
.M3

The Conceptual Basis of Language

DAVID MCNEILL
The University of Chicago

 LAWRENCE ERLBAUM ASSOCIATES, PUBLISHERS
1979   Hillsdale, New Jersey

DISTRIBUTED BY THE HALSTED PRESS DIVISION OF
JOHN WILEY & SONS
New York   Toronto   London   Sydney

Lawrence Erlbaum Associates, Inc., Publishers
365 Broadway
Hillsdale, New Jersey 07642

Distributed solely by Halsted Press Division
John Wiley & Sons, Inc., New York

Library of Congress Cataloging in Publication Data

McNeill, David.
   The conceptual basis of language.

   Bibliography: p.
   Includes indexes.
   1. Psycholinguistics. 2. Semiotics.
3. Concepts. 4. Grammar, Comparative and general
—Syntax. I. Title.
P37.M3   401'.9   78-32105
ISBN 0-470-26663-5

Printed in the United States of America

This book is dedicated to my wife and children.

Contents

Preface

The problem considered in this book is the relationship of speech to thought as it is involved in general adult linguistic processing. Nonetheless, I have been guided by two observations that have their most direct manifestations in the ontogenesis of language. One of these observations is that language is a *form of action.* The second is that many utterances are constructed in terms of *concrete models* of reality, or *sensory-motor representations.* Such concrete models are part of the meaning structure of utterances and also, by virtue of their sensory-motor quality, simultaneously part of action. (This is a second sense in which language is a form of action). Sensory-motor representations provide the crucial link between the action taken during speech output and the organization of abstract conceptions. This process of relating concrete models to abstract conceptions is called *semiotic extension.* Concrete models of reality are extended to abstract conceptions through a kind of reference of signs.

I have followed three approaches to these questions. The first and most fundamental is to view the relationship of speech to thought as a *network of signs.* This view brings out indexical and iconic aspects of speech in relation to thought, as well as symbolic aspects. The indexical aspect can be identified with the sensory-motor component of meaning. Indexical signs interlock with iconic and symbolic signs through the relationship of semiotic extension. Such interlocking creates a chain of signs connecting the indexical level to the more abstract meanings represented at the iconic and symbolic levels. All of these signs are internal, and they are a way of describing the process of programming speech output.

The second approach is to view the organization of speech as taking place within functional units called *syntagmata*. A syntagma is one meaning unit pronounced as a single output. Within a syntagma, speech output is based directly on meaning in the sense that the speaker, choosing an organization of meaning, is led automatically to an organization of articulatory output. Sensory-motor representations are basic to the structure of syntagmata, and the direct connection of meaning with articulation is provided by the relationship of semiotic extension.

The third approach is complementary to the first two. It views the organization of conceptions in terms of *conceptual structures*. Conceptual structures are represented in the form of labeled directed graphs, and this provides a mathematical definition of semiotic extension and of a number of other properties of the conceptual structure of utterances with consequences for the organization of speech.

Since I am concerned with verification of the empirical consequences of these views, I present a number of tests and illustrations, particularly evidence concerning speech timing, speech dysfluencies, intonation, ontogenesis, and gestures.

It is my pleasure to thank a number of individuals who helped me in a variety of ways as I worked on this book. First in terms of the magnitude of their help and my debt is my family, who endured uprooting and displacement to Princeton while I started work at the Institute for Advanced Study. I am very grateful to each of them for their love and support. It is to them that I dedicate this book.

I wish to thank George A. Miller for initially inviting me to the Institute for Advanced Study, and the Director of the Institute at that time, Carl Kaysen, for extending my visit there for a second year. I wish to thank two successive Deans of Social Sciences at The University of Chicago, Robert McC. Adams and William Kruskal, for allowing me a two year period away from my university obligations.

Financial support during the years I have worked on this book has come from several sources. I wish to thank the John Simon Guggenheim Memorial Foundation, the Alfred P. Sloan Foundation (to the Institute for Advanced Study), the National Institute of Mental Health, and The University of Chicago. A biomedical research grant administered by The University of Chicago supported the preparation of the many figures in the book.

Several generations of students in classes at The University of Chicago have received lectures based on different versions of this book. They have played a greater role in shaping it than perhaps they can realize. I also wish to thank a number of individuals who have read or discussed with me parts of the book and whose comments I have attempted to incorporate: Jerome Bruner, Frank Harary, Philip Johnson-Laird, Klaus Kirchgässner, William Marslen-Wilson, Nobuko McNeill, George A. Miller, and Victor Yngve. The drawings in Chapter 11 were done by Donald Novotny, and the figures throughout the book by Christopher Müller-Wille. James Galambos and Lee Mann compiled the references. James Bone typed the final manuscript and helped me in producing the book in many other ways.

The title of this book has posed endless problems. No single phrase less than 100 words long that I have discovered exactly corresponds to the content of the book. The title was finally chosen by empirical methods. Students taking my courses also had the problem of referring to the book, and "Conceptual basis of language" is the title they coined.

My contribution, therefore, is limited to simply inserting the article and this I must explain. In English one can express a triumph of certainty and finality with *the,* or express what in a scientific work is a becoming modesty with *a.* I have written *the* into the title for a reason that has nothing to do with this contrast. If one is looking for a lost house key, one would refer to it as "the key," for one is surely not looking, in this case, for "a" key. In similar fashion, with "The conceptual basis of language" I mean to express the idea that there is such a thing as the conceptual basis of language; but not that what follows is at long last "the" description of it.

David McNeill

INTRODUCTION

1 Introduction

The sun rose on the frozen scene. The men stopped their cars beside the river. Bacon started to walk. He barely escaped a fierce winter storm. In addition to relating a story, each of these sentences corresponds to the idea of an event. An event, according to von Wright (1963), is a change of state that takes place through an interval of time. In the foregoing sentences, for example, one state is that the sun had not risen; then it had risen. This change of state is an event. The idea of an event is an example of what I will refer to as a sensory-motor idea. The reason for this terminology, which will be explained in more detail later, has to do with both the origin and function of such ideas. A characteristic of sensory-motor ideas is that they are present in speech in much the same form regardless of the literal meaning. In the foregoing example the literal meaning consists of physical events, but in the following sentences this meaning is more abstract: *Time no longer seemed to move. History had stopped. Men placed their trust in the officials of their government. Memories of past glories replaced hopes for the future.* These sentences also refer to events, but none refers literally to the event described in the sentence. Time does not actually change. History does not really move. Trust cannot truly be placed into anything, certainly not into such containers as the officials of government. Memories do not replace hopes in any concrete sense. Yet, as we can see, these sentences do convey the idea of an event, and they do so as clearly as the physical events described in the first story. (An event, as von Wright points out, can consist of stasis through an interval; and *the times no longer changed* is an event of this type.) However, the events denoted are not actually physical, but abstract.

The omnipresence of concrete sensory-motor ideas in speech is a phenomenon that has received almost no attention from linguists or

3

psychologists. Philosophers have discussed these ideas only insofar as they wish to remove them from abstract meanings (e.g., Price, 1953). I intend to develop a theory of these meanings in which they play a fundamental role in speech programming and articulation. That they appear in much the same form regardless of the literal meaning in utterances leads us to recognize a hitherto unnoticed aspect of language, which I will call semiotic extension; this refers to the extension of sensory-motor ideas to meanings which are not sensory-motor. Given the role of sensory-motor ideas in the programming of speech output, semiotic extension is part of a theory of the relationship between speech and thought.

It is important to stress that sensory-motor ideas are not metaphors in any sense. In a metaphor, a term is used in a new way that is not literally connected to its original meaning. In semiotic extension, a sensory-motor idea appears with its own meaning applied to other meanings that are not equivalent to it.

Sensory-motor ideas occupy a unique position epistemologically. They are simultaneously part of action and part of meaning. Sensory-motor ideas are meanings which can be represented with action schemes. For example, the idea of an event (one type of an event) can be represented in a causative action sequence involving an object and a person who is the agent of the change in state. *The men stopped their cars* is an event of this kind. Not all events can be represented in this kind of action scheme, and the ones that cannot may require semiotic extension of the scheme. *The sun rose* is a physical event which requires a minimal semiotic extension consisting of abstraction from personal causation. Abstract events such as *Men placed their trust in government officials* require greater semiotic extension. We will regard the zero point, i.e., the point that demands the least extended meaning, to be the sensory-motor representation itself. Other meanings relate to this basis via semiotic extensions that are larger or smaller depending on the literal meanings invovled.

Among the ideas which are representable as sensory-motor action schemes, together with a brief definition of the scheme itself, are the following:

event—causative action squence;
action—the performance due to an agent or actor;
state—condition before or after an event;
property—condition on an event;
entity—the object concept (cf. Piaget, 1952);
person—animate being (cf. Piaget, 1952);
location—terminus or source of an event (cf. Piaget, 1952).

These schemes are discussed in detail in later chapters.

Ontogenetically, sensory-motor ideas most likely emerge initially from action schemes involving the child's own behavior, and gradually extend analogically to the behavior of other organisms and objects.

Signs

One approach to understanding semiotic extension in the speech process is to describe it in terms of an interrelation of different types of sign. In this description Peirce's theory of signs (Peirce, 1931–1958) is used to model semiotic extension. In terms of this theory the sensory-motor content of speech is most naturally regarded as indexical. An indexical sign is a sign that is actually connected to its object. The sign may be a part of its object (as with a facial expression), or it may be caused by its object (as with a footprint). (In some interpretations of causation this distinction may disappear.) Sensory-motor ideas, insofar as they are the foundations of integrated speech output, can be said to be objects causally connected to their signs (i.e., to the integrated speech output). The sensory-motor idea, in this definition, is indexed by the integration of speech output.

In addition to indexical signs formed from sensory-motor ideas, other aspects of the speech process may be represented as iconic or symbolic signs. An iconic sign can be diagrammatic, and many word-order sequences appear to be diagrams of conceptual interrelations. In this interpretation, such word-order sequences are iconic signs of the relations among ideas (sensory-motor or other ideas). A symbolic sign is an arbitrary and conventional (in the sense of socially determined) representation of whatever it represents. Certain syntactic devices (such as the passive, the relative clause, nominalization, etc.) appear to be symbolic signs in this sense. For example, the passive in English introduces certain sign characteristics (*be* or *get*, the past participle inflection) which conventionally refer to a fixed arrangement of concepts (having the logical object in initial position, or the idea of an asserted property introduced by *be* or *get*). As a social convention this sign functions as a whole. Although there are parts of the sign which refer to parts of the conceptual organization of the passive, these parts are not "little passives," for only the entire complex functions as a single arbitrary sign, used as determined by a social convention.

Semiotic extension is modeled in this framework in a way that depends on the epistemological duality of sensory-motor representations. Sensory-motor representations, as noted, are the *objects* of indexical signs. To model semiotic extension, we will say that sensory-motor representations also appear as the *sign vehicles* of iconic and symbolic signs. According to this model, therefore, semiotic extension requires the language user to interpret sensory-motor ideas as the signs (iconic or symbolic) of other, non–sensory-motor ideas. Sensory-motor representations, being indexed by the occurrence of integrated speech output as well as standing for other ideas, connect the non–sensory-motor meanings to the organization of speech output, as required of a theory of the speech-thought relation.

One can conceive of the organization of speech output as proceeding along the following lines. The speaker's processes of thought produce concepts that are represented in the form of symbolic and iconic signs. These signs have as their sign vehicles sensory-motor ideas, and these sensory-motor ideas are represented indexically by speech programs. In this way, an unbroken chain of signs connects the speaker's thought processes to his or her speech output. The entire process of organizing speech is itself a meaning structure.

The Syntagma

The integration of speech output can be said to take place within syntagmata. This term has been used by Kozhevnikov and Chistovich (1965), who defined it as one meaning unit pronounced as a single output. It can be compared to Lashley's concept of an organizational scheme (Lashley, 1951). The syntagma, as a theoretical concept, unites the articulation of speech with meaning. In other words, the organization of integrated speech articulation occurs within a single meaning structure, the syntagma. Measures of output integration (phonemic clauses, temporal control, etc.), therefore, should be expected to coincide with meaning integration (e.g., the idea of an event) as speech is produced. If speakers do generate speech output from syntagmata, we can describe the speaking process in the following terms: The speaker organizes and moves from one meaning unit to another. This includes sensory-motor meanings. As these new meanings are organized in the speaker's conceptions, fresh syntagmata become available via semiotic extension. Hence there is an integrated articulation of speech output that coincides with the expression of meaning, based on sensory-motor ideas.

In contrast to linguistic entities such as phrases, sentences, sentoids, etc., the syntagma is a unit of speech functioning. It may or may not correspond to the familiar structural units of linguistics, and it varies widely in size relative to linguistic levels of description.[1] My assumption is that functional and structural units need not correspond in any fixed or obvious way, and that units of functioning must be approached on their own terms, without a priori expectation of a correspondence with linguistic units.

Origin of Syntagmata

To further explain the function of sensory-motor ideas within syntagmata, it is necessary to consider the basis of sensory-motor representations in the organization of action, as well as the basis of this organization in hierarchies of control over motor processes. According to Bernstein (1967) and other action theorists (e.g., P. Greene, 1972), the performance of a coordinated action is the result of a hierarchy of control processes. The most subordinate

---

[1]In general, linguistic descriptions of competence must be distinguished from descriptions of the conceptual basis of language. The two types of description have different aims and distinct empirical domains. This question is discussed at length in Chapter 12.

levels in this hierarchy are the localized actions of specific muscle-articulator groups. Higher levels are characterized by a domain limited to activating and controlling the processes that are immediately below them. Successively higher levels are associated with increasing remoteness from the actual musculature and with increasing generality of the control mechanisms. At the most superordinate levels the scale of generality can be equated with that of an action scheme, i.e., an overall plan of the action as one of a certain type, free of the details of actual operations. A scheme of this kind has been called the concept of the action (Turvey, 1975).

An advantage of viewing action schemes in terms of hierarchies of control processes is that it becomes possible to see how two initially distinct hierarchies can be combined. For example, the lower levels of processes from hierarchy B can be inserted under the upper level of processes from hierarchy A. The result is a new hierarchy, AB, the concept of which is A, and the motoric effect B.

During the sensory-motor period of a child's development (Piaget, 1954), there is a convergence of two separate action systems, and the AB model appears to describe this situation. One system consists of sensory-motor action schemes of the type already mentioned. These schemes provide the principal basis of representation at the sensory-motor stage. We shall call this system A. The other system, B, is the basis of motor control over the speech musculature itself. This system passes through a complex development of its own during the same period (Jakobson, 1968). Systems A and B are not isolated from each other during this time. Contacts occur quite early and there may be AB fusions even during the first year. However, for reasons to be described later, these initial contacts are limited in their effects. By the end of the sensory-motor period, however, there emerges what can be called a developmentally new form of action and meaning based on by then widespread AB fusions. Sensory-motor action schemes come to function as the highest levels of the control hierarchies of articulatory actions. These fusions make possible syntagmata in which meanings (sensory-motor representations) organize articulation and speech output; they form meaning units pronounced as single outputs. From the point of view of the theory of signs, the AB fusion creates indexical signs in which B is the sign of A. From the point of view of action control, it creates a mechanism whereby a meaningful representation A dominates the control hierarchy for speech action B.

This step itself can be further analyzed. The fusion of these hierarchies depends on a new development in the capacity to form sign relationships. This development is triggered by the interiorization of sensory-motor schemes. Although the production and comprehension of single words emerges at a very early point (about 1 year or less) and the comprehension of some relations among words only somewhat later, the production of multiword utterances is delayed until nearly 2 years. The reason for this is as follows: The earliest examples of comprehension and production require only a relationship of signs with external referent objects. Although earliest word uses are strongly tied to the co-occurrence of external referents (deixis), the production of integrated sequential speech requires forming indexical signs with internal referent objects. These objects become sign vehicles in semiotic extension. The referent objects of the indexical signs are sensory-motor schemes. This new type of sign and the semiotic extension that depends on it should therefore be largely inaccessible before sensory-motor schemes can be represented mentally. Thus, the production of multiword utterances depends on an extra step developmentally: the interiorization, or mental representation, of sensory-motor action schemes. This can explain the widely noted but hitherto unexplained correlation between this interiorization process and the emergence of multiword utterances (Bloom, 1973; Brown, 1973; Piaget, 1962; Sinclair-deZwart, 1973). The new indexical signs amount to a new form of meaning in which sequences of words denote (among other things) *internal processes*. This particular relationship seems to be the essence of productive and conscious language use.

The terminology whereby ideas such as event, action, state, property, entity, and location are called sensory-motor has now been motivated in two ways. These ideas emerge from sensory-motor representations, and they function to control speech actions.

Representation of Conceptual Structures

The organization of utterances apparently takes the following form, conceptually. There is a structure of concepts and relations corresponding to the meaning. This structure has mapped onto it one or more sensory-motor ideas (semiotic extension) which are the basis of syntagmata and organized speech output. The process of mapping can be viewed as an interaction of indexical, iconic, and symbolic signs, but a more precise form of representation takes the form of labeled, directed graphs.

The use of graphs for representing conceptual structures makes only three assumptions regarding the meaning of utterances, and each of these can be motivated. The assumptions are that the meaning can be resolved functionally into (1) concepts that are (2) connected by relations, and that (3) the relations are oriented with respect to the encoding of speech. Given these assumptions, we can interpret graphs in the following terms:

1. The points in a graph correspond to concepts and are labeled with concept names.
2. The lines in a graph correspond to relations and are labeled with relation names.
3. The direction of the lines corresponds to the orientation of the relations and shows the direction of speech encoding.

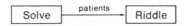

FIG. 1.1. Graph structure (simplified) of *solves a riddle.*

For example, the phrase *solve a riddle* contains two concepts (Solve, Riddle) and one relation between them (*patients*).[2] That is, the meaning is that *solve* has *riddle* as its patient. The indefinite article behaves as a relation (according to a test described in Chapter 8) but belongs to a second system of deictic and anaphoric reference. Ignoring this second system for the time being, the graph representation of *solve a riddle* is shown in Fig. 1.1.

The *patients* relation has an orientation which will be called operative, meaning that in the underlying logical form of the relation, [*patients* (Solve, Riddle)], the first encoded concept (Solve) is the referent and the second encoded concept (Riddle) is the relatum (Reichenbach, 1947). In the receptive orientation this order is reversed, for example, *the riddle is solved;* here, the first encoded concept is the relatum and the second encoded concept is the referent.

The word-order sequence of *solve–riddle* is an example, therefore, of an iconic sign of the diagrammatic type. The *sequence* of concepts is a diagram of the *operative orientation* of the *patients* relation (and the reverse *sequence* of "riddle-solve" is a diagram of the *receptive orientation* of this relation).

Such iconic signs build up indexical signs in the following way: If a sensory-motor idea can be related to two or more iconically related concepts so as to form a strong component in a graph (in a strong component all points are mutually interconnected), a new graph can be constructed in which this strong component is replaced by a single point (that is to say, a concept) labeled with the name of the sensory-motor idea. This new graph is called a contraction of the first graph. The contraction can be superimposed on the original graph. The result is a three-dimensional graph in which the contracted point has a sensory-motor meaning based on labeled relations among the lower points and includes the lower points (one of which also has the same sensory-motor meaning). This process therefore models the semiotic extension of the higher sensory-motor concept to the lower mutually connected concepts.

For example, Solve and Riddle are already related by *patients.* But this relation is unidirectional and therefore does not form a strong component. The concepts can be related to the sensory-motor concept of Action in such a way that all three concepts are mutually interrelated. Following the model above, we can replace this strong component with a single point labeled Action, superimpose it over the three lower points, and show a complex three-dimensional graph in which $Action_0$ on the upper level is semiotically

---

[2]The names of relations are in italics, those of concepts are capitalized.

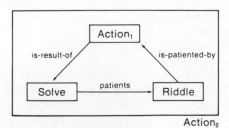

FIG. 1.2.   Graph structure model of semiotic extension (the idea of Action).

extended to Action_1 + Solve + Riddle on the lower level (Fig. 1.2). This graph shows the conditions that must be met for Action_0 to semiotically extend to Solve + Riddle, namely, that these latter concepts should relate to Action_1 by the relations *is-patiented-by* and *is-result-of*, and that all relations should be so oriented that the lower level concepts are mutually interrelated.

Quite complex graphs can be built up with this device. At each level of the graph there is a single point (concept) which has internal structure except at the bottom level. Here, too, further analysis may be possible, but these lower levels involve lexical knowledge beyond the network of iconic signs on which graph representations of semiotic extension are based (and consequently are excluded).

Symbolic Signs

Symbolic signs are conventional, hence easier to delimit. It seems feasible with certain symbolic signs, at least, to describe "devices" which could be employed to construct the signs. Such devices should construct not only the sign proper but also the conceptual structures to which they refer. I have attempted this with three signs: the passive, the restrictive relative clause, and the pseudocleft. The format of these devices is based on the ATN (augmented transition network) formalism, modified so as to permit parallel tests and actions (called PATNs). One can imagine a more complete formalism in which iconic and indexical signs also are constructed with PATNs, but this level of analysis is quite unreachable with iconic and indexical signs at present.

Each PATN introduces, among other structures, sensory-motor ideas. There is therefore a direct semiotic extension of these sensory-motor ideas to the conceptual structure that the device causes to be related to them. For example, the passive can introduce the idea of an Event, which is extended to the literal content in such constructions as *the riddle got solved*.

Syntagmata Based on Conceptual Structures

Conceptual structures consist of the three kinds of sign interconnected by semiotic extension. Typically a given conceptual structure contains several sensory-motor ideas, each extending to different strong components of the conceptual structure. Some strong components are included within others, and these are alternative bases for syntagmata. In any particular utterance only one such syntagma can be selected for a single output. The process whereby such activation is carried out is known as *ecphoria* [ec (out) + phoria (carry)]. The activation of a semiotically extended sensory-motor idea by ecphoria leads to a syntagma based on this idea. The semiotically extended sensory-motor idea is part of the conceptual structure of the utterance. Thus, with the addition of ecphoria, we have a theory about the relation between speech and thought applied to particular utterances. This theory may be diagrammed as in Fig. 1.3.

Data

Four kinds of data are considered in this book. One class consists of information about the organization of conceptual structures themselves. Such data can be used during the analysis of utterances. For example, the pseudocleft construction probes the conceptual structure of various utterance types. Another example is direct ratings of words and constituents in terms of relatedness (Levelt, 1974).

The remaining types of data tend to validate one or another theoretical claim or assumption. The assumption that the earliest multiword utterances of children are produced from syntagmata based on sensory-motor ideas tends to be validated by the nearly perfect classifiability of children's early utterances in terms of the sensory-motor ideas of Event, State, Action, Entity, and Location. The assumption that early syntagmata function as indexical signs with sensory-motor action schemes as the referents tends to be validated

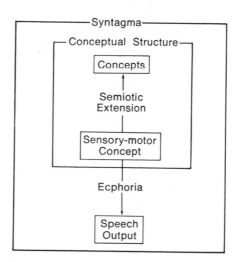

FIG. 1.3.   Logical arrangement of processes within a syntagma.

by the congruence of word-order sequences with (overt) action sequences based on the same schemes. For example, English-speaking children sometimes produce utterances in which locative words occur in initial position (*out train*) when there is a corresponding action that starts from the location (removing the train out from under a tunnel).

The assumption that adult utterances at every level of abstract meaning are still based on sensory-motor content tends to be validated by the correspondence of output segments in adult speech with sensory-motor content. Speech output segments can be recognized in several ways. Speech dysfluencies (errors, hesitations) strongly tend to co-occur with the boundaries of sensory-motor ideas (and also tend to interrupt certain grammatical constituents—in particular, verb phrases, prepositional phrases, and noun phrases with indefinite articles). Phonemic clause segments (Trager & Smith, 1951) similarly tend to correspond to sensory-motor ideas and may interrupt grammatical constituents. In these cases not more than a weak equivalence can be claimed between grammatical descriptions and perform-ance structures (Chomsky, 1965).

A different form of evidence is that speech segments which coincide with sensory-motor ideas are relatively more stable temporally than segments which coincide with surface or underlying grammatical clauses. The latter typically include several sensory-motor ideas. If speech programs change between sensory-motor ideas, each grammatical clause is likely to include the output of several such programs, and the unprogrammed change of programs hence would produce additional sources of variance.

A final form of data is that the encoding of sensory-motor ideas coincides with spontaneous gesticulations during speech. The interpretation of this correspondence is quite straightforward. Since syntagmata are held to be based on fused AB control hierarchies, it is necessary only to suppose that both hierarchies can continue to have something like their original motoric effects. Hierarchy B regulates the speech articulators, while hierarchy A continues to regulate movements of the hands which have generally been associated with the action scheme in question. (Hence, ideographic gesticulations can be explained.) Both channels are outputting parts of the same syntagma, and they thus are temporally linked but maintain their identities. In this way gesticulation can be viewed as an external dynamic trace of the internal speech program.

2 Previous Work

This book is concerned with the relationship between speech and thought, and especially with this relationship as found in the process of producing speech, but the ultimate emphasis is on the speech–thought relationship, not on speech production. In this chapter, half of the discussion deals with speech understanding. The purpose of the review that follows is to extract from current psycholinguistics any information about speech processing that may shed light on the relationship between speech and thought. The following statements appear to be supported:

1. Listeners are constantly guided by an attempt to organize meaningful representations in speech as they hear or produce it.
2. There is not a stage of speech processing which corresponds to a single linguistic representation; rather there is a multifaceted representation in which various levels are corepresented. The units of processing vary in scope and often appear to be quite small.
3. The units of processing correspond to concepts.

These properties of speech processing are easily expressed in terms of syntagmata and thus lead to a consideration of the relationship between speech and thought. It is difficult, though, to express these properties in terms of grammatical constituents. The latter have quite different descriptive functions (and are discussed in Chapter 12).

SPEECH COMPREHENSION

Functions of Tranformations

A starting point for the review of current research on speech comprehension is provided by the following quotation from J. Greene's (1972) text:

... neither syntax nor semantics can be understood in isolation, since the only purpose of using different syntactic transformations is to communicate some particular aspect of meaning. When transformations are being used to perform this natural function of conveying a meaningful relationship... they will be produced and understood perfectly easily. The special difficulties with them in psycholinguistic experiments are explained by the fact that transformations are being used in contexts in which they are not performing their natural semantic function [p. 116].

Greene rightly indicates an experiment by Wason (1965) as the pioneer work in establishing the conclusion she describes. Wason devised a situation where a negative sentence would be the more appropriate form and found that, in this situation, negative sentences were easier to complete than affirmative sentences.

On the basis of experiments of her own, J. Greene (1970, 1972) concluded that one natural use to which the negative is put is to contradict a prior assertion. In contrast to the affirmative form, therefore, which carries no presupposition of an earlier assertion, the negative should be made easier to understand when it appears in a context of a change of meaning, and this is in fact the result that Greene found.

From Wason's and Greene's findings, we should expect that whenever the situational context permits the negative to be understood with something like its normal semantic–pragmatic function, a negative sentence will be no more difficult than a non-negative sentence, and may be easier. Does the reverse hold? That is, if the negative is used in a situation that interferes with its normal semantic–pragmatic function, is a negative sentence more difficult? If the normal semantic–pragmatic content of a negative sentence includes the presupposition that a prior assertion exists whose meaning is different, then using the negative in a context in which there is no prior assertion to which it can be related may interfere with this part of the sentence content. It is not merely that the negative sentence is neutralized. It may be disrupted to an extent that corresponds to the mismatch between the context of no prior sentence and the presupposition that there is such a sentence with a different meaning. This disruption would then increase the difficulty of the negative sentence. In contrast, a simple declarative sentence, the form that is most neutral and presupposes the least, would suffer relatively less interference. Therefore, comparing "kernel" to transformed sentences in typical experimental contexts would create the incorrect impression that the transformed sentences are more difficult.

Many of the early psycholinguistic experiments can be reinterpreted in the light of this hypothesis. In particular, the finding described as "additivity of transformational effects" follows from it (Gough, 1966; McMahon, 1963; Mehler, 1963; Miller, 1962; Miller & McKean, 1964; Savin & Perchonock, 1965; Slobin, 1966). According to this finding, the psychological difficulty of sentences increases as a linear function of the combined difficulty of the separate transformations that they include. However, since all experiments purporting to show additivity have presented sentences in more or less inappropriate contexts (e.g., lists), one must assume that the semantic–pragmatic function of the transformations was interfered with. Each interference adds an increment of difficulty. It does not follow, therefore, that under natural conditions, transformed sentences create greater difficulties of perception than simple affirmative "kernel" sentences.

This reinterpretation assumes that listeners, even in experimental situations where speech is hardly being used normally, attempt to extract meaning from the incoming speech signal. More direct evidence of such an ongoing process can be found in other psycholinguistic experiments, in particular the so-called "click" experiments of Fodor, Bever, and Garrett (1974).

Perceptual Segmentation

A Model for "Click" Location.   In the first of the "click" experiments, Fodor and Bever (1965) used such sentences as the following:

That he was happy   was evident from the way he smiled.
      ↑   ↑   ↑
      a   *b* *c*

Audible clicks were placed opposite points *a, b,* or *c* on an audiotape track, and subjects performed the task of locating the click relative to the speech. The discovery by these authors was that the reported location of a click tended to be displaced into the clause boundary at *b*. That is, *a* was postposed, *b* was heard more or less accurately, and *c* was preposed. A model of what transpires in this situation is shown in Figs. 2.1, 2.2, and 2.3. In Fig. 2.1 are

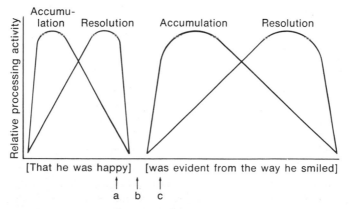

FIG. 2.1.   Hypothetical processes during speech understanding. Arrows indicate the positions of superimposed clicks.

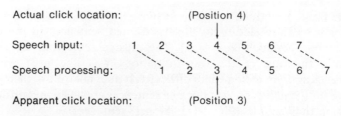

FIG. 2.2.   Click preposing at the beginning of a perceptual unit.

two processes, "accumulation" and "resolution," which are presumed to take place concurrently but peak at different points, as shown. At the start of a perceptual unit most of the incoming speech is accumulated, and at the end of the unit this accumulation is evaluated and all speech including currently incoming speech is resolved into a structural image. Then a new cycle begins, in this case with the next clause.

Although the model describes a continuous change of balance between accumulation and resolution, at the very end and beginning of a perceptual unit the imbalance is maximal. We may simplify the picture by considering these two extreme situations and relating the Fodor and Bever experiment to them. The model, the rest of which is in Figs. 2.2 and 2.3, assumes that the click and speech are not processed together. At the beginning of a perceptual unit, where speech processing is delayed, the click can be processed immediately, and its location is *preposed* (Fig. 2.2). The click is objectively at position 4 but appears to be at position 3, corresponding to the movement of click *c* above. At the end of a perceptual unit, when speech analysis is carried out, click perception is delayed, and click location is shown to be *postposed* (Fig. 2.3). The click is objectively at position 4 but appears to be at position 5, corresponding to the movement of click *a* above.

The model in Figs, 2.1–2.3 does not define the scope of the perceptual units over which accumulation and resolution alternate. According to the clausal hypothesis of Fodor, Bever, and Garrett (1974), this unit is the internal grammatical clause. However, the evidence of the click experiments themselves suggests that this cannot be the sole processing unit.

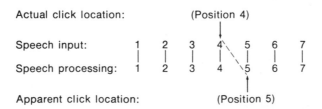

FIG. 2.3.   Click postposing at the end of a perceptual unit.

Determining Factors in "Click" Location.   Bever, Lackner, and Kirk (1969) discuss three hypotheses concerning the subjective location of clicks superimposed upon speech:

1. Click location errors move toward points that correspond to the boundaries between internal clauses (i.e., the clausal hypothesis).
2. Click location errors move toward surface structure boundaries in proportion to the number of simultaneously terminating constitutents at the boundary (i.e., its depth [Yngve, 1960]).
3. Click errors move toward surface clause boundaries. (Unlike the clausal hypothesis, this requires that the division into internal clauses should also be marked at the surface.)

The Fodor and Bever (1965) result is consistent with each of these hypotheses, since click movement was simultaneously toward all three types of boundary mentioned. Using sentences such as *In addition to his wives the Prince brought the court's only dwarf,* Bever, Lackner, and Kirk (1969) found that the subjective location of clicks was drawn toward the deeper surface phrase less than half the time. Therefore, they reject hypothesis 2. Their data take the following form: For each magnitude of click mislocation, they found the percentage of mislocations that went into the deeper of the two surface boundaries on either side of the click. For example, a click that coincides objectively with *wives* in the sentence above would be considered to be displaced one half-syllable if it was reported as either just preceding or just following the word *wives.* In this case a postposing error would be the one into the deeper surface boundary. The click would be displaced one full syllable if it was reported as coinciding with *his* or *the.* In this case a preposing error would be the one into the deeper surface boundary. Bever et al. found that 52% of the half-syllable errors, 41% of the one-syllable errors, 33% of the one-and-one-half–syllable errors, and 36% of the two-syllable errors were toward the deeper surface boundary. In all cases, therefore, hypothesis 2 is supported at a chance level or less.

However, matters change when we learn that "…one-half syllable errors in response to a click located objectively two words before or after the clause break confirmed the within-clause phrase-structure hypothesis 71%" (Bever et al., 1969, p. 234, note 9). That is, the phrase structure hypothesis apparently holds outside the immediate vicinity of the clause boundary (surface clause boundary in these sentences). It does seem to follow that surface phrases can form perceptual units if they are not in direct competition with a more powerful source of click movement. Therefore, hypothesis 2 cannot be categorically dismissed on the evidence of this experiment, although it must be considered in relation to the other hypotheses about click location.

To compare hypotheses 1 and 3, it is necessary to find sentences in which there are two internal clauses but only one surface clause. Bever et al. claim to have done this with the following NP-complement:

The general preferred the troops to fight

↑

The internal clauses correspond to *The general preferred it,* and *The troops fight.* Thus a click at the position shown should appear to be postposed into the clause boundary between the verb and the NP, although there is not a surface clause boundary at this point. Thus, any selective displacement to the position between the verb and the NP would be evidence for hypothesis 1.

Bever et al. argue that this type of sentence contains a single surface clause because there can be a reflexive pronoun in its grammatical object, a form possible only when the verb and object are within the same surface clause:

The general prefers himself to fight.[1]

Not everyone, however, accepts sentences of this kind (Chapin, Smith, and Abrahamson, 1972). In several lectures I have found that more than half the audience could not accept these reflexive pronouns. On the other hand, no one seems to reject the reflexive in other types of complement:

The general forced himself to fight.

The results of the experiments do show a greater postposing error for clicks objectively on the main verb in the NP-complement. However, almost certainly some (presumably at least half) of Bever et al.'s subjects treated the NP-complements as if a surface clause boundary existed after the main verb. Thus, the result of the experiment cannot be said to support hypothesis 1 over hypothesis 3. The most that can be claimed is that clause boundaries can attract nearby clicks, but we cannot say what kind of clause boundaries these are (surface or internal).

Putting Bever et al.'s two experiments together under the above interpretation, as seems to be appropriate, we conclude that a variety of perceptual units actually have been demonstrated. Not only are these units clauses or (still more restricted) internal clauses, but possibly both of these and surface structure phrases as well.

The picture becomes more focused if we take into account the results of another click experiment by Chapin et al. (1972), who used sentences such as the following:

---

[1]Bever, Lackner, and Kirk (1969) actually use this example: *John can't bear himself to be seen.*

1. The chairman of the board // should give ([whoever invented that process]) a prize.
2. The chairman of the board // should give [the inventor of the process] a prize.

In these examples, the double slash marks the major subject–predicate division of the sentence, the brackets mark internal clause boundaries, and the parentheses mark surface clauses boundaries. Thus (1) and (2) differ in that (2) omits a surface clause boundary. Unlike NP-complements, reduced relative clauses seem to be a uniformly acceptable means of eliminating surface clause boundaries. The clicks were objectively located temporally midway between the major subject–predicate boundary // and the internal clause boundary [. With sentences of this type, clicks were preposed by the subjects, i.e., mislocated *away from* the clause boundary, either internal or external.

Chapin et al. also used sentences in which the positions of the internal clause boundary and the subject–predicate boundary were reversed, such as:

3. Cars ([which are longer than 12 feet]) and trucks // should stay in the right lane.
4. Cars [longer than 12 feet] and trucks // should stay in the right lane.

Clicks objectively midway between the internal clause boundary] and the subject–predicate boundary // in these sentences were neither postposed nor preposed, i.e., they were not drawn toward the clause boundary, internal or external, or toward the subject–predicate division.

Fodor et al. (1974), however, have pointed out that many of the sentences that produced this result contain, in fact, *three* internal clauses. For example, in the underlying structure of the sentence

[Everybody tired-looking] over there // drank too much last night,

there are the following clauses: *Everybody is tired-looking, Everybody is over there,* and *Everybody drank too much last night.* In such a sentence any mislocation of clicks toward the subject–predicate point marked with the double slash is movement toward an internal clause boundary as well. These sentences, therefore, provide an ambiguous test. Since the click is objectively midway between two internal clause boundaries the equal preposing and postposing tendencies that are observed can be explained.[2]

A generalization that includes the results of all these experiments is that the unit of processing, rather than any particular linguistic entity such as the

---

[2]Fodor, Bever, and Garrett (1974) criticize other sentences in which Chapin, Smith, and Abrahamson (1972) claim that there is an internal clause boundary, but in which in fact there is none. I can find only two examples out of 20 for which this criticism is valid.

internal or external clause, is a conceptual or meaning unit. The listener perceives speech input in terms of coherent meanings. Sometimes this leads him or her to group the words as they are heard into phrases, subjects and predicates, or clauses (not to mention other possibilities). In many sentences the major meaning units indeed seem to correspond to clauses, but this correlation is not perfect. Sentences exist where the major meaning units map onto the sentence structure in other ways, and a number of the Chapin et al. (1972) sentences appear to have the property that the meaning and clause structures do not precisely coincide. For example, in

> The chairman of the board / / should give ([whoever invented the process]) a prize,

the basic meaning appears to be *The chairman of the board + should give someone a prize.* A plausible perceptual segmentation based on this meaning would divide the subject from the predicate, as Chapin et al. (1972) observed. In this case, the embedded clause does not coincide with the semantic division. In other sentences there is a correspondence between the boundaries of clauses and the major meaning units. For example, in

> The chairman of the board ([who was enriched by the process]) / / should give the inventor a prize,

the basic meaning appears to be *The chairman of the board + should give the inventor a prize,* and here the embedded clause coincides with the semantic division of subject and predicate. In the triple clause sentence of Chapin et al. (1972) mentioned previously the basic meaning seems to be *Everybody tired-looking + drank too much* in which the principal segments are *everybody tired-looking* and *drank too much.* The embedded clause boundary therefore coincides with the first segment and the subject–predicate boundary coincides with the second, and no click displacements were in fact observed.

If the perceptual unit in these experiments is a meaning structure rather than primarily a syntactic structure, the results could be explained in terms of the model proposed earlier. Clicks that objectively precede the close of a major meaning unit are postposed while the listener resolves this meaning, and clicks that objectively follow the start of a major meaning structure are preposed while the listener accumulates information about this meaning.

Memory

A striking phenomenon has been reported by Jarvella (1971; Jarvella & Herman, 1972), which also shows a correlation with conceptual organization. In these experiments, subjects listened to passages that are interrupted at various points. The subject then tries to recall as much as possible. The materials are so designed that before each point of interruption the identical string of words could be grammatically segmented in either of two ways, depending on the antecedent context, as in the following example (from Jarvella, 1971):

1. The tone of the document was threatening. Having failed to disprove the charges, Taylor was later fired by the President.
2. The document had also blamed him for having failed to disprove the charges. Taylor was later fired by the President.

Jarvella found that the ability to recall the text verbatim extended farther back in (1) than in (2). In both (1) and (2), the accuracy of recall dropped precipitously at the sentence boundary—*Having failed* in (1), and *Taylor was* in (2).

Clearly, the string of words, *having failed to disprove the charges Taylor was later fired by the President,* forms an integrated idea more readily in (1) than in (2). In (1) it combines into a single (complex) Event, whereas in (2) there are separate Events. The ability to recall the text verbatim parallels this segmentation.

Inasmuch as recall is an off-line measure, Jarvella's experiments cannot be taken to reveal that the immediate result of speech processing does not include semantic structure. Rather, they show that, beyond the boundary of a sentence, only semantic structure remains in memory. (These points are made by Tyler, 1977.)

The "click" experiments as well as Jarvella's experiments have used an off-line methodology. In this methodology the measure of the listener's processing activity is taken some time after his immediate perceptual response is made. In the click experiments, for example, the listener indicates the apparent click position after hearing the entire sentence and writing it down. In some cases, several seconds have elapsed. When an on-line response measure such as reaction time is used with the click paradigm, the result is not consistently related to the clausal structure (Abrams & Bever, 1969).

On-Line Processing

Shadowing. Research by Marslen-Wilson (1973) employs shadowing as an on-line methodology. This study shows convincingly that a semantic representation of speech is available within a few hundred milliseconds of hearing the relevant acoustic signal. Marslen-Wilson used subjects who were able to shadow speech with an average delay of only 250 msec, which is equal to about one syllable. All the information these subjects could receive about the signal at any moment therefore had to be processed within this short time. A variety of effects showed that within this time the incoming speech could be related to a semantic representation. For example, errors tended to correspond to the semantic and structural arrangement of the sentence up to the point of the error, and semantic anomalies disrupted the shadowing performance of these subjects as much as they did more distant shadowers. These findings have been confirmed and extended by more recent experiments (Marslen-Wilson, 1975). He has shown that shadowers (both close and distant) initiate the utterance of trisyllabic words in shadowing connected text on the basis of only the information contained in the first syllable. Although possibly lagging as much as 700 or 800 msec behind the input, these subjects were able to integrate a shadowing response with as little information as the close shadowers had used.[3] Thus the listeners were able to integrate each new word into an intact semantic and syntactic structure of the sentence within the duration of one syllable. This rate of structural integration conflicts with one assumption of the clausal hypothesis, that such integration takes place primarily at the ends of clauses. It suggests, instead, that the listener more nearly constantly adds information to a developing structure which includes a semantic representation.

Research by Lindig (1976) has shown that shadowers are able to integrate speech input into a *thematic* structure which covers an entire text of several sentences. Within 600–800 msec (the shadowing latency in this experiment), the listeners could place the input into its syntactic, semantic, and pragmatic context.

Multifaceted Representations. Using another on-line technique, Tyler (1977) has shown that concurrent reaction time measures are affected in the same way by semantic and syntactic anomalies, despite variations in the amount of semantic predictability deliberately introduced into the sentences. That is, although her experiment attempted to achieve a separate manipulation of semantic and syntactic structures, it was not possible to do so. Since the experiment measured reaction time on line, this result implies that differences in level of representation (semantic, syntactic), insofar as these have psychological reality, emerge only *after* incoming speech has been understood. This interpretation is consistent with the unit of processing having been a syntagma, where rather than several levels of representation there is a single, multi-faceted representation.

The status of the model presented earlier in connection with the click experiments (Fig. 2.1) now appears to be somewhat in doubt. A single representation which can be constructed on line does not seem to require extensive accumulation of unprocessed speech information followed by resolution. However, Marslen-Wilson, Tyler, and Seidenberg (in press) point out that the amount of information that the listener must carry with him may

---

[3]The critical words contained phonological distortions in the first, second, or third syllable. Listeners corrected the distortions in the second and third syllables more often when the word was semantically consistent with the text than when it was semantically inconsistent.

depend on what they call the relative determinacy of the information flow within the sentence. This is regarded as variable among sentences. In most sentences information early in clauses seems to be relatively underdetermined and information late in clauses seems to be relatively overdetermined by the prior sentence context. (The validity of this supposition has been demonstrated by Harris, 1978.) In this situation, the model of alternating accumulation/resolution might apply at clause boundaries, even though the explanation assumes that the clausal hypothesis is false. Marslen-Wilson et al. were able to show that the magnitude of clause boundary effects is reduced when the end of a clause is sufficiently underdetermined (e.g., *even though he hasn't seen many,...*), suggesting that it is the information flow rather than the clause boundary itself which is critical for determining whether there is resolution (and by implication accumulation).

Also, should the model of accumulation/resolution hold within syntagmata, the small size of this unit in most cases (see following discussion) would create the appearance of a continuous construction of an internal representation, although there would be cyclic peaks of activity as the internal structure of each syntagma in succession is resolved and as groups of syntagmata are related to each other.

Summary of Speech Comprehension

This review of research into speech comprehension has tended to establish the following points:

1. The listener is constantly guided by an attempt to extract meaning from speech. Processing steps tend to correspond to the reconstruction of meanings. This correspondence appears in several forms—transformations such as the negative are associated with particular meanings and apparently add to psychological difficulty only when this meaning is interfered with (as it usually has been in most experiments); click mislocations are associated with points of major change of meaning in test sentences; and memory for speech undergoes a qualitative change at the boundaries of major meaning changes.

2. The listener responds to the speech signal on line, in the sense that he makes a semantic analysis of the incoming signal in as short a time as possible; according to current estimates, this occurs within one syllable.

3. The listener computes a single, multifaceted representation in which syntactic and semantic information are not functionally distinguished. This form of representation is naturally provided by the concept of a syntagma, and is shown most directly in the apparent difficulty of manipulating syntactic information separately from semantic information. Memory of speech from the most recent clause, moreover, apparently consists of a mixture of surface and underlying information changing to more purely underlying information for more distant clauses, consistent with an initial multifaceted representation.

4. The size of the processing unit varies, relative to levels of linguistic representation, apparently corresponding to the importance and scope of the conceptual structure on which it is based. The evidence for this comes from the click studies undertaken so far; additional evidence of the variability of the unit of speech production is discussed in Chapters 8 and 9. The size of the production unit apparently extends from a single syllable to several clauses. On the basis of this degree of variation, there is little hope of reaching a consistent theory of speech processing expressed in terms of a single level of grammatical constituent structure (e.g., some form of the clausal hypothesis). The concept of a syntagma, in contrast, does provide an account of this variation, as described in succeeding chapters.

SPEECH PRODUCTION

Theories of Speech Production

Theories of speech production tend to deal with the same question: how far ahead do we plan speech output? On this point, there is surprisingly little variation.

Theories Based on the Sentence.   Theoretical assumptions regarding the size of the planning unit have been made by Fromkin (1971), Garrett (1975), and MacNeilage (1973). Their assumptions are essentially the same: They assume that the planning unit corresponds to a clause or sentence. The choice of a unit this large is due in part to an attempt to accommodate a type of speech error in which words are displaced between phrases, and in part to an attempt to account for intonation contours which are definable over entire clauses.

Fromkin (1971), for example, proposes that the speech production process begins with a syntactic structure generator which produces (along with a semantic feature generator) syntactic–semantic structures. These are then the input for a process of generating the intonation contour. Thus, the initial planning unit is something like an entire sentence, within which word exchanges can occur. MacNeilage (1973) makes a similar assumption. For him, the first step after conceiving of the meaning of an utterance is to decide the general syntactic form; subsequent steps generate the intonation contour and the lexical choices. Garrett (1976), whose interests focus more on the semantic–syntactic end of the speech process, proposes the hierarchy of stages in the generation of a sentence shown in Fig. 2.4. In this model, like Fromkin's and MacNeilage's, the production process is planned on the level of the sentence as a whole. M_1, M_2, M_3, ..., M_n represent different messages. Only one is involved in a given utterance, and it determines the lexical choices and the grammatical relations. The latter establish the general syntactic form of

Level of Representation	Function	Type of Error
Message source		
	Semantic factors	Exchanges
Functional level		
	Syntactic factors	Shifts
Positional level		
Sound level		
	Phonetic detail	Deletions, additions
Instruction to articulators		
		Tongue twisters
Articulatory systems		

FIG. 2.4.   Hierarchy of stages in speech production proposed by Garrett (1976).

the sentence. The next step is to select a "positional frame." Then the process moves down to decide the phonological properties of the utterance. These various steps are carried out at every level for the sentence as a whole.

Fromkin's, MacNeilage's, and Garrett's theories are alike in another respect. They each assume the existence of separate levels or stages of production. In Garrett's model, for example, the syntactic level is reached only after the semantic level has been resolved, and the phonological level is reached only after the syntactic level has been resolved. This is the clausal hypothesis of comprehension reversed for production. These models make the same assumption, that there are functionally distinct processing stages which correspond (more or less) to the levels of linguistic description. (The syntagma theory, in contrast, proposes a unit of processing which encompasses several of these levels in one function.)

Critique.   As mentioned above, Fromkin's, MacNeilage's, and Garrett's models have been motivated in part by an attempt to accommodate certain types of speech errors, and in part by an effort to provide a basis for intonation contours definable over clauses. There are several difficulties with the assumption of clause-level planning, however, which become clear when other factors are considered:

1. The first factor is the extremely low frequency of errors that show planning at the clause level. Examples of such errors (from Garrett, 1976, but following Fromkin's, 1971, convention of writing "intended" → "produced") are the following:

I broke a stay in the dinghy yesterday → I broke a dinghy in the stay yesterday

Although suicide is a form of murder → Although murder is a form of suicide

I've got to go home and give my back a hot bath → I've got to go home and give my bath a hot back

To understand these exchange errors, it seems necessary to argue that not only were the two words involved simultaneously activated, but their grammatical positions were to some extent already decided within a larger structure. In these errors, planning appears to have been at a clause or other major constituent level. However, such errors are extremely rare, and it does not follow that the planning level of these exchanges is a fixed property of the speech production process.

People who take note of speech errors often remark how surprisingly "common" exchange errors are. While the word "common" is not defined, even if we assume that there are two or three such errors a day in the speech of a particular individual, the frequency is still extremely low relative to the number of times distinct speech programs are used in the course of a day. One must raise a question of research strategy. Could it possibly be correct to build a theory which can only form speech plans at a clause level when such plans apparently occur in a tiny fraction of all speech plans? A theory so severely restricted simply has no way to account for the vast majority of speech plans.

2. A second consideration is the result of the speech-shadowing experiments mentioned earlier (Marslen-Wilson, 1973; 1975). The shadowing task provides information about both comprehension and production of speech. From the point of view of comprehension, the shadowing latency (the average interval between input and output) determines the longest amount of time the subject has to assimilate the input. From the point of view of production, the shadowing latency gives the shortest possible interval for planning the output. (However, this does not mean that there could not be longer intervals, in which, for example, the subject could successfully forecast the input.) The shortest intervals through which speech planning could take place were, on the average, 250 msec, or one syllable. Certain of the errors the shadowers made seem to have been the result of such a small planning interval, while others imply planning of greater scope. In Marslen-Wilson's (1973) example, output A and output B imply larger and smaller planning units, respectively:

Input: He heard at the brigade that the...
Output A: He heard that the brigade had...
Output B: He heard it...

The shadower with output A has formulated a plan corresponding to an entire subordinate clause. This error induces a further sympathetic error downstream (*that* → *had*). In this case the planning unit may be at the level described by the models of Fromkin, MacNeilage, and Garrett. But output B is apparently formulated at a lower level of structure, and in fact requires us to credit the subject with nothing more than one syllable's worth of planning. Hearing *heard,* the shadower plans only the next constituent (NP) and responds with *it* (which no doubt is an assimilation of *at* from the input, as was the output of *that* in A). In shadowing, then, we find evidence of various levels of planning, but not evidence that forces us to assume planning is always at the highest level.

In terms of possible syntagmata, the basis of planning in output A could be an Event (*the brigade had done X*), whereas in B it could be a State (*he heard it* is a State in the sense of being a condition which results from some Event). These syntagmata are comparable to each other as programming mechanisms in that both rest upon sensory-motor content.

3. A third relevant consideration is that phonemic clauses in spontaneous speech tend to be very short. In many utterances, therefore, intonation contours do not have to be defined over entire grammatical clauses at all. (A phonemic clause is, by definition, the range of an intonation contour.) In a corpus analysed by Duncan and Fiske (1977), the distribution of phonemic clauses is highly skewed (see Table 9.7, a tally made by the present writer), and the median length is only 2.6 syllables. The utterances below the median correspond to just one or two word phrases. Thus, there does not appear to be phonological speech planning at the level of clauses for most utterances. Nonetheless, planning at this level is required for a few examples, and for explaining the ability of speakers to produce citation forms where the intonation pattern does form over a whole sentence. A model of speech production should therefore provide a flexible basis for speech programming in which no single linguistic level has priority status. The syntagma provides this flexibility, because the sensory-motor content can be complex or simple and the scope of the phonological program can vary correspondingly.

The models of Fromkin, MacNeilage, and Garrett describe speech planning at the sentence level, because they assume that the speech producer is, in fact, directly producing sentences. However, if the unit of speech production is functional, not structural, the speech producer may not directly produce sentences or constituents of sentences at all. After the speaker has generated speech from syntagmata, it may be possible to describe the structures that appear in terms of sentences and their constituents, but this description will not correspond to the functional units of production.

A related theoretical claim in the models of Fromkin, MacNeilage, and Garrett is that speech production takes place in a succession of stages. Each stage is thought to correspond to a level of linguistic representation. Rather than being a succession of stages, however, speech production may work with a single more complex representation. This can be compared to the development of multifaceted representations during speech comprehension (Tyler, 1977).

Multifaceted Representations

Danks (1977) attempted to separate two stages in the generation of utterances, namely, an initial stage of conceptual generation, and a later stage of syntactic formulation. His evidence convinced him, however, that this separation is impossible to achieve. The experiment had two stages, one for each of the two hypothetical stages of sentence generation. In the first stage the subject (ignorant that he or she would have to produce sentences in the second stage) mentally "related" sets of words, e.g., *animal* and *tent,* or *mother* and *ring.* The subject did not say or write anything but only indicated when these terms had been mentally related. Thus there was recorded a latency of response that could be compared to the latency of response in the second stage. This second stage consisted of producing sentences that incorporated the same words as had been presented in the first stage (the words were presented again, and the latency for starting the sentence was noted).

Assuming that in the first stage the subject works out a semantic structure and in the second stage produces a sentence based in part on this structure, the first stage latency should correlate more strongly than the second with measures of the semantic complexity of the sentence produced (number of semantic roles, etc.), whereas the second stage latency should correlate more strongly than the first with measures of surface complexity (length in syllables, etc.). In Dank's experiment, however, semantic and surface indices correlate with both first and second stage latencies to the same extent. When given words to relate in the first stage, subjects apparently cannot avoid incorporating them into a linguistic form, contradicting the assumption that there are different levels of processing.

Kempen (1977) provided subjects with sentences to memorize that were in either a main clause or subordinate clause form. In Dutch, the language of the experiment, a VO order is observed in main clauses and an OV order in subordinate clauses. Half of the memorized sentences were, therefore, VO and half OV. For testing, the subjects were given the subject noun phrases of these sentences and were asked to complete them as either VO or OV (cued indirectly by manipulating the initial conjunction, which required a main or subordinate clause). Sometimes, therefore, a subject would have to complete a sentence he had memorized in the VO order as OV and sometimes one memorized in the OV order as VO. In addition, following instructions, subjects had to produce either a complete (VO or OV) predicate or just a partial predicate consisting of the first word of the full predicate (i.e., they had to say the V or the O, respectively—the latter not grammatical).

The latencies for making these completions were shortest when the produced order was the same as the memorized order (VO or OV); it was longest when these orders were opposite; and it was intermediate when only V or O was produced. This seems to indicate that V and O are retrieved together by the speaker and in a specific order. Depending on whether this order corresponds to the completion response the subject must make, the latency is larger or smaller. This picture is predicted from the syntagma theory, according to which the speakers in Kempen's experiment would not be able to retrieve a structure from memory without at the same time formulating an output; there is a single, more complex step, not a succession of functionally distinct steps, in this theory.

To summarize the discussion so far, we have considered three theoretical models (Fromkin, MacNeilage, Garrett). These have made similar assumptions regarding sentence-level speech planning and the existence of stages of successive speech programming. The first of these assumptions appears to be so restrictive that most speech production simply fails to be covered by the theory. The second assumption appears to conflict with evidence of multifaceted single-stage speech production.

Empirical Studies of Speech Production

There is also a more empirically oriented speech production literature that bears on the issue of the speech planning unit. My discussion of this literature begins with studies that show speech planning in a relatively global way and proceeds to those that show it more specifically.

Hesitation Phenomena. In a series of investigations, Goldman-Eisler (1968) and her colleagues (Henderson, Goldman-Eisler, and Skarbeck, 1966) have attempted to show an alternation between "hesitant" and "fluent" periods of speech output. This classification has been criticized by several authors (Boomer, 1970; Jaffe and Feldstein, 1970; Rochester, 1973), and it does appear to be rather arbitrary. The longest speech burst in a "hesitant" phase, according to a graph in Henderson et al. (1966), is 2.5 sec, while the shortest speech burst in a "fluent" phase is 0.5 sec. One should not wish to have categories which admit exceptions as large as these. In order to use these findings to estimate the extent of speech planning, I have considered all stretches of uninterrupted speech, regardless of duration, to be the output of single production plans. This definition surely errs in overestimating the duration of longer plans, since there can be changes of speech programs without measurable hesitations, but it probably gives a fair estimate of the duration of shorter plans. (But without knowing the text and the location of the pauses within it, even this estimate is problematical). The definition avoids assuming that any phase of speech is "fluent" or "hesitant" and thus is free from the criticisms which have been made of this distinction. The result is shown in Table 2.1. This table shows that nearly a quarter of the speech bursts are only one-half second long (presumably single words), but that occasionally much longer bursts apparently occur (14% are 3 sec or more long). Subject to the foregoing caveats, this again is evidence of flexible speech programming.

A Conditioning Study. Faile (1972) has used conditioned hand retractions to detect the onset of speech planning units. The hand retraction was first conditioned to the occurrence of particular words that were likely to be produced in a story the subjects were to tell. These responses tended to occur in advance of actually saying the word and at the beginning of what Faile termed phonological phrases. The following would be an instance, where *dark* is the conditioned stimulus:

it was [an unusually dark night]

↑

hand retraction

Brackets indicate a phonological phrase. (This example is based on but does not actually appear in Faile.)

Anticipatory conditioned responses thus seem to show activated lexical items at the beginning of phonological phrases. Although Faile speaks of these phrases as planning units, actually the experiment shows only that lexical choices may take place at the onset of phonological phrases. Whether more of the structure of the phrase is available to the speaker at this point is not known. That there is some independence of lexicalization and the

TABLE 2.1
Duration of Speech Bursts (Based on Henderson,
Goldman-Eisler, and Skarbeck, 1966, Fig. 1.b)

Duration (sec)	Frequency	Cumulative %
0.5	5	23
1.0	2	32
1.5	2	41
2.0	6	68
2.5	3	82
3.0	1	86
3.5	1	91
4.0	1	95
4.5		
5.0	1	100

evolution of the rest of the structure is suggested by occasional examples in which the conditioned responses occurred two or more phonological phrases before the critical word, suggesting premature activation of the word in a context where integration with ongoing structure was unlikely. (Lexicalization, of course, can also lag behind integration of structure.)

Phonological phrases in Faile's definition strongly correlate with grammatical constituents,[4] and of these a wide variety is represented. In one experiment, 19 different constituents of various sizes coincided with the conditioned response.

Speech Errors. Several discussions of speech errors have appeared in recent years (Fromkin, 1971; Garrett, 1975, 1976; MacKay, 1970). Much of the credit for stimulating this new interest must be given to Fromkin. She has been able to show clearly how speech errors can be interpreted as revealing one or another aspect of the structural organization of speech. However, the most elaborate classification of speech errors from a semantic and syntactic point of view appears to be Garrett's, and it is his terminology and examples that I use in this discussion.

1. *Exchange Errors.* As a general hypothesis regarding the source of exchange errors, I am adopting the suggestion of Baars and Motley (1976), that exchanges are the result of competition between alternative forms. Baars and Motley have actually been able to induce exchange errors at both a sound and word level by establishing conflicts between source words through artificial means. They would, for example, explain *both of enough* (see below) as the result of a conflict between simultaneously activated *enough* and *both*.

Garrett (1976) lists the following examples of exchange errors involving words (the classification in terms of sensory-motor content is explained later):

Slips and kids—I've got (enough of both)$_{Entity}$ →
  I've got *both* of *enough*

I broke a (stay in the dinghy)$_{Entity}$ yesterday→
  I broke a *dinghy* in the *stay* yesterday

Although (suicide is a form of murder)$_{Existence}$→
  Although *murder* is a form of *suicide*

I've got to go home and (give my back a hot bath)$_{Action}$→
  give my *bath* a hot *back*

---

[4]A weakness of this study is that in most experiments the subjects themselves, and in another experiment a panel of partially trained undergraduates, determined the boundaries of the phonological phrases. It is quite possible and seems likely that these inexperienced raters would confuse grammatical criteria with phonological criteria, increasing the correlation of the two spuriously.

McGovern favors (busting pushers)*Action*→
McGovern favors *push*ing *bust*ers

I hate working on (two-letter words)*Entity*→
I hate working on two-*word letter*s

It just (started to sound)*Event*→
It just *sound*ed to *start*

Oh that's just a (truck backing out)*Event*→
Oh that's just a *back truck*ing out

Each of these is plausibly the result of competition between the two words involved in the exchange. For example, *enough* and *both* are each quantity words and could be in competition as alternative specifications of this idea. This conflict may have been induced by stress on *both*. A further assumption is that the two words are simultaneously activated. This is possible in these cases because the words are within the same potential processing unit. In the examples above, in fact, the words that are exchanged appear as elements of speech sequences that have the same sensory-motor meaning and could have been programmed as single outputs, and hence they are words that would have a natural basis for being simultaneously activated. (The definitions of sensory-motor content were introduced in Chapter 1 and are discussed further in Chapter 5.)

The scope of the speech programming units evidenced by the word exchange errors cited by Garrett covers a range of degrees of internal complexity. At the simplest level is a single NP, *two-letter words,* and at the most complex are embedded clauses, *stay in the dinghy* and *started to sound.* Nonetheless, these are all interpretable as single programming units based on syntagmata.

2. *Shift Errors.* Garrett describes a second category of errors (with various subdivisions not discussed here), which he calls shift errors. In these errors a bound morpheme is shifted one or more words. For example,

They get weirder every day→ They get weird ever*ier* day
He gets it done→ He get it*s* done
He goes back to→ He go back*s* to

Some of the exchange errors previously cited also involve bound morphemes. In those cases the bound morphemes themselves did not move but were attached to one of the exchanged words. For example,

It just sound*ed* to start

It seems possible that shift errors and the behavior of bound morphemes in exchange errors are related phenomena. If there is a connection, however, we must assume that bound morphemes arise from a process that is separate from the process of controlling the word order (Garrett, 1975). Under this assumption we suppose that bound morphemes are inserted into the speech output by separate devices which are synchronized by the speech program to fire at particular points. In a shift error, the synchronization is less than perfect. For example, if there is a device for introducing tense marking (taking into account temporal reference, etc.) that could be out of phase with the rest of the programming process, there could be an error such as *he go backs to* or *he get its done*. In the reverse case of an exchange error the device again appears to be separately programmed. Thus, *start* and *sound* exchange places but the past-tense inflection is still correctly inserted into the overall syntagma. In principle, there should be "double" errors consisting of an exchange and a shift such as *it just sound to started* or *he back goes to,* but apparently none has been noted. Whether this absence is merely due to a sampling problem or to something deeper is unknown. The hypothesis of separate devices for inserting bound morphemes is not without its own problems. In particular, the basis of the synchronization is obscure. Because shifts can occur onto the ends of words of greater syllabic length (e.g., *weird everier*), mere output duration would not seem to be a good candidate for this basis. Somehow the device "knows" where the ends of words are, and when it is out of synchrony, it is off position in terms of these word units. Yet it does not seem to specify very precisely what the syntactic and semantic properties of the word unit should be (e.g., *get its* shifts tense to a pronoun).

The evidence of speech errors reviewed here points to two conclusions. First, the speech planning process flexibly covers a range of structures. This variety can be understood in terms of syntagmata. Second, the speech program is complex enough to coordinate at least two separate mechanisms that on occasion become out of phase with respect to each other.

Studies of Speech Latency. The logic of the type of study described in this section is the following: By introducing variations of the amount or kind of information to be included in utterances that subjects must produce, one can look for variations in onset latency to see if these information variables are part of the process of readying the speech program or are introduced as the program is running. Information that is part of the readying process will delay speech onset, whereas information that can be introduced into a running program will not have this effect.[5]

---

[5]A critical assumption is that the utterance is the output of just one speech program; this assumption has not been validated with (for example) phonological evidence in either of the studies described below.

Taylor (1969) has found that the "abstractness" of cue words is a major factor in determining the latency with which subjects commence producing sentences that incorporate the cue word (not necessarily in first position). On the other hand, surface depth (Yngve, 1960) did not correlate with this latency. One could consider the possibility, therefore, that relating certain words (critical words in the sense that they must appear in speech) to syntagmata is part of the preparation process, whereas structural decisions corresponding to left or right branching (which determine the depth) are made on-line. "Abstractness" of words should roughly correspond to the level of representation required to incorporate and make use of the words in speech output. A concrete noun, for example *car* or *pen,* can be incorporated and properly used at a representational level of functioning (Piaget, 1954); a more abstract noun, for example *insertion,* can be incorporated and properly used only at a higher level of concrete operations; and still more abstract words, for example *compensation* (in its physical sense), seem to require a coordination of concrete operations. These differences in level of representation induce different degreees of semiotic extension of the sensory-motor syntagmata to the literal meanings of the words. Semiotic extension may therefore be part of the speech preparation process.

Lindsley (1975, 1976) has described several experiments in which the pre-utterance preparation appears to encompass aspects of the verb in NV(N) sequences but not the entire lexicalized verb. Conceivably, the subject selects the meaning of the verb just before he or she begins to produce the initial noun and completes lexicalizing the verb as the utterance of the noun proceeds.

Lindsley's results suggest that the complete lexicalization step corresponds functionally to inserting information into a running articulatory program, as distinguished from specifying the organization of the program in advance in terms of meaning. In Faile's (1972) study mentioned earlier, conditioned hand withdrawals occurred at the onset of the phonological phrases which contained the conditioned stimulus word. To reconcile this observation with Lindsley's findings, we have to assume that the actual conditioned stimulus was the meaning of the word, not necessarily including the lexicalized word itself, and that the lexicalization of this meaning did not necessarily occur until later.

Summary of Speech Production

The foregoing review of speech production research has consistently brought us to the following conclusion (as had our earlier review of speech comprehension research): The unit of speech processing is complex in terms of linguistic levels, flexible in terms of surface scope, and, in many utterances, quite small. From these facts, one can infer that much of the time *speech is produced as it is organized.* The capacity to produce speech as the internal structure of the utterance is being built up is exactly what the models of Fromkin, MacNeilage, and Garrett deny, because for them planning is always at a major constituent level. The syntagma theory, on the other hand, provides a flexible basis for speech planning, and can accommodate units (sensory-motor ideas) which differ in scope, including ones sufficiently small to explain how speech output can occur as the internal structure of the utterance is worked out by the speaker. The remaining chapters of this book present and elaborate a theory of the relationship of speech to thought in which the concept of a syntagma plays a central part.

II THEORY

3 Sign Structures

The purpose of this chapter is to analyze the relationship of speech to thought in terms of the interaction of different varieties of sign (Peirce, 1931–1958). This analysis yields a description of semiotic extension. Semiotic extension refers to the process by which the sensory-motor content of syntagmata makes contact with more abstract non–sensory-motor meanings. This process can be viewed as an interaction of signs. Viewing semiotic extension in terms of signs affords a comprehensive picture of the speech–thought relationship and provides a framework within which a more precise representation of semiotic extension (in terms of graphs) can be developed.

Considered as an interaction of signs, semiotic extension consists of linking indexical signs to iconic or symbolic signs as follows: sensory-motor ideas are the *objects* of indexical signs and are the *sign vehicles* of iconic and symbolic signs. Symbolic signs also can have iconic signs as sign vehicles. Thus, there are two categories (iconic and symbolic) of interlocking signs that parallel the semiotic extension of sensory-motor ideas to different types of sign. This description of semiotic extension as a pattern whereby the object of one type of sign (indexical) is the sign vehicle of other types (iconic, symbolic) emphasizes that semiotic extension is itself a kind of meaning relationship. Bearing in mind the dual role of sensory-motor ideas (they are both signs and schemes for actions), we can say that, due to semiotic extension, there is a meaning relation between abstract content and the organization of speech output within syntagmata, and the form of this meaning relation is analyzed in terms of symbolic, iconic, and indexical signs.

THE THEORY OF SIGNS

According to Peirce,[1] every sign involves three elements that are related to each other as a triad. This triad cannot be reduced to its three separate constituent pairs, for no one of these pairs has in itself the quality of being a sign. Only the three elements taken together make a sign possible. The elements of this irreducible triadic relation are what Peirce calls the sign or representamen (and which I will call the sign vehicle), the interpretant (anything that is the outcome of interpreting the sign), and the object. The sign vehicle is the word, sentence, sundial, diagram, etc., that conveys the meaning of the sign. The interpretant is the result of interpreting the sign vehicle as referring to the object. Peirce writes, "For the proper significate outcome of a sign, I propose the name, the *interpretant* of the sign. The example of the imperative command shows that it need not be of a mental mode of being" (5.473); i.e., it can be a concrete action. Note that an interpretant is not an interpreter. Interpreters have no systematic role to play in this theory of signs. The object is what the sign vehicle is interpreted as referring to. The object can be anything; it is not necessarily a physical object and might be a mental process or a conception.

The mechanism of the sign is that the object–sign vehicle relation is duplicated by the object–interpretant relation. The sign vehicle determines the interpretant to be related to the object in the same way as the sign vehicle is related to the object.

A sign vehicle is "...[a]nything that determines something else (its *interpretant*) to refer to an object to which itself refers (its *object*) in the same way, the interpretant becoming in turn a sign. . ." (2.303).

"A sign is only a sign *in actu* by virtue of its receiving an interpretation, that is, by virtue of its determining another sign of the same object" (5.569).

"A *sign* is a representamen of which some interpretant is a cognition of a mind" (2.242).

For example, if the sign vehicle is iconic, that is, if the sign vehicle resembles the object in some respect, then the interpretant of this sign vehicle, which is the interpretive response, itself resembles the object. For instance, a diagram refers iconically to its object by arousing a mental representation (an interpretant) that also resembles the object. If the following diagram represents a road from A to B,

$$A \rightarrow B$$

---

[1] The parenthetical references that follow are to the collected works of Peirce (1931–1958). These are given in the form of decimal numbers. The number to the left of the decimal designates the volume and the numbers to the right the paragraph. Thus 2.280 refers to paragraph 280 of volume 2.

the interpretant (an image, perhaps) also represents the road from A to B in the same way, by resemblance. For example, the interpretant might be a conception of spatial orientation that has a certain extent, a beginning, and an end—i.e., a conception that results in another iconic sign for the road.

Peirce's theory, then, is that the sign vehicle creates or causes the interpretant to stand in the same relation to the object as the sign vehicle itself does. This relationship may be iconic, indexical, or symbolic, depending on the sign relationships in question.

An important caveat is that signs are often said to perform a certain function with respect to an external and socially shared reference field. For example, a pointing finger may function as an index of an external event for an interlocutor in the same situation. The internal signs resolved here in speech production are functional in exactly the same sense, but there is no external reference field. The field is entirely internal, consisting of mental and other processes. The shift of emphasis does not seem to disturb the logical structure of Peirce's theory, so even sign vehicles will be conceived of as being internal. An utterance, even viewed as a sign vehicle, is not open to direct observation except for those signs reflected at the most external acoustic or myographic levels (from which follows an ocean of methodological grief for psycholinguists). In fact, the only truly external signs in the speech formation process as discussed in the present context are these final acoustic and muscular effects of the speech programs. Otherwise the interlocking signs are always internal.

The triadic relationship of object, sign vehicle, and interpretant can be represented as follows:[2]

Index: O → S ——— I   a significate outcome is
                                             produced in the interpreter's
            real connection   mind by "noticing" the object

Icon: O → S ——— I   a significate outcome is
                                             produced in the interpreter's
            resemblance   mind by forming a relationship that resembles the object

Symbol: O → S ——— I   a significate outcome is
                                             produced in the interpreter's
            rule   mind by forming a structure that refers to the object

---

[2]I am indebted to C. Schmidt for this notation.

In these diagrams the interpretant is related to the object in the same way as the sign vehicle is. For instance, in reading a diagram of a road, the interpretant, as a significant outcome, might be a mental representation of the road, an outcome that is related to the road in the same way as the diagram is.

Peirce casts the discussion of signs in the context of a general epistemological theory in which knowledge is gained through sign interpretations. The glosses above reflect this in speaking of forming a significate outcome in the mind of an interpreter. This function of the sign in the acquisition of knowledge introduces an asymmetry wherein the recognition of signs is favored over the construction or emission of signs. This asymmetry, however, presupposes a corresponding analysis of sign construction. It is logically anomalous to say that one produces a sign by interpreting it. Once a sign is produced it can lead to an interpretant, and in the speech production process there are both a producing and an interpreting of interlocking signs. But producing any one sign cannot sensibly involve its own interpretant. Because the interpretant reproduces the relation between the object and the sign vehicle in intepreting a sign, it is required that in producing this sign there is something that is also capable of accomplishing exactly the same thing as a construction. Let us say that this element (to maintain the Peircian flavor) produces a significate input, which I will call the productant. Like the interpretant, the productant is not to be confused with the producer of the sign. The producer (an individual) relies on both interpretants and productants in constructing utterances. The productant as an input introduces exactly the same relation between the object and the sign vehicle that the interpretant duplicates as an outcome. The mechanism of producing a sign according to this theory is also triadic. There cannot be merely a single link of the object to the sign vehicle (as this would lack the quality of a sign) but a triadic one that includes the productant. This productant then differs according to the type of sign involved.

Thus, we can match the foregoing diagrams with the following, which show the relationships of sign vehicle, productant, and object involved in sign construction:

Index: P ——— O → S   a significate input is produced in the producer's mind by attending to the object

                  real connection

Icon: P ——— O → S   a significate input is produced in the producer's mind by forming a relationship that resembles the object

                  resemblance

Symbol: P ——— O → S   a significate input is
                          produced in the producer's
       rule   mind by forming a structure
                          that refers to the object

The productant and interpretant are related, because the interpretant is a reproduction of the sign vehicle–object relation, which (in the case of a sign that is produced) is the result of an input, the productant. Hence the full sign structure should be represented as:

P ——— O → S ——— I

As with the interpretant, the productant also is a sign of the object. It differs from the interpretant only in being involved in a position logically (not necessarily temporally) anterior instead of posterior to the sign vehicle. For example, in producing an indexical sign, "noticing" or attending to the object causes a productant which is the input for emitting the sign vehicle, e.g., attending to moving the fist against a door is the productant for producing the sign vehicle of a rapping sound. The productant is not supposed to be temporally prior to the sign vehicle in any of the speech situations discussed in the following paragraphs.

In the case of speech, the productant of an indexical sign is the process of activating and coordinating the speech output. It could be a set of neural commands based on a sensory-motor idea (the object) that leads into a hierarchy of processes and to eventual speech coordination. With an iconic sign, the speaker assigns temporal valence to two or more interrelated concepts. This process of assignment is the productant, which is the input for the iconic sign vehicle. The latter, in the case of an iconic sign, includes a temporally ordered sequence of concepts. With a symbolic sign, the productant is a set of procedures which constructs the sign vehicle, including both indexical and iconic elements. These types of sign interlock, and all three are involved in the production of particular utterances.[3]

If the productant and interpretant are merged (overlooking the distinction between production and interpretation of signs), the foregoing diagrams become the familiar meaning triangle:

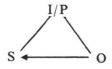

---

[3] I am indebted to J. Galambos for raising these issues.

Iconic Signs

An iconic sign vehicle "...is a sign [vehicle] which refers to the Object that it denotes merely by virtue of characters of its own, and which it possesses, just the same, whether any such Object actually exists or not. It is true that unless there really is such an Object, the Icon does not act as a sign; but this has nothing to do with its character as a sign. Anything whatever... is an Icon of anything, in so far as it is like that thing and used as a sign for it" (2.247).

Examples of iconic sign vehicles are images in paintings, maps, diagrams, metaphors, the bracketing of algebraic formulas, and many word-order sequences of speech. The latter are icons in which likeness is aided by the application of rules. The iconic aspects of speech have been vastly underestimated in previous linguistic and psycholinguistic discussions, presumably because the question had been considered in terms of sensory images, such as sound symbolism and onomatopoeia (Werner & Kaplan, 1963). However, iconic signs of a non-sensory kind play a major part in many or all utterances. These signs can be compared to diagrams, and it is on the diagrammatic aspects of speech that many word order sequences depend. Peirce (2.280) describes sentences as logical icons supplemented by conventional means: "...[I]n the syntax of every language there are logical icons of the kind that are aided by conventional rules." Other logical icons are, for example, mathematical formulae: "...an algebraic formula is an icon, rendered such by the rules of commutation, association, and distribution of the symbols" (2.279).

Word sequences can be regarded as iconic diagrams of oriented logical relations. The significance of the term "oriented" is discussed in the next section. As diagrams, word-order sequences function like other iconic signs. They refer to their objects by virtue of a resemblance. The arrangement or sequence of words resembles the arrangement or orientation of related concepts, and the temporal word sequence can therefore be regarded as diagrammatic. Peirce wrote that "Many diagrams resemble their objects not at all in looks; it is only in respect to the relations of their parts that their likeness consists" (2.282). Oriented pairs of related concepts are what we should call the objects of these temporally ordered concepts. The temporally ordered sequence is the sign vehicle. (This is not quite the full sign vehicle, as it is necessary to add the sensory-motor content on which the process of contraction depends. The full sign vehicle is a sensory-motor idea specified for this temporally ordered sequence. Cf. the discussion in Chapters 1 and 6.) The productant of an iconic sign vehicle consists of a rule whereby one orientation is given one temporal valence and the opposite orientation is given the other (often with the aid of a symbolic device). Such rules differ between languages. Therefore, as Peirce recognized, a convention is involved in these icons. An example of an oriented logical relation of English is "A *patients* B." This is the Object of an iconic sign vehicle, e.g., the conceptual structure underlying a verb phrase, "A the B." The sign vehicle is produced by the productant, causing the oriented relation to have a temporal valence, such that concept A precedes B. The opposite orientation of the same logical relation is "B *is-patiented-by* A." This is the object of another sign vehicle, e.g., the conceptual structure underlying "B is Aed," which is produced by giving to the oriented relation a temporal valence that is opposite from the first valence.

At an abstract level, the above explanation of concept sequences interlocked with indexical signs based on sensory-motor schemes clarifies the problem of serial order in speech (Lashley, 1951). That is, it points to one possible solution. The temporal order is first determined iconically, and this then becomes a parameter of the speech program that denotes the temporally specified sensory-motor scheme. The speaker determines word order from the orientation of the relations between concept. This process is discussed further in various places in this book.

In terms of the notation given previously, iconic sequences of concepts can be represented as follows:

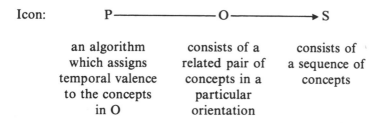

Icon: P————————————O————————▶ S

an algorithm which assigns temporal valence to the concepts in O	consists of a related pair of concepts in a particular orientation	consists of a sequence of concepts

Orientation.   To understand and evaluate the claims made regarding the iconic aspects of speech, it is necessary to understand the concept of orientation. The following explanation is of necessity rather lengthy, and this may seem to emphasize iconic signs over indexical and symbolic signs. To do so, however, would be a mistake. As noted before, all types of sign are involved in every utterance. No single type is more important than the others.

The concept of orientation applies to logical relations and refers to whether the referent or the relatum of the relation is the point of focus (Reichenbach, 1947). Either the referent or the relatum may receive focus. The referent of a logical relation is the starting point, so to speak, of the relation. The relatum is the terminal point. If the relation is *is-father-of* (father, child), the referent is the father and the relatum is a child. If the relation is *is-child-of* (child, parent), the referent is a child and the relatum is a parent. (Therefore, these relations are not converses.) In general, for any two-place relation, f(x, y), the first argument (x) is the referent and the second argument (y) is the relatum. In the case of the direct object there are two possible relations based on the same objective situation: *patients*(A, B) and *is-patiented-by*(B, A).

Knowing the referent and relatum of a logical relation is basic to defining the orientation of the relation. This orientation is called *operative* if the focus is on the referent. It is *receptive* if the focus is on the relatum. These terms therefore refer to whether the focus is the source of the relation (operative) or the recipient of the relation (receptive). In English speech and that of many other languages, focus correlates with temporal order, as first elements tend to be focal (Halliday, 1967a). Thus orientation interacts strongly with the temporal order of utterances in these languages. The orientation tends to be operative when the speech order is referent-relatum, and receptive when it is relatum-referent. In principle, other focusing devices also can induce different orientations of logical relations. For example, a cursor does so:

patients(A, B)   *patients*(A, B)
       | |
(operative)   (receptive)

The logical relation is not different between these examples, but the point of focus, and hence the orientation, is different. One might naturally express the second example in the form of a passive, "B is patiented by A," which is the second alternative version of the relation mentioned at the end of the previous paragraph. I will say that *patients* (A, B) is operative and *is-patiented-by*(B,A) is receptive. I now have to motivate this nomenclature.

It is necessary to decide which of two converse logical relations underlying speech shall be the *basic form*. Once this is decided, the question of orientation will be settled. The basic form of two converse relations designates one of the arguments as the referent and the other as the relatum, even though the converse relation is also true. The rule followed makes use of the fact that iconic and symbolic signs interact. The basic form of a logical relation will be said to be that form which corresponds to utterances that do not employ orientation-changing syntactic devices. The term "corresponds to" in this context means that the name of the relation (*patients* or *is-patiented-by*) expresses the meaning of the relation in the utterance. An example of an orientation-changing syntactic device is the passive; there are others with the same effect. For example, the following will be said to be the basic form of a direct object relation:

patients(Writing, Letter)

This form of the relation corresponds to *writes the letter*. Because this phrase does not employ an orientation-changing syntactic device, this version of the logical relation is basic. On the other hand, the passive, *the letter is written,* involves an orientation-changing syntactic device, and the version of the logical relation to which it corresponds is therefore not basic. A nominalization, *the letter's writing,* has a similar effect. The important point is that the basic form is able to correspond to some utterance without the use of any orientation-changing syntactic devices, whereas the nonbasic form is able to do so only with the use of some such device. The basic form, of course, also can appear with a syntactic device, as in *the writing of the letter*.

Given the basic form, it is then automatic to determine the orientation. When the focus is on the referent of the basic form, the orientation is operative; when the focus is on the relatum of this form, it is receptive. The version of the direct object relation in *patients*(A, B) is therefore operative, and the version in *is-patiented-by*(B,A) is receptive. Thus, *writes the letter* and *the writing of the letter* [= (Writing) *patients* (Letter)] are operative, and *the letter is written* and *the letter's writing* [= (Letter) *is-patiented-by* (Writing)] are receptive.

Using the same standard for designating the basic form of logical relations, Table 3.1 lists several examples in both their operative and receptive orientations. We can take fragments from this table and work out the orientation of relations within simple sentences. For example,

1. Albert writes the letter
2. Albert talks while writing the letter
3. Writing the letter takes all afternoon

Example (1) is the combination of two operative orientations, and Example (2) is the combination of three, one of which, (Albert) *performs* (Writing), is discontinuous at the surface. Example (3) presents a receptive relation between *writing the letter* and *all afternoon*. The argument for this classification refers to the impossibility of passivizing (3)—*all afternoon is taken by writing the letter*. The application of an orientation-changing device is blocked with the relation underlying (3), which could be explained if this relation is *is-duration*(A, B) and thus (3) is receptive to begin with. (This argument assumes that the passive device is incompatible with operative orientations; that this may be the case is discussed in Chapter 7.)

From the point of view of programming speech output, the theory so far comes to this: The speaker is constantly choosing which of two related concepts is focal; this choice determines the orientation and therefore the object of an iconic sign. When this object is connected to a suitable sensory-motor idea, an iconic sign vehicle is created that can become the object of an indexical sign. This can activate a speech program that will have a temporal order of concepts based ultimately on differences in focus between logically related ideas. (Although this description sounds like there should be a temporal sequence of sign types as well as of concepts—iconic preceding indexical—this is merely a convenience of exposition; in fact, since the analysis of signs takes place within a syntagma, it is natural to suppose that all three types of sign coexist in time.)

TABLE 3.1

Derivation of Orientation

Relation (Referent, Relatum)	Operative	Receptive
performs (Albert, Writing)	(Albert) performs (Writing)	(Writing) is-performed-by (Albert)
performs (Albert, Talking)	(Albert) performs (Talking)	(Talking) is-performed-by (Albert)
patients (Writing, Letter)	(Writing) patients (Letter)	(Letter) is-patiented-by (Writing)
is-duration (Time, Event)	(Time) is-duration (Event)	(Event) takes-duration (Time)

48

Indexical Signs

An indexical sign vehicle ". . . is a sign [vehicle] which refers to the Object that it denotes by virtue of being really affected by that Object" (2.248). "In so far as the Index is affected by the Object, it necessarily has some quality in common with the Object, and it is in respect to these [sic] that it refers to the Object. It does, therefore, involve a sort of Icon, although an Icon of a peculiar kind; and it is not the mere resemblance of its Object, even in these respects which makes it a sign, but it is the actual modification of it by the Object" (2.248). For example, the sound of a rapping on a door is an indexical sign of someone knocking. There is "a quality in common" between the blows of this someone and the sound of the rapping, but the character of the sign as an index does not depend on this resemblance. In the same sense there is "a quality in common" between a sensory-motor scheme which functions as the object of an indexical sign vehicle and the articulatory programs it coordinates (for example, the order of words) but the indexical relationship lies in the real connection (ecphoria) of the articulatory programs to the sensory-motor scheme.

The characteristics of an index (listed in 2.306) are the following:

1. There is no significant resemblance to the object (although Peirce presumably means to allow "qualities in common" such as those described in the preceding paragraph).

2. Reference is to an individual existing object. For example, a rap on the door indicates a concrete single incident of a blow falling on the door. An integrated speech program similarly indicates an individual activated sensory-motor scheme.

3. The sign vehicle refers to the object by "blind compulsion." A pointing finger indicates what it is pointing at, for example, by "blind compulsion" of attention onto the object. The relation between the organization of speech output and a sensory-motor concept is likewise one of "blind compulsion," in which producing and activating the sensory-motor scheme of an utterance leads to a productant and to the programming of the utterance. This is a correct analysis given our argument that there is a real connection between the coordination of speech action and the sensory-motor scheme; that is, the speech program includes the sensory-motor content which initiates and controls the output.

Examples of indexes are a symptom of a disease, damage as a sign of some destructive agent, the deictic pronouns (*I, you, this, that,* etc.), and other signs actually connected with their objects in some way.

The deictic pronouns are connected to their objects in that they force attention onto the object; the connection in this case arises because the deictic pronoun is part of the act of referring. The connection is apparently not causal. The connections in the case of sensory-motor concepts and speech programs are more correctly called causal. The deictic words of language have become the prototypical examples of indexes for many linguists and psycholinguists, although they are only one type, and not necessarily the most representative type, of index.

A sensory-motor idea can "cause" the integration of speech output in one sense of causation, because the sensory-motor idea is part of the speech program itself. The sign vehicle is in part composed of the object. Through the process called ecphoria, activating the sensory-motor idea triggers the rest of the program. The situation is reversed for the deictic pronouns: the sign vehicle (the pronoun) is the part, and the object (the act of referring) is the whole.

The view of deictic pronouns and other so-called shifters assumed in this discussion is related to that proposed in Silverstein (1976): "So we must distinguish between semantically-constituted symbols, the abstract propositional values of which are implemented in actual referential events, and the shifters, or referential indexes, the propositional values of which are linked to the unfolding of the speech event itself [p. 25]." I take this statement to be consistent with the view that the shifter or deictic pronoun is a sign of the speech act of referring itself, and the occurrence of the deictic pronoun is part of this act. So if we say *I,* this utterance is part of the act of speaker reference, and insofar as there is a referential value of the *I* it is *this act.* This speech act, in turn, refers to the individual speaker, but that is an analytically separate step. It is incorrect, in this view, to say that *I* refers directly to the speaker, since what is referred to directly is a speech act of self reference. One might argue instead that the deictic pronoun is caused by the speech act of referring, but this would be a quite different view, in which the deictic pronoun is a kind of symptom of the act of referring, and still the pronoun would not refer to the speaker directly. It is worthwhile to examine these classifications in more detail.

One can distinguish at least four varieties of indexes, three involving causation and one the relation of parts to wholes, as in Table 3.2. The use of the word "cause" in this table is best interpreted as having the meaning of "power to bring about."

The terms "abstraction," "reaction," and "composition" need not be defended to the bitter end. However, the pattern of statements in the table is important, for it defines the different categories. Note that both the presence or absence of causation and the relevance and direction of the part-whole relationship must be taken into account in each of these categories. Causation by abstraction refers to a situation where the effect is abstracted from the cause, such as a symptom of a disease or the rapping sound that results from knocking. (It is not knocking unless there is a rapping sound; it is not jaundice

TABLE 3.2
Varieties of Indexical Sign Relationships

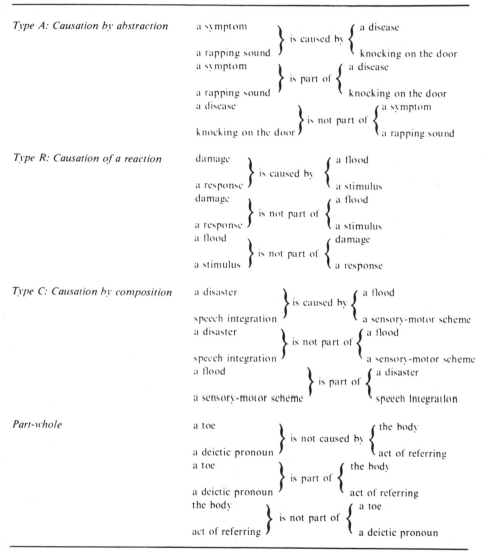

Type A: Causation by abstraction

- a symptom } is caused by { a disease
- a rapping sound } { knocking on the door
- a symptom } is part of { a disease
- a rapping sound } { knocking on the door
- a disease } is not part of { a symptom
- knocking on the door } { a rapping sound

Type R: Causation of a reaction

- damage } is caused by { a flood
- a response } { a stimulus
- damage } is not part of { a flood
- a response } { a stimulus
- a flood } is not part of { damage
- a stimulus } { a response

Type C: Causation by composition

- a disaster } is caused by { a flood
- speech integration } { a sensory-motor scheme
- a disaster } is not part of { a flood
- speech integration } { a sensory-motor scheme
- a flood } is part of { a disaster
- a sensory-motor scheme } { speech integration

Part-whole

- a toe } is not caused by { the body
- a deictic pronoun } { act of referring
- a toe } is part of { the body
- a deictic pronoun } { act of referring
- the body } is not part of { a toe
- act of referring } { a deictic pronoun

51

unless there is a yellowish tint of the skin.[4]) The relationship of a sensory-motor scheme (activated) to a speech program (operating) is compositional, like that of a flood (unleashed) to a disaster (suffered). It is not abstractive, like that of a rapping sound to knocking; reactive, like that of a response to a stimulus; or whole to part, like that of the act of referring to a deictic pronoun. By "compositional" I mean that the cause (activating a sensory-motor scheme) is part of (helps compose) the effect (running the speech program). This differs from abstractive causation in that the part-whole relationship is reversed; from reactive causation in that there is a part-whole relationship of any kind; and from the part-whole relationship in that there is a causative relationship. Activating the part can trigger the whole in compositional causation.

A well-known example of the compositional variety of causation appears in the James-Lange theory of emotional reaction (cf. James, 1890). According to this theory, an emotional reaction, such as fear, is caused by the performance of some component of the reaction, e.g., by trembling or running away. Doubtless there are other examples of compositional causation. It may be that this variety is well represented in psychological causes and effects. All of these categories of causation, as well as the part-whole relationship, are nonetheless capable of becoming interpreted as indexical signs. But it is the triggering relation (ecphoria) that is relevant in the case of speech output, and this form of causation is compositional in the above classification.

In terms of the notation used previously, indexical signs can be represented as follows:

Index:

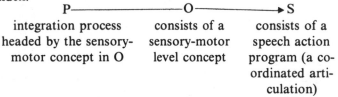

P	O	S
integration process headed by the sensory-motor concept in O	consists of a sensory-motor level concept	consists of a speech action program (a co-ordinated articulation)

Symbolic Signs

A symbolic sign vehicle "...is a sign [vehicle] which refers to the Object that it denotes by virtue of a law, usually an association of general ideas, which operates to cause the Symbol to be interpreted as referring to that Object"

---

[4]The disease example does not work out properly if too much modern technology is allowed. For example, it seems wrong to say that an abnormal X-ray picture is part of a disease, although it is (in some sense) caused by the disease and is a symptom of it.

(2.249). A symbol depends crucially on the interpretant (and productant). Symbols are signs "...by virtue of being represented to be signs" (8.119). " A symbol is a sign which would lose the character which renders it a sign if there were not interpretant. Such is any utterance of speech which signifies what it does only by virtue of its being understood to have that signification" (2.304). Examples of symbols are words and sentences, although both also have indexical and iconic aspects.

Various parallels support the identification of syntactic devices as a type of symbolic sign. The manufactured sign vehicle denotes its object "by virtue of a law," that is, a rule or convention. It is a sign "by virtue of being represented to be [a] sign," and depends crucially on an interpretant/productant (namely, the procedure) for its character as a sign. Peirce clearly intended a wide range of signs as symbolic. However, the term "symbolic sign" will be used in the specialized sense as referring to syntactic devices.

The objects of symbolic signs in this sense are conceptual structures or parts thereof. These conceptual structures may be simple or complex and may include other concepts and interrelations. The sign vehicle is also a conceptual structure manufactured by the syntactic device, but it can include morphological features as well, when these are generated by the device. The interpretant/productant is the device itself. An aspect of meaning can be symbolized by the structure (the sign vehicle) created by the syntactic device. For example, a receptive orientation of the *patients* relation can be symbolized by the passive. Other symbolic signs can represent the same meaning relation. For example, one form of nominalization also represents focus on the relatum of the *patients* relation (*the army's training,* etc.). But since symbolic syntactic devices are conventions which must function as a whole, typically each one conveys more than a single item of information. The passive, for example, introduces a concept of an Event or State that, through interlocking with other sign modes, becomes part of the overall conceptual structure of the utterance. A nominalization introduces a concept of an Entity in a similar way. A speaker thus has a range of choices for the object of the symbolic sign when using many syntactic devices.

Using the notation employed earlier, a symbolic sign can be displayed as follows:

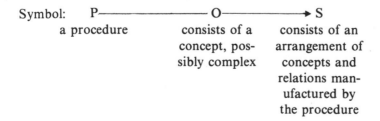

Symbol: P———————— O————————→ S
    a procedure   consists of a   consists of an
                   concept, pos-   arrangement of
                   sibly complex   concepts and
                                    relations man-
                                    ufactured by
                                    the procedure

SUMMARY

Factoring the relationship of speech to thought into its components, we isolate indexical, iconic, and symbolic aspects. The meanings of utterances are expressed through all of these sign modes at once. Such signs are to be regarded as internal. Semiotic extension is also a meaning relation, in which sensory-motor representations stand for other meanings while they are themselves represented by speech programs. The sensory-motor representation is the object of an indexical sign and is the sign vehicle of an iconic or symbolic sign. The connection between abstract meaning and organized speech output therefore runs through the sensory-motor level as an essential link. Detailed analyses of each type of sign show that (1) the indexical signs involved in speech production rest upon a type of causal connection between sensory-motor schemata and motor-control hierarchies; (2) iconic signs relate word-order sequences to oriented logical relations; and (3) symbolic signs are constructed by devices which relate meanings to conceptual structures according to conventional rules.

4 Basis of Syntagmata

It is possible to analyze the basis of syntagmata further, and this will be done using two approaches. The first considers syntagmata from the point of view of the control processes involved in speech output. The second considers them from that of sign relations, building on the results of the preceding chapter.

SYNTAGMATA FROM THE POINT OF VIEW OF SPEECH OUTPUT CONTROL

Sense Indications and Sense Units

Kozhevnikov and Chistovich (1965) develop the following argument on the basis of the work of Yngve (1960). They consider a theoretical device for producing speech which follows rules of the following kind:

1. $A = B$
2. $A = B + C$
3. $A = B + C + D$
4. $B = M + N$
5. $N = X$

In the generation of any sentence, only one expansion of a given symbol on the left, such as A, is permitted to occur. There must be some basis for selection, therefore, when the same symbol appears on the left of more than one rule. Kozhevnikov and Chistovich propose that this basis is a *sense indication*. That is, it is an element of meaning that corresponds to one expansion of a symbol on the left. They next define *a sense unit*. This is a set of sense indications where all of the sense indications are mutually compatible and thus can be given simultaneously. Examples of compatible sense indications, hence of sense units, are (4), (5), and any one of (1–3); examples of incompatible sense indications, hence not of sense units, are any combination of (1–3). The effect of such a "machine," where the possible expansions of symbols are selected on the basis of sense indications and those that are compatible are all expanded at once, would be to introduce cycles of operation corresponding to the sense units. Kozhevnikov and Chistovich (1965) connect these cycles with units of articulation planning in the following passage:

> These conclusions are very important to us since they make it possible to assume that the grouping of output symbols of an automatic machine synthesizing sentences which is necessary for the construction of an articulatory program does not require any additional mechanism. This grouping should already be at the output of the automatic machine itself, thanks to the presence of sense cycles in its operation. If this assumption is correct, then one articulatory program should correspond to one sense unit [p. 74].

A syntagma refers to this correspondence of an articulatory program with a sense unit: "[I]t is natural to assume that [a syntagma] is both a sense unit and simultaneously an articulatory unit" (Kozhevnikov & Chistovich, 1965, p. 74).

It is now necessary to relate this view to the theory of semiotic extension. This can be done with the hypothesis that one sense indication corresponds to one sensory-motor scheme plus those ideas that the sensory-motor scheme encompasses via semiotic extension. It is the latter ideas that differentiate alternate expansions of the same symbol (corresponding to A = B, A = B + C, etc.). Following this line of thought, different semiotic extensions of the same sensory-motor scheme should not appear within a single speech program (sense unit), as this would lead to incompatabilities. A speech program could, according to this hypothesis, consist of:

Entity
Entity + Action
Action + Entity
Action + Location
Event + Location

but not of different semiotic extensions of:

Entity + Entity
Entity + Action + Action
Event + Event.

There is some support for this hypothesis in the grammatical organization of complex sentences, for example of complements, which appear to be devices for interrelating events; e.g., *I forced him to march.* The structure of the complement is thought to be such that a sentence is embedded in an NP (Rosenbaum, 1967, preface). This structure has the following effect: If a speaker produces an utterance consisting of a main clause and its complement clause as a whole, he or she would not be sending sense indications corresponding to Event + Event in a single production, but ones corresponding to Event + Entity. The existence of NP properties in the complement clause, therefore, may reflect the Kozhevnikov and Chistovich performance constraint that there cannot be repetitions of different semiotic extensions of the same sense unit within a single speech program. The NP makes possible the production of the two clauses as one output. A similar argument can be extended to restrictive relative clauses, which also interrelate events and do so by making the embedded clause into an NP (see Chapter 12).

Motor Control Hierarchies

A sense unit, or syntagma, organizes a sequence of articulations. A model by which this may be done will now be developed. On the basis of evidence in Kozhevnikov and Chistovich (1965), we will assume that the elements that the syntagma organizes are syllables. However, the model that follows could be reformulated for other elementary units without jeopardizing its basic structure.

The point of view of this model first appeared in the 1935 writings of Bernstein (1967), who was concerned with the co-ordination of movements. It has since been adopted by P. Greene (1973) in his theory of action control in complex automatic systems (computer networks, robots, etc.). Some quotations from Bernstein will present this point of view:

> [T]here exist in the central nervous system exact formulae of movement... or their engrams, and... these formulae or engrams contain in some form of brain trace the whole process of the movement in its entire course in time [p. 37].

> If a guiding engram of this type exists (we may refer to it as the motor image of a movement) it must have a dual nature; it must contain within itself... the entire scheme of the movement as it is expanded in time. It must also guarantee the order and the rhythm of the realization of this scheme [p. 39].

> This motor image corresponds to the real, factual form of the movement, that is, to the curve B... and in no way to the curve of the impulse [p. 40, italics omitted].

The last remark refers to a theoretical graph (Bernstein, 1967, p. 20, Fig. 14) in which the time course of a movement B is shown to be the composite of two factors: (a) forces acting on the movement from the exterior, and (b) the activation level C from the central nervous system. The motor image, therefore, corresponds to the intended final action, rather than to the neural means of achieving this action (which will vary with the external field of forces).

P. Greene (1973) describes action control in terms of hierarchies of processes in which each higher-level process manages (that is, monitors, directs, supplies information to, and initiates and terminates activity in) a small number of lower-level processes. The number of degrees of freedom controlled by each higher-level process is relatively small, and its domain of effect is limited to the level just below it. The depth of the hierarchy, however, can be quite extended, so that a very complex action can be controlled through a hierarchy of processes, no one process of which controls more than a few degrees of freedom. The highest-level processes have no direct contact with the lowest levels of the effectors. Rather, the highest levels specify the behavior of other high-level processes, which in turn control lower levels. The highest levels can be equated with Bernstein's "motor images of the movement." Turvey (1975) has coined the term "concept of the action" which can be referred to this same level; Lashley's (1951) "organizational scheme" and Kozhevnikov and Chistovich's (1965) "syntagma" can also be referred to this level. All of these expressions convey the notion of a scheme or plan of action. The upper level(s) of the hierarchy of control processes are naturally regarded as this scheme or plan. From the point of view of the uppermost level of control, most of the action output is the result of automatic lower-level processes that the executive sets in motion and instructs, in global fashion, but cannot directly control.

Among the aspects of performance that the plan of the action must specify are the following, according to P. Greene (1973):

1. *The purpose of the action.*   "Systems having many degrees of freedom should be guided and regulated by controllers to which commands are given in purpose-oriented form [p. 431; cf. Bernstein's curve B, above]." The executive controller is aware of only the intended final form of an action. Its commands to the rest of the action system are formulated in terms of such goals. For example, a command representable as "jump!" should be sufficient for initiating the programming of an action sequence that will result in a number of coordinated postural changes, propulsion with the legs, preparation for alighting, etc. In the case of speech, the purpose of the action is to express such and such a meaning or to achieve such and such an effect. The initial commands to the speech apparatus should be given in terms related to this purpose. The final chapter of the book contains a discussion of the relationship between speech processes and speech use.

2. *Feedforward.*   These are adjustments of a present state that are based on information from earlier states. "Even a crude estimate of a control signal

can eliminate so much of the output error that the remaining compensation is likely to be within the powers of a feedback system that is much simpler than would be required in the absence of feedforward" (P. Greene, 1973, pp. 432–3). The distinction between feedback and feedforward refers to whether the information on which control is based is derived before or after the initiation of the action being controlled. In feedback this information is derived after initiation of the action; it is output-based, as in the familiar example of a thermostat–furnace–heating system, and supplies correction of further output. In feedforward, the control information is derived before the action is initiated; it is input-based and defines the broad limits within which the action will take place. An example is provided by the regulation of arm movements. Feedforward specifies the destination of the arm movement, the orientation of the arm and hand with respect to the rest of the body, the destination, and any other factors associated with the goal of the action. Feedback then takes care of the precise execution of this movement by converging onto a point within the broad region defined through feedforward.

In the case of speech, feedforward appears to be involved in determining the articulatory sources of stress, the intonation contour, the terminal juncture, and other properties of the output which are captured in a suprasegmental description (Halliday, 1967a; Lehiste, 1970). With all of these properties of the speech output, the information can be specified, within broad limits, in advance through feedforward.

The lower-level control process must be able to carry out further steps, given information from the higher control levels. In particular, three further processes can be mentioned: detection, tuning, and changes of length of output.

3. *Detection.*   The lower-level process must contain sensors, or detectors, that are capable of monitoring deviations from the conditions assumed by the higher-level processes. These sensors generate signals which are input to further corrective mechanisms, two categories of which are discussed later. An example of a sensor of this type would be the proprioceptive feedback receptors that enable the muscles that are controlled during the execution of a movement to produce a response. In the case of speech, articulatory gestures generate proprioceptive signals that are available to the control process through feedback loops (Ohala, 1970). Presumably there are also detectors (sensor may be the wrong word) for such properties of the speech program as length and rhythmic structure. The importance of these (purely hypothetical) detectors will be seen later.

4. *Tuning.*   The information from the higher-level controllers, which is the information fed forward, must be "tuned" or adjusted to the specific conditions of the movement, for these conditions vary from performance to

performance. For example, depending on the initial posture of the body, the position of the limbs, the relative location of the intended landing place, and a host of other factors, the numerous autonomous mechanisms activated by the command "jump!" must be given more exact values than can be supplied at the highest control levels.

In speech, there are many examples of tuning. The specific syllabic position of the stress points, the placement of the intonation contour across syllable positions, and many other details of the speech output can be regarded in this way as the result of tuning.

A rather different process that also can be regarded as a form of tuning is lexical insertion. Notice that this tuning process refers only to the insertion of lexical items into the speech stream. The semantic choice of lexical items (retrieval) is not a tuning in this sense. The articulation of individual words clearly is integrated into the whole syntagma, as many phenomena show. The formation of enclitics and vowel and consonant reductions depending on stress, in particular, show this integration. Viewed as a form of tuning, lexical insertion adjusts the running of the speech program, so that it performs a specific ordered sequence of articulatory gestures. For example, the word *intonation,* when retrieved, directs the speech program to produce a specific sequence of articulatory gestures, i.e., moving the blade of the tongue forward to contact, then back, etc. This tuning is always part of a larger running program, a nontrivial fact when more than one word is involved. The concept of tuning seems to be appropriate for the process of lexical insertion, because the composition of the lexical item tells the processor how to modulate its operations.

5. *Changes of length.* The lower-level control processes must have the capability of following instructions to extend or contract the basic motor image of the movement, while keeping this image topologically intact. Adjustment for length also is a kind of tuning but more qualitative in its effect. Thus the control equivalent of "extend the arms slightly farther than usual" should be a directive that can be interpreted at the lower levels of the control hierarchy for arm movements.

In the case of speech, variations in the length of the output arising from syntagmata have to be taken into account in determining stress and intonation contours, among other things. This adjustment could be given as a gross instruction, for example, to extend the part of the intonation contour before the position of the tonic stress as a flat line; then further adjustments could be introduced into this flat line if conditions warrant.

Model for a Syntagma

An event is defined as a change of state, or as a stasis, through an interval of time (von Wright, 1963). One sensory-motor action scheme that corresponds to this abstract formulation is that of a causative Event. If an agent P causes a change of state in an Entity E by performing an Action A, we can speak of this as one kind of an Event. The model that follows assumes this type of an Event.

Is important to be clear regarding the implications of this definition of an Event for our assumptions concerning the form of the syntagma. Syntagmata are said to arise from a fusion of sensory-motor action schemes with hierarchical control processes for movements of the articulators. The motor image of the articulatory movements corresponding to an Event syntagma, therefore, should contain the same parts as the action scheme for a causative Event. We cannot say a priori what these parts are. However, for the sake of an example, let us assume that something in the articulation corresponds to each of the parts P, E, and A. Also there should be a relationship among these parts (e.g., contiguity). The motor image will contain three contiguous elements.

A further assumption in this example is that when less than the full transitive Event scheme is represented, the reduction should be achieved by letting P = E, and the parts that remain should be the change in this (P = E), and the A the part to which this change is due. The syntagma below is based on this latter, shortened (intransitive) version of the full Event scheme, and thus contains only two elements (see Chapter 6 for further discussion). Numbered notes on this syntagma follow.

Label	Event
1. Scheme:	[person changes]
2. Semiotic extension:	[(Jack) *performs* (Sitting)]
3. Morphological device:	[+ s]
4. Feedforward stress:	[ ]
5. Feedforward contour:	[────────────────↓]
6. Tuning with lexical items:	[jæk sɨt]
7. Tuning the device:	[jæk sɨts]
8. Tuning the stress:	[jæ̂k sɨts]
9. Tuning the contour:	[jæ̂k sɨts]
10. Tuning the length:	none
Output:	jæ̂k sɨ tₜ s

Notes:

§1. The scheme is a fixed formula which calls for the idea of a Person and the idea of some change of state. The use of English words here has no systematic significance; it simply designates the meaning of the sensory-motor idea in this instance.

§2. Semiotic extension of this Event scheme to (Jack) *performs* (Sitting) is assumed to be possible (a mechanism for this process is discussed in later chapters). The semiotic extension establishes the order of concepts and words (an iconic sign).

§3. The morphological device shown produces an inflection on whatever is the last element of the syntagma. This device has an internal structure, not shown, that may be rather complex and is sensitive to number. As far as its output is concerned, it places a marker (s) at the end of the syntagma; this position will always be correct for this type of sensory-motor scheme (an Event limited to P and A) so long as no orientation-changing syntactic devices are used.

§7. Tuning the morphological device is necessary in order to convert the marker (s) into an appropriate phonetic realization, in this example [s], and to find the end of the word on which it goes. If the latter aspect of this tuning process should fail, shift errors are possible (*he get its,* etc., Garrett, 1976), in which the suffix is inserted into the speech output at the wrong place. The tuning could be based on the grammatical properties of word classes, among other things.

§§4 and 5. The formula for the movement specifies targets for movements in the form of stress and intonation patterns. The ones assumed above are based on Halliday's (1967a) discussion and represent, in his terms, neutral tonicity and tone, with a pretonic segment. (For an explanation of these terms, see Halliday, 1967a.) Only a relatively small number of intonation and stress patterns exists; it is entirely within the realm of possibility that each one is produced by a fedforward pattern programmed by a different syntagma. Thus, there may be Event syntagmata based on the concept of "person changes" for each different intonation pattern. The patterns are fedforward, that is, set up in advance by the syntagma, and then are tuned for the lexicalizations when words become available and for the effects of any morphological or syntactic devices that have been applied (§§ 8 and 9). Since Steps 4 and 5 are distinct steps from Steps 8 and 9, when there is competition during lexical insertion, and an exchange error takes place (Garrett, 1976), the stress and intonation contours should be tuned to the exchanged rather than the original words.

§10. There is no tuning required for length, two syllables being considered to be the basic output length of this syntagma. This length is assumed to be basic for the following reason: There are two parts of the sensory-motor scheme (P and A), and since this scheme is, by our hypothesis, a motor image of articulatory movements, the length of the utterance should be two basic output elements (assumed to be syllables). This particular proposal is very possibly not correct, but I am trying to make concrete the claim that the form of the sensory-motor scheme should have an effect on the phonological output. The hypothesis, that this effect is felt on the minimum length of the output of the syntagma, predicts that any utterance whose meaning corresponds to "person changes" would have at least two syllables, one for each element of the syntagma.[1] (Indirect evidence that different sensory-motor schemes have distinct effects on the programming of speech or gestural output is given in Chapters 8 and 11.)

When words are more than one syllable long, such as *Albert* or *dances,* the output of the syntagma must be extended in length. This can be done by a low-level instruction to the effect that if there is more than one syllable in the first part of a two-part syntagma, the *level* portion of the fedforward intonation contour is extended, whereas if there is more than one syllable in the second part, the *falling* portion of this contour is extended. For example,

ǽlbert si-ts

ǽlbert dǽnsez

Feedback. All of the adjustments described above as tunings are accomplished through feedback loops. These are not shown in the example but must be presupposed. For example, the tuning of the intonation contour depends on information concerning the number of syllables (as well as the rhythmical structure), which becomes available when the lexical items are retrieved.

Summary and Comment

This chapter has so far shown how sensory-motor schemes can correspond to the "motor images of movement" used in coordinating the action of the speech articulators. Such sensory-motor schemes have the special additional property of being meaningful in terms of the speaker's conceptual processes while simultaneously serving as schemes of movements. They are therefore a natural basis for syntagmata.

The example of a syntagma that we have discussed does not go very far. The conversion of global instructions, such as those for stress and intonation, into motor commands, given to specific muscle-joint effectors, simply does not appear. And one would have to be a physiologist to carry the example further in this direction. Nonetheless, I hope that it is clear that, to understand fully the goings on at the neuromuscular level of speech articulation, it may be necessary to consider the entire control hierarchy for speech co-ordination. This means that the speaker's intended meaning should not be left out of account even in a neurophysiological investigation. When interpreting

---

[1]The converse proposition, of course, is not expected to hold; there is no reason to suppose that all two-syllable utterances have the same sensory-motor content.

myographic recordings, for example, it would seem to be important to consider the semantic structure of the speech, at least its sensory-motor component, as this structure may have an effect on patterns of neuromuscular integration within the syntagma.

THE AB MODEL

The AB model describes the ontogenesis of syntagmata as follows: There is a process of convergence between different motor control hierarchies such that the processes of one hierarchy (B) are placed under the highest-level processes (scheme) of another hierarchy (A). This creates a new type of motor control hierarchy, AB, in which the motor output is through the B channels, while the motor image or concept of the action is established in A. In the example of the Event syntagma, A corresponds to the sensory-motor scheme of the Event representation [person changes], and B corresponds to Steps 3 through 10 of the syntagma.

The first contacts between the A and B systems seem to occur quite early in life. Lewis (1936), for example, described vocalizations as early as 8 months in which he found "some traces" of objective reference, and there may be contacts even before this. But these early AB contacts are, per force, limited from the point of view of the meanings represented and also of controlling speech output. These limitations of meaning and control have in part the same source. They exist because the sensory-motor schemes themselves are not fully differentiated from overt action performance. The AB hierarchy requires that A should correspond to an internal representation, and this presupposes a differentiated sensory-motor scheme. In fact, the differentiation of sensory-motor schemes follows a lengthy process, traced in detail by Piaget (1954), which is completed only in the second year of life, typically around 18 months. By the end of the sensory-motor period, with this differentiation well established, there are widespread AB fusions, shown in the expansion of the meanings that a child may express and in the first appearance of multiword utterances. These fusions open the way for meaning (in the form of sensory-motor representation) to co-ordinate articulation; that is, they open the way for the formation of syntagmata.

The motivation for the fusion of representational schemes with the control hierarchies of articulation is presumably innate in the species. There are no obvious functional reasons in terms of psychological organization for movements of the lips, jaw, tongue, velum, uvula, larynx, etc., to be connected with representational processes. That there is a universal connection, which always appears in ontogenesis at approximately the same time, is plausibly treated as an innate characteristic. This may have evolved in the species due to selection pressures that have little or nothing to do with the functional organization we are describing. The connection, whatever it is, apparently is lacking in neighboring species, such as the chimpanzee, who otherwise show similarities of representation and even of language capacities (cf. Premack, 1976).

SYNTAGMATA FROM THE POINT OF VIEW OF SIGN RELATIONSHIPS

Interlocking Signs

The preceding chapter established that the internal organization of the speech production process could be analyzed as an interlocking of three types of sign: indexical, iconic, and symbolic. A deeper insight into the concept of a syntagma now can be gained by applying this analysis. The ontogenetic fusion of systems A and B are viewed as resulting in indexical signs; in these signs the running of the speech program (B) constitutes the sign vehicle denoting the activation of a sensory-motor idea (A) that triggers the program. Semiotic extension enters the picture in that this sensory-motor idea (A), when semiotically extended (Step #2 in the syntagma model), is at once the object of the indexical sign vehicle (B) and the sign vehicle of an iconic and/or symbolic sign object. (In the syntagma model above, the morphological device for inserting (s) is an example of a symbolic sign and the Event sensory-motor structure with s is the sign vehicle.) Thus syntagmata have an internal structure that can be mapped onto the interlocking of signs with which we model semiotic extension.

Ontogenesis of Indexical Signs

In terms of ontogenesis, this formulation expresses an effect that the child's cognitive growth during the first two years will have on its speech and on the interpretation that can be given to its speech. The interiorization of sensory-motor schemes that gradually takes place during this period permits the indexical component of syntagmata to develop. At the earliest stages, when the sensory-motor representation is not differentiated from overt action, internal indexical signs cannot be said to exist. As the ontogenetic process of differentiation proceeds, the possibility of indexical sign vehicles (system B) developing internal referent objects (sensory-motor ideas) grows stronger. There is an emergence, during this period of cognitive growth, of a new type of meaning, which is this indexical relation between speech and thought that is generated when speech programs are activated. Speech output comes to denote internal mental representations, whereas previously it had only denoted the concurrent motor activity of which it was a part. There is thus a gradual shift, corresponding to the emergence of internal indexical signs, in the function of speech, which is motivated by the developing interiorization of sensory-motor schemes.

It becomes possible for these signs to be semiotically extended only when the internal objects of the signs (sensory-motor schemes) are established. Only after sensory-motor schemes are mentally representable can the child begin to treat them as the sign vehicles of other signs—iconic or symbolic signs. For this reason, I suggest, the correlation noted by Piaget and many others does exist, between the interiorization process and the appearance of organized multiword utterances (cf. Bloom, 1973; Brown, 1973; Piaget, 1962; Sinclair-deZwart, 1973). These multiword utterances depend on the appearance of semiotically extended sensory-motor ideas, which function as the sign vehicles of iconic or symbolic signs and as the objects of indexical signs. (This explanation corrects and supplants one given in my earlier paper on this subject, McNeill, 1975a.)

At the same time, and as part of the same process of cognitive change, the character and range of meanings in the child's speech increases during the sensory-motor period. Thus, there is a two-fold effect of mental growth on language. Speech comes to denote (indexically) thought, and thought is refined to accommodate a variety of relations that expand the range of the child's meanings. The child develops parallel and linked sign systems. Those signs that have the external world as their objects correspond to the social, objective referent field; those that have the inner world of thought processes as their objects correspond to the mechanisms of speech. These signs emerge together. In one sense they are the same system, but analytically we can see that there are the two poles mentioned, internal and external. Together they bring about the possibility of programming multiword utterances that are used for the expression of meanings that are objective and socially shared.

The utterances of very young children seem to be part of the child's overall behavior as much as, or more than, part of any linguistic system (Rodgon, 1976; Rodgon, Janowski, & Alenskas, 1977). When the process of interiorization has carried the formation of indexical signs further, however, utterances appear to have, to an adult, increasing semantic value. This phenomenon is demonstrated with examples below. The adult is responding to the cognitive changes taking place within the child, specifically to the expansion of meanings and to the increasing clarity of the indexical sign relationships in the child's utterances, which permits these utterances to denote thought processes. We can represent the relationship of the child's production to the adult's comprehension of a given utterance with two meaning triangles as follows:

Adult   Child

where S is the utterance program and O is a sensory-motor scheme. I and P refer to the interpretant and productant, respectively. The adult will recognize semantic value in the child's production to the degree that these sign structures are equivalent. Clearly, this depends on the development of the O—S connection, which in turn depends on the extent of interiorization.

Some Observations.   Lewis (1936) traced the changes of meaning in several words that appeared at an early age in the speech of one child and were used by this child continuously for more than a year. The vocalization *mama* is one such word, and it developed as follows:

1. The earliest vocalization, which was *m m m m* at 5 months, had only an "affective-conational function."
2. By 8 months *mammam* and its variants was used when the child was "mildly lacking something," e.g., was reaching for a plaything or requesting that some attention be paid him.
3. At 12 months he made his first overt response to *mama* (to the request, "Baby, give mama crustie [crust of bread]," the child held up the crust he had been gnawing on). Note that this response shows an association of *mama* with giving or displaying an object, not necessarily an association with the child's mother. Lewis concludes that the word, in fact, does not yet refer to the mother.
4. At 14 months *mama* was more specifically associated with attempts to obtain objects. For example, having dropped a favorite toy, he looked for it unsuccessfully, then looked at his mother and said "mama." Also, when he was asked to find some object which he could not see, he said "mama" as he looked for it. Also, he said "mama" as he brought toys into the room, and when he woke up in the morning.
5. At 18 months when he saw a picture of a smiling woman he said "mama."

This series of examples is particularly useful, because there are related vocalizations throughout. There is increasing semantic value in the sense that we are more and more certain, as the child becomes older, that the utterance denotes internal mental representations. This shift in the quality of the meaning of the word underlies the possibility of an indexical sign relationship of the type necessary for semiotic extension.

Greenfield and Smith (1976) have written at length of these kinds of changes of meaning. Their results are based on observations of two children, both English-speaking, and the observations commence in each case before the 12th month. Greenfield and Smith catalogue their examples according to what seem to them to be the semantic case relations in which the words are involved (cf. Fillmore, 1968); these classifications appear in Table 4.1. However, it must be said that it is premature to agree with certain of their classifications; it is quite possible that the child's conceptions are not sufficiently well differentiated for us to speak of semantic case relations at all, particularly with the very young examples. For example, Greenfield and Smith propose that *dada* at 13-3 (13 months and three weeks of age) is an example of the agent relation. This was said when the child heard but did not see that someone had entered the house. It is not proven, however, that the child had differentiated agents from actions within events; if the child's conceptions were limited at this point to events conceived as wholes, the vocalization could have been attached to this, for there was a change of state, and such a description of the child's word usage, at the level of undifferentiated events, would be closer to the picture of its intellectual functioning at this level (Piaget, 1954).

Table 4.1 is based on Greenfield and Smith's (1976) Tables 8 and 9 (pp. 60 and 70). Child A and Child B refer to the two children in the study.

Both children begin with expressions which are always part of a larger action. For example, Child A says "dada" to accompany every kind of action. Child B says "hi" as it waves. These are comparable to the use of *mama* when retrieving objects at 14 months, as described by Lewis. Slightly more advanced, but still of very limited semantic quality, are Child A's indicative and volitional uses of *dada* and *nana*. Such utterances are indexical signs with external objects, but apparently not signs with internal objects. In comparison to the earlier examples, however, the volitional and indicative examples are slighly more connected or conventional meaning. Instead of saying "dada" to accompany every action, the child says it to accompany only actions which include the father. This tendency is sharpened further in the rest of Table 4.1 for both children, and it is to this development that Greenfield and Smith attribute a growth of semantic cases.

It appears that several of the more focused uses, nonetheless, may not yet be signs with internal objects. The following were produced with a concurrent action and consequently do not show definite evidence of relating to interiorized representations: *do(wn)* at 14-21, *down* at 18-1, *poo* at 18-8, and *bap* at 18-19, for Child A; and *ba(ll)* at 13-0, *up* at 13-16, *down* at 14-6, and

TABLE 4.1
Examples of Single Word Speech from Two Children (Based on
Greenfield and Smith, 1976)

Semantic Function	Child	Age[a]	Example
performative	A	8–19	*dada,* to accompany every action
	B	7–22	*hi,* waving
indicative	A	9–8	*dada,* looking at Fa.
	B	8–12	*dada,* looking at Fa.
Volition	A	11–28	*na, na* (= negation), crawling to forbidden bookcase
	B	11–24	*nana* (= negation), turning from stairs
Agent	A	13–3	*dada,* hearing someone enter
	B	13–3	*daddy,* hearing Fa. enter
Action or state of agent	A	14–21	*do(wn),* when sits or steps down
	B	13–16	*up,* reaching up
Object	A	16–19	*bar* (= fan), asking for it to be on
	B	13–0	*ba(ll),* having just thrown one
Action, or state of object	A	18–1	*down,* shutting cabinet door
	B	14–6	*down,* having just thrown object down
Object in location	A	18–8	*poo,* putting hand on bottom
	B	14–29	*caca* (= cookie), pointing to kitchen door
Person in location	A	18–19	*Lara,* seeing empty bed
	B	15–29	*fishy,* pointing to empty tank
Location	A	18–19	*bap* (= diaper), showing where feces go
	B	15–20	*bo(x),* putting crayon in box
Modification[b]	A	19–29	*more record*
	B	18–1	*again*

[a]Age in months and weeks.
[b]This is the term used by Greenfield and Smith; however, recurrence would seem to be a better choice (Brown, 1973).

bo(x) at 15–20, for Child B. All of these examples are indexical signs in the external sense, but we have no evidence that they are indexical in the internal sense.

Other utterances from Table 4.1 show differentiation from action, however, and are closer to being signs denoting internal mental representations. Among these we find the following: *dada* at 13–3, *bar* (= fan) at 16–19, and *Lara* at 18–19, for child A; and *daddy* at 13–3, *caca* (= cookie) at 14–29, and *fishy* at 15–29, for Child B. There is apparently some degree of internal representation in these cases, and there is no accompanying action which serves as a representation. It is impossible to discover from the examples, however, how far we should go in saying that the child has differentiated its conceptual representations from its overt actions. As the final section of the chapter demonstrates, there are degrees of this interiorization.

Summary.   According to our anaysis so far, multiword utterances become a possibility for a child when its interiorization of sensory-motor schemes has reached a sufficiently advanced stage for semiotic extension to take place. This process presupposes some ability for representation in the sense of Piaget. Thus, multiword utterances are withheld until the beginnings of representational intelligence, as many observers have noted. At the same time, children's utterances gain in semantic value, in that they refer more precisely to objective referents and become interpretable as signs that denote internal mental representations.

ARTICULATION GROWTH
(GROWTH OF SYSTEM B)

The system we have been calling B, for controlling the co-ordination of the movements of the articulators, undergoes a development that begins at least as early as 5 months of age. The first identifiable AB fusions occur a few months later, around 8 months of age. There is continued development of articulation right up to and well beyond the first appearance of multiword speech.

The question of whether there exists an independent ontogenesis of articulatory patterns that is not guided or motivated by the baby's attempt to organize meanings has not been answered, and opinions on this subject vary. It does seem to be the case that children will babble without any communicative attempt being made (vocalizing in isolation, etc.) but this does not necessarily suggest that there is no organization of meaning going on at the same time. Moreover, even though the earliest traces of objective reference appear at 8 months (Lewis, 1936), while the earliest traces of phonological simulation appear at 5 months or so, to establish that there is autonomous development of articulation during these three months would at least require looking for meanings of the kind that 5-month-old babies could possibly organize. One would have to exclude the possibility that these meanings are supplying the basis for AB fusions.

This issue is not yet resolved, and I do not discuss it further here. Instead, I shall consider the growth of system B without regard to potential AB contacts.

Weir (1966) observed differences in the babbling of five infants, 5 to 10 months old, who were being raised in different linguistic–cultural environments. Babies exposed to Chinese (Cantonese) speech produced more monosyllabic and vocalic sounds and greater pitch variation over single vowels, than did babies exposed to English or Russian speech. These linguistic–cultural differences were apparent as early as 5 months. The Russian and English infants, in contrast, showed more consonant–vowel reduplication, and stress and intonational patterns extended over several syllables. Thus, apparently, some of the processes represented in the example of a syntagma above, such as the feedforward of stress and intonation, were being developed in the latter half of the 1st year by these children.

Cruttenden (1970) noted a number of changes before the 1st birthday in the vocalizations of his twin daughters, including the appearance of a ⁻⁻ intonation pattern which seemed to be an imitation of the mother's way of saying "allgone." There was apparent responsiveness to intonation patterns in adult speech in the 8th month. The distribution of the consonantal sounds [b, d, g, n, l] shifted gradually toward that of English during this period. This drift was completed well before the occurrence of the first imitated words. The drift suggests that the baby introduces at least part of the tuning mechanism of system B in its 1st year of life. Cruttenden makes the observation that the range of babbling sounds was not nearly as inclusive as has been believed (not approximating the range of speech sounds used in various languages of the world), but was, rather, limited to a small number of phonetic categories. Viewing sequential speech sounds as tuning of output programs, this observation suggests that initially children have the capacity to make a relatively small number of adjustments of speech programs, and they apply these to an equally restricted set of fedforward intonation and stress patterns. In other words, they simply have at their disposal a small number of speech programs.

The first identifiable AB contacts involve utterances with some form of objective reference, although, as suggested above, these contacts may not actually be the first. By 8 to 12 months with many children, nonetheless, vocalizations occur in which the child directs its attention and behavior toward an object or other person. Lewis (1936) lists three functions of intonation in 9–10-month-old babies: (1) delight at getting something; (2) dissatisfaction; and (3) rage at being reprimanded. Even here, there is some degree of objective reference. By 12 to 18 months, these functions are replaced or elaborated on: (1) a sound pattern made while reaching for objects; (2) a demonstrative sound pattern; and (3) an interrogative sound pattern. Lewis considers this development to involve an increase of definite reference that takes place in the absence of conventional words. The underlying explanation presumably has to do with the child's concurrent cognitive development, a matter to which I return in the next section.

An interesting example of phonological patterning has been described by Ingram (1974) and can be mentioned as an example of what appears to be a feedforward process set up at an early stage of phonological development. This pattern or "strategy" appeared in the speech of two children as follows: In words with more than one consonant, no matter what the first one was, the following one(s) was (were) articulated either at the same point or at a point more posterior. Thus, utterances were programmed to move from the front to the back of the mouth, as they proceeded in time. This strategy is quite naturally conceived of as a fedforward instruction established in advance of the onset of articulation. The strategy appeared clearly in the speech of two children (at 21 and 17 months, respectively), one English-speaking and one French-speaking, but Ingram proposes that other children may apply it also, though not necessarily so consistently. Examples from the English-speaking child are as follows (the adult model on the left, the child's version in the middle, and the proscribed sequence in the adult model that the child changes on the right):

alligator [dæge] *g—d
animal [mænu] *n—m
candle [naŋu] *k—nd
candy [naŋi] *k—nd
cream [miŋ] *k—m
hammer [mænu] *h—m
coffee [baki] *k—f

And examples from the French-speaking child, recorded in the late 19th century, are the following:

carbone [bõ] *k—b
soupe [teteč] *s—p
couteau [koko] *k—t
garde [dā] *g—d
café [pɛtɛk] *k—f
cuiller [bedeč] *k—y

Summary. There is, as the above sketch suggests, considerable evidence that the processes involved in system B start emerging in the 1st year of life at least as early as 5 months of age. Whether this emergence involves only system B, or a fusion of A with B, is not entirely clear. By 8 months, nonetheless, most observers agree that there is some trace of what Lewis terms objective reference, implying AB contact. However, these AB hierarchies are limited by the meaning representations of which children at this age are capable. Not only is this a limitation on the range of content that a child expresses, but a limitation on the possibility of semiotic extension. This limitation is not lifted until the process of interiorizing sensory-motor schemes is completed; at this time indexical, iconic, and symbolic signs become possible, and through these signs multiword speech following the processes described in Chapter 3 becomes possible.

COGNITIVE GROWTH
(GROWTH OF SYSTEM A)

The full interiorization of sensory-motor action schemes is the final phase of an ontogentic process that runs continuously through approximately the first 2 years of life. Piaget (1954) traces this emergence for several categories: objects, causation, space, and time. Each of these, when fully constructed, corresponds to a general sensory-motor idea—respectively, the ideas of an Entity, an Event, Location in space, and Location in time. These are stable schemes differentiated from the actions performed in relation to them. The examples below relate to the construction of the concept of an Entity (the object concept), but are representative of intellectual growth in this period in general. The differentiation of causality, space, and objects in fact occurs as part of a single process. We shall see that the changes engendered by this process of construction simulate the development of meaning in word usage mentioned previously. This underlying cognitive development provides an explanation of the changes of meaning in single-word speech that passes beyond the linguistically based account of Greenfield and Smith (1976), and shows how speech relates to the child's mode of intellectual functioning.

The genesis of the object concept (and the others mentioned above) can be regarded from two points of view. On the one hand, there is the emergence of the mental category of objects. From this point of view (emphasized by Piaget), we trace the growth of the logic of this form of mental representation. On the other hand, there is the process of control over the child's actions. From this point of view, we trace the ability of the child to plan and carry out more and more complex actions that relate to objects (reaching goals that are increasingly remote and hidden, using means that are increasingly distant from the action itself, and so forth). These two points of view emphasize, in the same genetic process, one or the other side of the epistemological duality of sensory-motor representations. Thus, as we read Piaget's account of the genesis of the object concept, we should not forget that this is also the gensis of control over more and more complex goal-directed actions.

According to Piaget's terminology, at 5 or 6 months the child is in Stage 3. This is the time at which the first evidence of phonological patterning appears, as noted previously. Stage 3 representations should therefore be sought in these vocalizations, if any evidence of AB fusions is to be found this early. At Stage 3 the permanence of objects is an extension of *actions in progress*. Thus, for example, Lucienne is playing with a box; she stops to play with her father and drops the box at the same time; she then returns her hand to the exact spot where the box had been when she dropped it, apparently believing that it will be where it was when she used it before.

By the time that most investigators of child speech recorded that they recognize the first sound–meaning correlations, the child's conception of objects has achieved a certain independence from action, but this is limited to the context in which the object has been previously experienced and manipulated (Stage 4). It is easy to see how this form of representation is expressed in concurrent word usages. For example, Jacqueline at 10 months finds a toy hidden under her father's hand, which is on her lap. Then he hides the toy under a rug a short distance away and returns his hand to her lap. The movement of the toy had been visible to the child, but she lifts her father's hand and searches for it there. Utterances such as "dada" only while looking at the father or "nana" only while crawling to a forbidden object, also context-bound, appear to involve representations at the same level.

The 5th stage, between 1–0 and 1–6 (1 year and 1 year and 6 months) approximately, is characterized by a progressive acquisition of the spatial relations of objects. The child no longer makes the mistake of believing that objects exist only in the same contexts. If the experiment above is repeated at this stage, the child will search for the object directly in the second hiding place and will not return to the first place even if the object cannot be found. The object has an independent reality to the extent that it is no longer just an aspect of an undecomposable context. However, this is a limited and fragile kind of freedom. If the object is displaced in a more complex way (for example, by making the displacements invisible), the child will retreat to his earlier dependence on context. One of Piaget's examples that demonstrates both the achievements and limitations of this stage is the following: At 1–6 Jacqueline watches as her father hides an object in a box that has no lid, and then watches as he hides this box, with the object inside, behind a screen. Then the box is brought out empty. The child does not understand that the object must have been left behind the screen. Now, if the box contains the object, as before, but both the box and object are left behind the screen. Jacqueline will fetch the box and ipso facto the object.

Speech based on this level of representation could produce several of the examples cited by Greenfield and Smith and the most advanced use of "mama" described by Lewis. In each of the examples, the utterance presupposes an ability to represent absent objects. For instance, *ca ca* (= cookie) pointing to the kitchen door, *Lara* when seeing an empty bed, *fishy* pointing to an empty tank, and *bo(x)* putting a crayon in the box could all be produced at this level. The earliest such example is at 14–29, as is appropriate for the 5th stage of object representation.

By the 6th stage in Piaget's description, the child's process of constructing the object concept is complete. For example, Jacqueline at 1–7 could follow invisible displacements behind as many as three screens successively. Sometimes she would touch the screens in order as she recreated the sequence of displacements, and then she would turn over only the last screen. Piaget (1954) writes of this stage regarding the scheme of an object, that the object is no longer, as it was during the first four stages, merely the extension of various accommodations, nor is it, as in the fifth stage, merely a permanent body in motion whose movements have become independent of the self but solely to the extent to which they have been perceived; instead the object is now definitely freed from perception and action alike and obeys entirely autonomous laws of displacement. [p. 84].

It is this representational scheme of an object, developed out of fully developed action co-ordinations, that the child may enter into semiotic extension, using the scheme as an iconic and/or symbolic sign of other meanings, as described in the preceding chapter.

SUMMARY

In this chapter we have considered how syntagmata may be based on a fusion of motor control systems. This has led us, in turn, to consider the origin of syntagmata ontogenetically.

Any action control system is supposed to consist of a hierarchy of processes arranged so that each level controls only a few degrees of freedom on the level below it; complexity and flexibility are provided in these hierarchies through depth. The highest level, called the motor image of the movement, or scheme, may have no direct contact with the lowest levels which manage the effectors.

System A consists of these kinds of control hierarchies for actions performed in the external world. These are actions, for example, involved in the manipulation of objects in space. The motor images of such actions are eventually used to construct sensory-motor representations of reality. Thus, system A provides a collection of representational schemes. System B consists of control hierarchies for movements of the articulators. It organizes motor patterns such as those that result in intonation and stress patterns, sequences of syllables, etc.

A syntagma is defined as a meaning unit (sense unit) produced as a single output. In terms of our theory, this is produced by a fusion of systems A and B such that the motor image of A co-ordinates the output of B. Systems A and B may fuse as early as the child's 1st year of life. Appropriate meaningful representations clearly control the articulatory process by 8 or 9 months, and the possibility that there is such control at 5 months (the earliest evidence of phonological patterning) cannot be ruled out. However, the initial fusions are limited by the still insufficient differentiation of sensory-motor schemes from action control. This prevents there being internal indexical signs in which the articulatory processes of B are the sign vehicles denoting the sensory-motor schemes of A, and it also therefore prevents there being any semiotic extension. It is for this reason, I propose, that multiword utterances are withheld until the child has constructed interiorized mental representations based on action schemes.

5 Sensory-Motor Ideas

Sensory-motor ideas have appeared in several guises. They have been identified with the indexical component of the speech-thought relationship; with "images of movement" that guide articulation; with the basis of syntagma; and with elements of meaning that are semiotically extended to contact semantic content at other levels. All of these manifestations of sensory-motor ideas arise from the unique epistemology of the sensory-motor level of representation. Sensory-motor ideas alone exist simultaneously in the realm of action and the realm of meaning. It is this dual existence that gives them their central position in the speech-thought relationship. The sensory-motor meaning domain has direct access to the control of speech articulation.

SENSORY-MOTOR IDEAS BASED ON EVENTS

My purpose in the present chapter is to examine the meaning structure of this domain. For such an examination we must go beyond a description of the basis of sensory-motor ideas in the organization of action schemes. It is possible to show how a number of sensory-motor structures in speech are ultimately based on the idea of an Event (cf. Schank, 1972, for a related suggestion), and utterances tend to be organized around the concept of an Event. Speakers add information until they have built up an idea of an Event, and when they introduce complexities these too are of Events. Other sensory-motor ideas, moreover, can be shown to depend on or derive from the idea of an Event. By defining the idea of an Event, therefore, we can find our way into the meaning structure of the domain of sensory-motor ideas in general.

Definition of Event

Events may be based on causative action sequences, as in *the men stopped their cars;* or they may involve changes in which causation (as stated in the utterance) does not play a role (*it rained*). A logical formalism for events[1] introduced by von Wright (1965) is particularly useful in this context, because it applies in a variety of situations and contains within itself definitions that can be applied to sensory-motor ideas. This formalism is only a guide for thinking about the structure of Events and their relationships to other ideas. It is not a psychological model, and we will have to go beyond it in several respects in order to define certain sensory-motor ideas.

Von Wright has developed a calculus of events based on a connective, T, meaning "and next." An event in this calculus is conceived of as a change of state and is represented as two successive states separated by a moment of time (T) of unspecified duration. An elementary event is any one of the disjuncts in the following tautology, which is thus exhaustive:

$$(sTs) \text{ v } (sT{-}s) \text{ v } ({-}sTs) \text{ v } ({-}sT{-}s)$$

In these expressions, s is a proposition which describes a state. There are four elementary events, and these can be glossed as follows:

1. *s remains* (sTs)   "s, and next s"
2. *s disappears* (sT–s)   "s, and next not s"
3. *s appears* (–sTs)   "not s, and next s"
4. *s stays away* (–sT–s)   "not s, and next not s"

In two of these, the same state of affairs appears on both sides of the connective T (*remains* and *stays away*), and in the two others there are different states of affairs. Nonetheless, each of (1–4) is an elementary event.

English recgnizes Events corresponding to (1) and (4) as well as to (2) and (3). Of course, the form of the English sentence does not necessarily correspond to the form of the logical formula defining the event, and there is no reason to expect that such a correspondence would in general be possible. The following sentences are each based on the concept of an Event and illustrate the four elementary events:

1. *The bishop remained for the last speech.* This has the form of sTs (1). Let s_1 = *the bishop was present until the last speech,* and s_2 = *the bishop was present after the last speech.* Then, as far as his presence was concerned, the state of the bishop did not change.

---

[1]Lower case refers to real-world events, states, actions, and so forth, whereas upper case refers to concepts. This tedious device unfortunately is necessary.

2. *The bishop left the room.* This has the form $sT-s$ (2). Let s_1 = *the bishop was present in the room,* and s_2 = *the bishop was not present in the room.* Then, the state of the bishop changed such that he disappeared.

3. *The bishop arrived in the court.* This has the form $-sTs$ (3). Let s_1 = *the bishop was not in the court,* and s_2 = *the bishop was in the court.* Then, the state of the bishop changed such that he appeared.

4. *The bishop avoided the ceremony.* This has the form $-sT-s$ (4). Let s_1 = *the bishop was not at the ceremony,* and s_2 = *the bishop was not at the ceremony.* Then, the state of the bishop did not change, and he remained away.

This notation also provides a rationale for tense marking within the concept of Event. Tense marking establishes a relationship between the moment T and another reference point in time. For example, *I saw Max* relates the change of state involved in seeing Max to the later moment of speech. Reichenbach (1947) pointed out that in English and other languages there are *two* reference points. In *I had seen Max,* the event T is earlier than an anchor point, and the anchor point is earlier than the moment of speech. In *I shall have seen Max,* the moment of speech is earlier than the event T, and the event is earlier than the anchor point. In all, Reichenbach distinguished nine tenses within this framework.

The following examples of the concept of Event are taken from a sample of spontaneous speech reported by Terkel (1970), (which, however, may have been edited). Each is recognizable as an Event by there being represented in the meaning of the utterance a change of state.

they marched
they took your livestock
it got
a neighbor wouldn't buy

The last two examples illustrate Events in which the component Action is not completely specified (cf. the definition of Action discussed later in this chapter). The last example illustrates an event in which the same state is maintained ($-sT-s$). A theoretical possibility, not illustrated by anything in Terkel's sample, is that an Event is conveyed in speech by the juxtaposition of two States, but there is no speech fragment that corresponds to a change of state itself. Consider the sentence *I knew he was sick when I saw him,* or the reverse, *when I saw him I knew he was sick.* In either version, we could represent the meaning as s_1 = *I saw him,* and next s_2 = *I knew he was sick.* There is an Event, although nothing in the sentence corresponds to the change of state itself. The interval corresponding to T in this case may be infinitesimal, but there is still a succession. An actual example of this type is analyzed in Fig. 8.8.

Definition of State

Each of von Wright's logical formulae for an elementary event defines a real-world state derivatively, as either the condition that existed before the change of state, or the condition that existed after it. For example, either s_1 or s_2 is a real-world state:

$$s_1 \ T s_2$$

States (the concept) according to this definition would be *the bishop was not in the court* and *the bishop was in the court,* both of which are real-world states of the bishop. Similarly, the other examples of events derivatively provide two states each each, e.g., *the bishop was not present in the room, the bishop was present until the last speech,* etc. Both of these also is the concept of a State.

States can be recognized by two characteristics. One is lack of change. This characteristics does not mean that States are permanent Properties (in fact, that would contradict the role of states in events), but that change is not specified, or that nonchange is specified, in the utterance. In this way, an event can be made into a State. An example of a specified nonchange is *if they dump the produce.* This converts the event *they dump the produce* into a State of the referent of *they,* which is specified by the conditional as nonchanging within the utterance. The auxiliary *would* has a similar effect; for example, *they would dump the produce* is specified as a nonchanging State of *they,* in contrast to the event *they dump the produce.* Examples of change not being specified are *people were determined* and *it wasn't enough* (to do something), in both of which lack of change is part of the inherent meaning (both are s_1).

The second characteristic of States is that the unchanging state must be initial or final in a real-world event. It must be possible to link a State to an event as s_1 or s_2. For example, *it wasn't enough* is initial in an event of the form $(-sT-s)$, as we know from the second clause in the discourse, which is *to satisfy them.* On the other hand, it follows from this characteristic that the two clauses in *if they would dump the produce they would force the market,* are not individually States, because this sentence as a whole does not correspond to an event. (There is no change of state.) Both of the characteristics of States—an unchanging condition and a condition that is initial or final in a real-world event—must be present for a speech segment to be called a State. However, the two clauses in the last example considered together could qualify as the initial State of another event.

In general, complex sentences in the subjunctive mood, as in this last example, do not correspond to real-world events; hence constituent clauses in the subjunctive cannot be concepts of States. This contrasts with complex sentences in the conditional, where the conditional clause is a State and the nonconditional clause is an Event corresponding to a real-world event. For example, *if they dump the produce they force the market* corresponds to an initial real-world state and then a real-world event.

Examples of States in Terkel's (1970) speech sample are the following:

> people were determined
> it wasn't enough
> it's still hung over him
> if they would dump the produce they would force the market

Intuitively, these examples appear to be correctly classified as States. The basis of the classification is that each example meets the two criteria mentioned above; i.e., each is unchanging (in the context of the utterance) and each is the initial or terminal condition of an event. It should be mentioned, however, that data presented in Chapter 8 on the reliability of classifying speech segments into sensory-motor categories show that the least reliable such classification is that of State. This is hardly surprising, for although the abstract definition of a State in terms of events is straightforward, recognizing States in speech involves questions of considerable subtlety, and disagreements over these affect reliability values.

Definition of Process

The idea of a Process may be defined as the idea of a temporally extended (real-world) state. Given the formula for an event, $s_1 T s_2$, where s_1 and s_2 are states, the temporal continuation of s_1 or s_2 is a process, and the concept of a Process corresponds to this. Unlike a State, a Process includes the idea of continuous change corresponding to s_1 or s_2. We can see from this definition that there should be two kinds of processes corresponding to whether s_1 or s_2 is extended in time, and thus a distinction between types of concepts of Process. When s_1 is extended, the Process is one which ends in an event. There is an interval through which s_1 occurs and then, at the end, a change of state to s_2. An example is conveyed with the verb *bake* in *the cake baked until noon*. At noon, if there is a change of state, it is that the cake baked. When s_2 is extended, the Process begins with an event. Here the interval begins with a change of state, and the new state continues. An example is conveyed with the verb *sleep* in *Max slept until noon;* here the change of state creating the process of sleeping occurred before noon.

The distinction between these kinds of processes is reflected in language as brought out clearly when the process is negated. For example, *the cake didn't bake until noon* (with normal declarative sentence intonation) means that the cake finished baking at noon. *Max didn't sleep until noon* means either that Max woke up before noon, or after noon, or that sleep started at noon.

However, it does not mean that sleep ended at noon. The third meaning, that sleep started at noon, shows directly that *sleep* denotes a process which begins with an event. The meaning with *bake*, that baking finished at noon, similarly shows directly that *bake* denotes a process which ends with an event. Thus, *bake* and *sleep* convey two concepts of Process. Whether there are concepts of pure Processes only, which do not include events, is not as clear. Such meanings would be abstractions away from the underlying events. The identity of the real-world process (continuous state) would have to be provided from a source outside of this abstract process. *Continue* and its synonyms, such as *keep on,* may be examples of this kind, as in *the music continued (kept on) until dawn.* This sentence implies the occurrence of the events of the music starting and stopping, but these events are not incorporated into *continue (keep on)* in the way that the events of getting baked or falling asleep are incorporated into *bake* or *sleep.* Unfortunately, however, there is not a positive test of the concept of pure Processes. If we try negating *continue,* we find that it behaves neither like *bake* nor like *sleep.* For example, *the music didn't continue until dawn* does not mean either that the music ended at dawn or that it started at dawn, and perhaps this a weak negative test of a third concept of Process. Another possible example would seem to be conveyed by the verb *change,* except that *it didn't change until dawn* shows that this process, like sleep, begins with an event.

Examples of the concept of Process from Terkel (1970) are the following:

we can't stand (to have something done) (extends s_2)
the argument kept on (pure process)
you don't forget these things (extends s_1)

The second example is a component of another sensory-motor idea, State, which appeared as an example in the preceding section.

It seems to be the case that the sensory-motor idea of a Process is expressed only through certain process verbs. If one looks for expressions that denote processes but do not make use of these verbs, one is disappointed. Table 5.1 lists a number of examples of verbs of this kind. (A test that distinguishes a process meaning from a nonprocess one is whether the verb can appear in the affirmative form with *until;* Miller & Johnson-Laird, 1976). For example, **Max arrived until noon* shows that *arrive* lacks a process meaning. *The people arrived until noon* is acceptable but has an interative meaning. The nouns in parentheses in Table 5.1 distinguish the process senses of the verbs, some of which have nonprocess senses as well, e.g., *develop.*)

The transitive verb/intransitive verb distinction exists in both process verbs and nonprocess verbs. Examples of the latter are *arrive* (intransitive) and *transform* (transitive). Among the process verbs in Table 5.1 are

TABLE 5.1
Classification of Process Verbs[a]

Extension of s_1	Extension of s_2
(society) degenerates	(woman) labors
(photograph) develops	(attitude) develops
forget (facts)	(stone) falls
organizes (files)	(Max) sleeps
(glue) sets	(Max) lives (in Rome)
(wax) congeals	(Max) breathes
(ham) cures	(thing) changes
(whiskey) ages	(Max) dreams
(leaves) dry	(fluid) circulates
(water) evaporates	(it) rains
(cake) bakes	(Max) travels
(food) cooks	(fetus) gestates
consumes (food)	(Max) works
(meat) roasts	makes (objects)
(homo erectus) evolves	(Max) imprisoned (him)
(ice) melts	
(beer) ferments	
(snake) molts	
(caterpillar) metamorphoses	

$$(\text{agent}) \begin{bmatrix} \text{red} \\ \text{black} \\ \text{white} \\ \text{sad} \\ \text{glad} \end{bmatrix} + \text{ens (patient)}$$

[a]Examples were suggested by Gary Bond, James Bone, Franci Duitch, Starkey Duncan, Jr., Karen Lindig, William Marslen-Wilson, Cheryl McNeill, Nobuko McNeill, Lance Rips, Robin Rosenberg, Michael Silverstein, and Richard Wallstein.

degenerates, labors, develops, sleeps, etc., all intransitive; and *forgets, imprisons, organizes,* and the addition of the causative suffix to adjectives, all transitive.

Definition of Action

An Action is a *performance* due to an agent or actor. It is a kind of change of state, or real-world event, therefore, but includes only the change itself. The concept of an Action is always part of the concept of an Event. The isolation of the Action can be accomplished by omitting the performer; what is left is the Action. This form of organization is particularly striking in the speech of young children (cf. Chapter 10). There are syntactic devices (such as complement formation) that accomplish this same isolation in the speech of adults.

If the event conveyed is *the bishop left the room,* the bishop's Action is *left the room,* or simply *left* in the intransitive sense of "depart." These fragments correspond specifically to the real-world action that the bishop performs as part of the event of leaving the room.

The term *action* is generally used to mean intended action and to suggest the existence of a goal on the part of the performer. For example, if leaving the room is something the bishop did under his own power, it was the bishop's own action. However, if he left the room propelled by an explosion, we should not call this the bishop's action. Many utterances that include the concept of Action directly convey the performance a real-world action and imply the goal. For example, *the bishop left the room* presents the performance of leaving the room directly and implies the goal that the bishop should not be in the room. However, in some semantic domains the reverse exists. Here, the utterance, still including Action, may directly present the goal and imply a performance. G. Lakoff (1977) notes that many verbs of destruction suggest a change of state by describing the final State; for example, *smash, crush, squash, split, blister, disintegrate,* and many others. In terms of the analysis of actions given, these verbs describe the goal of the action by specifying the state (s_2) of the event of which the action is a part. Clearly, these verbs do not directly describe their performances, which are quite different from the outcome states and are only implied.

Examples of Actions from Terkel (1970) are all of the first type and specify the performance:

> met on the road
> buy groceries
> to withhold produce
> having a farm sale

Actions isolated from Events have a limited distribution in adult speech. In the speech of young children, in contrast, the idea of Action is highly productive in isolation. The last two examples illustrate syntactic devices (complements with *to* and gerundive nominalizations) in which the sensory-motor idea of Action can appear in adult speech without the idea of Event. A few other syntactic devices accomplish this as well, e.g., imperatives (*get the groceries*). Except for these specialized devices, however, adults are generally excluded (in English, at least) from access to the idea of an Action as a separate source of speech programming. All of the other examples of Actions above, as is typical, appear in the context of Events (*you couldn't hardly buy groceries,* etc.).

The difference between transitive and intransitive verbs, such as *buy* and *meet* (as in the examples above), is in part a difference in the internal complexity of the concept of Action. With a transitive verb this idea is more complex, since a patient is part of the Action. The idea of the Action includes the patient. (Real-world actions, of course, are independent of this distinction.) The sense of an incomplete proposition that comes from omitting the patient (*Oscar buys*) arises because the amount of detail of the idea of the Action is insufficient. Such expressions, however, include a performer and an Action and still correspond to an idea of an Event, even though they are incomplete on the lower level within the Action. As a consequence, they are possible Events consisting of performers and actions (and in fact, are common as segments in spontaneous speech, cf. Chapter 9).

Note on Verbs. In the framework of sensory-motor ideas, so-called action verbs and process verbs refer to real-world events. This is the case regardless of whether the verb is transitive or intransitive. These different types of verb all express changes of state. Process and nonprocess verbs, for example, differ in that the former are derived by conceiving of the temporal extension of the s_1 or s_2 of an event, but they still include this change of state in their meaning. Transitive and intransitive verbs distinguish events on the lower level of action, but both the transitive and intransitive types refer to real-world events. All of these verbs, in isolation, therefore can convey the idea of an Event; for example, *hit, run,* or *sleep,* each, by itself, refers to a change of state (a real-world event), although with minimal or insufficient specification.

Definition of Property—Event (State)

An Event Property is conceived of as a condition on the occurrence of a real-world event. (Properties of Persons and Entities are discussed in the next section.) Such real-world conditions are usually conveyed by adverbs. When there is modification of the idea of an Event, this means that the condition in the real world corresponding to the Property had to have been met in order for the event to have occurred. If the event is *the bishop left the room quickly,* the condition for the occurrence of this event is that it should have taken place within a certain range of speeds; the idea of the event having been within this range is then the idea of a Property.

Conceiving of Properties as conditions on the occurrence of events, rather than as attributes that intersect events, seems to be a superior interpretation of the logical structure of conjunction. This logical structure would be approximately as follows: the bishop moved from the room, and the movement *was* leaving, and the movement *was* speedy (Reichenbach, 1947). Such a logical conjunction is often interpreted as meaning there is an intersection—intersecting movement with leaving and with speed. However, if one conceives of *quickly* as denoting the attribute of speed regardless of any particular event, and explains *left quickly* as the intersection of *left* and *quickly,* there is no way to explain *evolved quickly* as being a similar intersection on a totally different time scale. For example, *the bishop left quickly* and *homo sapiens evolved quickly* have widely different meanings in terms of time. On the bishop's scale, the event of homo sapien's evolving was slow indeed. If we avoid the interpretation of modification as an intersection of attributes with events, however, we can explain how the same modifier can apply on quite different scales, because it can be interpreted as meaning a condition an event must meet. The condition for leaving a room quickly is that the movement should be a type of leaving, and this leaving should be speedy. The condition for evolving quickly is that the change should be a type of evolving, and this evolution should be speedy. This interpretation has the logical structure of conjunction, but it avoids some of the implications of the notion of intersection. Conceiving of *quickly* as a condition on the occurrence of events binds its meaning to the particular events it modifies. *Left quickly* doubtless involves meeting different conditions from *evolved quickly,* even though both have to do with speeds.

A criterion of the Property of an Event or State is a frame such as the following: the Event consists of leaving, and this leaving is speedy. More generally, p is a Property of an Event if we can state the Event as e, and state that e *is* p. So, the adverb of manner, *quickly,* is shown to be a property of the bishop's *leaving* in *the bishop left quickly,* because the above frame holds for it. On the other hand the locative adverbial, *home* is not a property of the bishop's *leaving* in *the bishop left home,* because we cannot state that the event consists of the bishop's leaving, and the bishop's leaving *is* home.

Only two examples of the Property of an Event or State appear in the samples from Terkel. One is *we were constantly being questioned.* This adverb of quantity is shown to be a property of the event, *we were questioned,* as follows: the event consisted of we-were-being-questioned, and the event we-were-being-questioned *was* constant. The other example is of a State. It is the *so* in *I never felt so old.* This is shown to be a State Property as follows: the state consists of I-felt-old, and the state of I-felt-old *was* extreme. Notice that to apply the test we have to disregard the negative of the original, and express *so* as *extreme.* However, these changes are apparently justified, because retaining the negative gives the wrong meaning, and the sense of *so* intended appears to be the reduced form of *so extremely (I never felt so extremely old).*

Definition of Property—Entity or Person

The definition of the Property of an Entity or Person is parallel to but simpler than the definition for the Property of an Event. A Property of an Entity or Person corresponds to a real-world condition on the existence of the entity or person. Generally, but not always, adjectives express this idea. As before, this definition is thought to be a superior interpretation of the logical structure of conjunction. If something is a red building, we can state this modification as follows: if x exists, x *is* a building, and x *is* red. If some person is fat we can say: if m exists, m *is* a person, and m *is* fat. The conjunctions are simpler in these cases than in Events, since they do not contain higher-order predicates (*the leaving is speedy* is a higher-order predicate).

The same advantage over intersection associated with the interpretation of a property as a condition holds also, as each type of entity or person can have its own condition. The condition for being a fat gorilla can be diferent on a scale of volume from the condition for being a fat mouse. One of these uses of *fat* is bound to be problematic if we think of modification as an intersection of entities and attributes.

The definition of the Property of an Entity or Person will apply to most adjectives, either when apposed (*the fat gorilla*) or introduced by the copula (*the gorilla is fat*). The criterion does not apply to other uses of *be,* such as class inclusion (*the gorilla is a vertebrate*) or identity (*Henry is this gorilla*). It does apply to predicate nominals (*New York is a city,* because a condition for x being New York is that x *be* a city) and to restrictive relative clauses (as demonstrated in the following discussion).

A criterion for a Property of an Entity or Person is the following: p is a Property of an Entity or Person if we can say of something x that x *is* this Entity or Person, and that x *is* p. For example, *large* is a property of *gorilla* (or *city* of *New York*), because we can say that x *is* a gorilla (x *is* New York), and x *is* large (x *is* a city).

Examples of Properties of Entities or Persons in Terkel (1970) according to this criterion are the following:

> *absolute* bottom (= *extreme* bottom)
> this is *my* court
> [people] *who were brought up as conservatives*

For example, x *is* the bottom, and x *is* extreme; and x *is* a court, and x *is* mine. (Thus, predicative possessive pronouns apparently behave as Properties of Entities or Persons.)

The restrictive relative clause (*who*) *were brought up as conservatives* is shown to be a Property of Person as follows: x *is* a person, and x *was* brought up to be a conservative. Restrictive relative clauses with verbs other than *be* similarly can be shown to be Properties of Entities or Persons. For example, *primitives who live in caves* (meaning the kind of primitive who lives in a cave) can be rendered as x *is* a primitive, and x *is* living in a cave. This states that a condition on being this kind of primitive is living in a cave. It shows a connection between restrictive relative clauses and conjunction at the level of Persons or Entities.

OTHER SENSORY-MOTOR IDEAS

Definition of Entity and Person

There is no definition of Entity or Person in terms of real-world events in the form these are represented in the von Wright formulae. These ideas can be described and defined in other terms, but they cannot be derived from or otherwise related to the idea of an Event. Why there is this gap in the framework based on von Wright's structure of an event is a puzzle; perhaps it is because the ideas of Entity and Persons are so important in human affairs that they have developed independent definitions and separate origins.

As first approximations I will attempt to characterize the ideas of Entity and Person in terms of psychological representations, considering Entity first. By the close of the sensory-motor period, objects are differentiated as stable schemes from the actions which are performed on them. This differentiation is most noticeable in the child's understanding of the spatial relations of objects and of their permanence regardless of the child's perception or action (Piaget, 1954; cf. the discussion of the object concept in the preceding chapter).

Using this characterization, we can describe the sensory-motor idea of an Entity as a relatively stable referent point that does not change form or identity as a function of one's own perception or action. Although this definition is based on the idea of an object at the end of sensory-motor development, quite abstract Entities are consistent with it (through semiotic extension). For example, *a hot day, recent events,* and *the sinking of the Bismarck,* are all regarded as Entities, meaning that they are relatively stable referent points that do not change in their essentials as a function of perception or action. Events, States, Actions, Processes, and Event Properties, on the other hand, are not Entities according to this definition, because change is a fundamental part of each of them. (Entity Properties, on the other hand, are stable if the Entities they modify are stable.) The effect of the nominalization of *sinking of the Bismarck* is to convert this event into a stable referent point; thus it can appear as the object of actions and otherwise find itself embedded into other Events.

An interesting question arises when we consider the lack of conservation of substances shown by young children. If a child believes that, by altering the shape of a substance, the substance is no longer the same, should it be considered an Entity according to the definition? Sinclair-deZwart (1967), in fact, has shown that nonconserving children do not modify nouns denoting substances in a way that clearly preserves the idea of a single object. For example, rather than saying of two jars of water, "this one is taller and thinner, and that one is shorter and wider," they say "this one is taller and that one is shorter, and this one is thinner and that one is wider," dividing their references to the same jars of fluid. While this undoubtedly also reflects the child's understanding of properties, it seems to show that the two jars of fluid were not entirely stable as reference points.

Examples of Entities from Terkel are the following:

> your household goods
> a bushel of corn

The idea of a Person differs from that of an Entity in being infused with animacy and consciousness. If we were so bold as to attempt a definition of this idea, we might say that it is a reference point that changes, but the change is not a function of perception or action on the speaker's part. In contrast to an Entity a Person undergoes change, and like an Entity this change is independent of the speaker's own actions. This definition is appropriate to the idea of a Person which exists at a certain level of mental development (for example, it includes most animals). Observations in Piaget (1960) suggest a course of mental evolution during childhood that points toward a concept something like the one described. Examples of Persons according to this definition include individuals but also collectivities when these are thought to be alive and conscious; for example, "a neighbor" or "the town" can be instances of a Person.

Some of Terkel's examples of the idea of a Person are the following:

> the rank and file people of this state
> a few judges

SPECIFICATION OF EVENTS WITH CASES

It has been noted that the so-called action verbs and the process verbs, by themselves, convey Events. For example, each of *hit, run,* and *sleep* refers to a real-world change of state. The ideas of Event that they convey, however, are minimally specified. We find from the verb only what is contained in the von Wright formula s_1Ts_2, and possibly the initial and/or final condition of this change of state.

Languages offer various refinements of this minimally specified situation. For example, transitive verbs can be viewed as one such refinement. The present section discusses the major refinements, which fall into a relatively small number of familiar categories. One refinement consists of specifying the cause of the change of state; another involves specifying the patient. Other refinements specify recipients, instruments, locations, and beneficiaries. In general, the semantic cases (Fillmore, 1968) can be interpreted as systematic codifications of the means used by speakers for adding specificity to the idea of an Event. Each case, according to this interpretation, applies to and specifies the idea of an Event, in a way that corresponds to the case meaning.

Starting from the bare change of state conveyed by the verb, the smallest additions would seem to be the cause, patient, and recipient of the change of state, corresponding to the agentive, objective, and dative cases (Fillmore, 1968). The reason for regarding these additions as minimal is that they correspond to arguments in the logical structure of verbs. If the change of state is *hit,* specifying the agent and patient provides information that identifies parts of the logical form; for example, in *hit* (x, y), specifying the agent provides the value of x and specifying the patient provides that of y. If the change of state involves a different logical form, a 3-place predicate, for example, *give* or *take,* the recipient or source z is part of the logical form. Specifying this recipient provides the value of z, for example in *give* (x, y, z), and would also be a minimal addition, according to this definition.

Thus, the agentive, objective (= patient), and dative (= recipient or source) cases can be singled out because they correspond to arguments in the logical structure of Events. The basic form of the Event is settled once these arguments are specified. Other cases, however, do not correspond to arguments in this basic logical structure. For example, the location, instrument, and beneficiary of the change of state (corresponding to the locative, instrumental, and benefactive cases) do not appear in the basic structure of Events. If there is specification of the location or instrument of *hit*, the logical form of the Event is not rendered more complete, although more information about it is provided. The difference between *hit* and *give,* in contrast, involves logical form (2-place versus 3-place predicate) as well as quantity of information.

We will use the logical structure of Events to provide a basis of classification of the means of specifying Events, and we will say the cases that correspond to arguments in the logical form of Events (agentive, dative, objective) contain information that *completes,* or fulfills, their Events, while cases that do not correspond to such arguments (locative, benefactive, instrumental, and others) provide information that *extends,* or elaborates on, their Events but does not complete them. This distinction between information that completes and information that extends Events will be of importance in the representation of conceptual structure, developed in the next chapter. Cases of the first type appear as part of the representation of ideas of Events themselves. Cases of the second type appear as additional meaning structures which are related to Events.

Examples of cases of the first type (involved in completing Events) include the following:

Agentive: *Max* in *Max felled the tree,* or *the tree was felled by Max.*
Objective: *mutton* in *the mutton roasted,* or *Max roasted the mutton.*
Dative: *Michael* in *Max gave the watercolor to Michael.*

Examples of cases of the second type (involved in extending completed Events) are the following:

Locative: *New York* in *they found it in New York.*
Instrumental: *forklift* in *he carried it with his forklift.*
Benefactive: *class* in *he did it against his class.*

OTHER BASIC IDEAS

Two concepts that play an important role in the organization of utterances derive from the idea of something existing. This idea is in some respects the opposite of the idea of an Event. Whereas the latter is based on succession and change, the idea of Existence is based on a lack of succession or change. (Existence is not stasis, because stasis, a type of Event, corresponds to a succession of the same state.) Existence is an independent fundamental concept, and enters into a different network of connections, for example, to deixis.

One such deictic usage based on existence is involved in the speech fragments of *it's, there's,* and the like. These are used deictically, with the meaning of Existence. The deictic function may be abstract or concrete. For example, *there's something I want to tell you* includes deictic reference to the existence of an idea or topic in discourse in precisely the same way that *there's something metallic on the table* includes deictic reference to the existence of a physical object on the table. Similarly *it's been a difficult time* refers to existence in the same way as *it's my screwdriver* does, although the deictic referent is abstract in the first case.

The second concept based on existence is, in a sense, the inverse of it, namely, an idea of *Unspecified* Existence. English speech uses this idea extensively, most importantly in forming questions and relative clauses. For example, *what* in *what did you see* indicates the idea of Unspecified Existence concerning the patient of *see,* and the archeologist's reply *wonderful things* specifies what it is that exists (none too precisely). In relative clauses, such as *primitives who live in caves,* the relative pronoun indicates the Unspecified Existence of the Entity or Event that the relative clause modifies (it also, of course, serves as a deictic marker of the onset of the relative clause). Unlike a question, a relative clause provides the information that specifies this Entity or Event immediately within the same utterance, but otherwise the two usages seem to be intimately related. Questions are not discussed in this book, but an analysis of (restrictive) relative clauses is given in Chapter 7.

SUMMARY

This chapter has been concerned with developing a meaning structure in which sensory-motor ideas are related based for the most part on the idea of an Event. This latter idea is regarded as fundamental in the sense that one can show how to reach most of the other sensory-motor ideas from it. The fundamental structural position of the idea of an Event corresponds to its central role in speakers' programming strategies, where utterances tend to be built up until the idea of an Event is complete.

To define an Event, I have made use of von Wright's (1965) calculus of events based on T: a real-world event is a change of state through an interval of time, $s_1 T s_2$. The concept of an Event refers to this. Different connections of sensory-motor ideas to this definition have been described. Collectively these connections represent the meaning structure of much of the sensory-motor domain:

1. Sensory-motor ideas which can be derived from the definition of a real-world event are *States* and *Actions*. A State refers to either the initial condition s_1 or final condition s_2 of an event. An Action corresponds to the performance that causes or motivates the event, and it is often described by omitting the performer.

2. Sensory-motor ideas that refer to temporal extensions of events are *Processes*. Two types are distinguished, depending on whether the extension is of s_1 or s_2, and correspondingly on whether the process ends in or begins with an event (e.g., *bakes* and *sleeps*, respectively). A third possible idea of a Process refers to an extension of a state but not to any specific change of state (*continues* and its synonyms).

3. Sensory-motor ideas that correspond to different forms of specification of Events are *locations, instruments, beneficiaries, causes, patients, recipients,* etc. Case grammar (Fillmore, 1968) can be regarded as describing the means of specifying Events, with the cases organized into two types: those that correspond to the basic logical form of Events and that complete Events, and those that do not correspond to this basic form and that elaborate on Events.

4. Sensory-motor ideas that refer to the conditions on the occurrence of events are *Event Properties,* and those that refer to conditions on the existence of entities or persons are *Entity* or *Person Properties.* These types of Property have different detailed logical structures, but in both, the structures rest on conjunction. This conjunction is interpreted as showing that if the condition is met, the event, or thing, exists and is represented by the corresponding Property.

The ideas of *Person* and *Entity* resist definitions in terms of the idea of an Event, perhaps because they receive enhanced importance if defined separately. In our discussion psychological interpretations were described in terms of reference points, in which Persons are reference points that are alive and conscious, and Entities are reference points that are inert and unchanging.

Two further basic ideas are Existence and Unspecified Existence. These participate in a second semantic system, separate from Event, that merges with the pragmatic effects on speech and appears in such fragments as *it's, there's,* and the *wh*-words in question and relative clauses (which have several deictic functions in discourse).

6 Conceptual Structure

The conceptual structure of speech can be said to be a network of related ideas, or concepts. The relationships are created during the speech event. The manner of connection of these concepts, hence their structure, can be studied. It differs in different utterances and thus is able to express distinctions of meaning. The conceptual structure includes both the sensory-motor content of speech and the non–sensory-motor content to which it is extended. It therefore summarizes all the components of meaning referred to previously in terms of indexical, iconic, and symbolic signs, as well as the interlocking of signs that models semiotic extension. As a form of representation the conceptual structure provides a means whereby we can grasp the total conceptual organization of utterances. Although this point of view may lose immediate sight of the sign structure of speech, it gains a layout or map of the ideas with which the speaker is engaged.

The conceptual structure is meant to be a model of the organization of concepts that the speech user manipulates. Built into the definition of the conceptual structure, therefore, is the assumption that the speech user functions on a single complex level of representation, which we will say is the conceptual structure; components of this structure, which we may analyze as belonging to different levels (for example, different types of sign), converge onto a single mode of representation, the conceptual structure level. The advantages of such a representation will become apparent as we proceed; they include (a) a hypothesis about the mental organization of speech perform-ance; (b) a model for the generation of speech sequences; and (c) a basis for a mathematical treatment of conceptual structure in terms of graphs.

The opening sections of this chapter present the general notion of the conceptual structure, and the main discussion thereafter develops a means for representing conceptual structure. This chapter is organized under three major headings: (1) basic representation of conceptual structures in terms of graphs; (2) extension of this representation; and (3) derivation of new results.

BASIC REPRESENTATION

A desirable feature for a method of representation would be that it is capable of showing directly the relations of concepts. This suggests some kind of diagrammatic model. The method also should have well-understood properties of its own, and it should, in an intuitive sense, be "fitting," appropriate for the conceptual information being represented. In explaining his choice of graph structures for representing the information contained in visual scenes, Winston (1970) writes as follows:

> In this connection, one hears such terms as lists, trees, rings, and nets, each of which suggests a form of storage. In selecting one, attention must be paid to several criteria. I have already mentioned the problem of rapid access. There may also be a need to use memory space efficiently. But in the research phase, perhaps it is most important that the storage format be in some sense natural with respect to the information to be stored. This means that the transformation from a situation to its representation should be simple, not awkward. Simple lists suffice for a list to the grocery store, while tree-like charts frequently picture command hierarchies or genealogical histories.... But many more complex situations require the net... [T]he network seems to have the appropriate blend of flexibility and elegance to deal straightforwardly with scenes... [where]... each object is naturally thought of in terms of relationships to other objects and to descriptive concepts... [pp. 17–18].

A similar rationale can be developed for the use of graphs in representing the conceptual structure of utterances. The descriptive problems are not at all dissimilar between visual scenes and the conceptual structure of speech, particularly in the emphasis on the relationships of concepts to each other and to descriptive terms.

Different examples of directed graph representations of conceptual structures are given in this discussion and in following chapters. The points of the graph (the nodes) correspond to the concepts of the conceptual structure, and the lines of the graph (the arcs) correspond to the relations between concepts of the conceptual structure. Directed graphs show relationships among points and hence relationships among concepts in the conceptual structure. The directions of the lines correspond to encoding sequences. Speech proceeds from the initial point (tail end) of a line to the final point (head end). This last property distinguishes the present interpretation of graph structures from the interpretations given by other authors, e.g.,

Anderson and Bower (1973), Kintsch (1972), Rummelhart, Lindsley, & Norman (1972), and Woods (1970).

The present interpretation of directed graph structure, then, has three basic elements:

1. Points in the graph are said to correspond to concepts in the conceptual structure.
2. Lines in the graph are said to correspond to relations in the conceptual structure.
3. The directions of the lines are said to show encoding sequences.

Labeling the graph appropriately at the points and lines completes the representation of the conceptual structure.

Interpreting directed graphs in the manner described rests on a minimal set of assumptions corresponding to points 1–3 above. That is, we have to assume that it is possible to analyze the conceptual organization of speech into (1) concepts, (2) relations, and (3) relations with specific orientations. A definitive test for concepts is described in Chapter 8. The same test for relations is not definitive but is applicable with high probability. The characterization of orientation was described in Chapter 3 and is discussed further in Chapter 8.

Utterance Path

An utterance path is a particular sequence of points and lines in a graph structure. The utterance path must be a connected (unbroken) sequence. A given graph structure may contain several utterance paths. A *complete* utterance path is one in which every point of the graph appears at least once. A given graph structure may have zero, one, or more than one complete utterance paths. In the case that there is not any complete utterance path, there is no single utterance possible that can completely reflect the conceptual structure. In the case that there is just one complete utterance path, the conceptual structure can be said to determine a unique utterance. If there is more than one utterance path, the conceptual structure can be said to offer the speaker multiple encoding strategies.

Examples of connected and disconnected sequences of points are given in Fig. 6.1. Only the connected sequences (whether or not complete) are utterance paths. The speech direction is always from tail to head, for example $(1)\rightarrow(2)$ underlies 1–2. Disconnected sequences may be indistinguishable from sequences produced in a backwards direction. For example, line 1–4 in G_2 of Fig. 6.1 is disconnected in that it omits point 2, and it is backwards in that it proceeds from 1 to 4 contrary to the direction of the line. Examples of complete and incomplete utterance paths in G_2 are (complete) 1–2–4–3 and

Structure	Connected sequence	Disconnected sequence
	1-2	1-3
G_1 1 —→ 2 —→ 3	2-3	
	1-2-3	
	1-2-4	1-4-3
G_2	1-2-4-3	2-3-2
	1-2-4-1	1-2-4-2
4	1-2-4-1-2	1-2-4-3-2

FIG. 6.1.   Examples of utterance paths.

1–2–4–1–2–3, and (incomplete) 1–2–3 and 1–2–4–1–2. In Fig. 6.2, graph G_1 has no complete utterance path, graph G_2 has exactly one complete utterance path (1–2–3–4), and graph G_3 has infinitely many complete utterance paths, e.g., 1–2–3–4, 1–2–4–1–2–3, 1–2–3–4–1–2–4–1–2–3–4, and so on.

Not every line in a graph must be transversed in order for the utterance path to be complete, although every point must be included in order for it to be complete. For example, graph G_2 in Fig. 6.2 does not include line 2–4 in its only complete utterance path. The shortest complete path in graph G_3 does not include two lines, 2–4 and 4–1. Including all the points determines a complete utterance; including different lines determines different complete utterances.

However, this does not mean that every concept or relation is necessarily encoded into vocal speech. Some concepts and most relations are latent in utterances and are brought out only via probes. Nonetheless, all the concepts present in the conceptual structure, including latent concepts, must be included in the utterance path for it to be complete. To omit any concept, and have the result count as a complete utterance, would introduce an element of arbitrary choice in the representation of conceptual structures.

In conceptual structures, disconnected utterance paths correspond to a common form of speech dysfluency (called a breakdown) in which the speaker abandons one utterance path and replaces it with another within the same conceptual structure. The conceptual structure itself is preserved. In these situations, we will say that the speaker is not following a single utterance

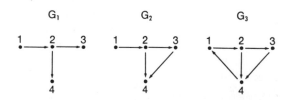

FIG. 6.2.   Complete and incomplete utterance paths.

path through the conceptual structure. *I feel that was definitely her um a characteristic of her kind of a defensive response* is an example of a disconnected utterance path.[1]

Such a disconnected utterance leaves out no concept but fails to relate one or more parts of the conceptual structure. In contrast, an incomplete utterance path occurs when the speaker leaves out one or more concepts necessary to carry the utterance to completion, for example, *She began to loosen up and was.* (Further discussion of disconnected utterances is found in later sections.)

Contraction

Within a graph there may be strong components in which every point is related to every other point. In a strong component, each point can reach any other point. A new graph can be derived by replacing each strong component in a graph by a single point in a new graph. This new graph is called the "contraction" of the first graph.

For example, the graphs in Fig. 6.3 demonstrate various possibilities of contraction. Graph G_1 may be contracted to G_2, G_3, or G_4; G_2 is the maximal contraction. In G_2, S_1 replaces the set $\{1,2,3,4\}$ in G_1, and S_2 replaces $\{5\}$. This contraction is maximal because S_1 and S_2 are the largest strong components in G_1.

In G_3, S_3 replaces $\{1,2,3\}$, S_4 replaces $\{4\}$, and S_2 replaces $\{5\}$. In G_4, S_6 replaces $\{3,4\}$, S_5 replaces $\{2\}$, S_7 replaces $\{1\}$, and again S_2 replaces $\{5\}$. It is true, of course, that the maximal contraction, G_2, describes all the mutually interconnected points of G_1. From the point of view of representing mutual interconnections, knowing the maximal contraction is necessary and sufficient. However, our concern here is with the interpretation of graphs.

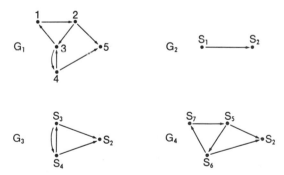

FIG. 6.3. Contraction of graphs.

[1]This example and others below are courtesy of S. Duncan, Jr., and are from a conversation (see chapter 9).

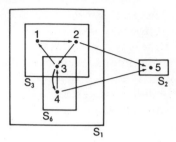

FIG. 6.4. Superimposition of degrees of contraction in a three-dimensional directed graph.

Different interpretations can be given to the different degrees of contraction, as explained in the following discussion; this leads to a natural representation of the sensory-motor content of utterances and to a model of semiotic extension.

Thus, unlike usual graph theoretic statements, ours retains intermediate degrees of contraction. For example, the series we have discussed can be shown in a single three-dimensional graph, as in Fig. 6.4. In other words, combining different degrees of contraction into a single graph provides a graph with a complex internal structure. The complex points of this graph are derived from the higher-order contractions of the graph in G_1 in Fig. 6.3: S_1 includes S_3 and S_6; S_3 includes points 1, 2, and 3; and S_6 includes points 3 and 4. In this way, the process of contraction can become a model for the representation of complex concepts that contain other concepts. Some of these complex concepts may have sensory-motor content. When a complex concept corresponds to a sensory-motor idea, contraction shows a mechanism for a semiotic extension of this sensory-motor idea to the other content at the "lower" (i.e., less contracted) level.

Model for Semiotic Extension

In order for such semiotic extension of a sensory-motor idea to occur, two requirements must be met. First, the sensory-motor idea must *encompass* the other content. This content is the information that differentiates (specifies) the speech program which is accessed via the sensory-motor idea; the other content thus has to be part of this idea. Second, the sensory-motor idea must be related to the other content. If the sensory-motor idea is that of action, for example, the other content to which it is extended has to have some relationship to the idea of an action. Both of these requirements are met by the model of semiotic extension to be described.

A sensory-motor idea is shown at two places in this model. It is introduced, to begin with, on the lower level along with the other content. This step requires that the sensory-motor idea should be related (by labeled lines in the graph) to the other content, and it thus ensures that the second requirement is met. If these relationships are also oriented correctly, it will be possible to form a strong component consisting of the sensory-motor idea and the other content. The contraction of this strong component to a point in a new graph will be labeled with the sensory-motor idea also. When the contracted and original graphs are superimposed, the new sensory-motor idea (a point in the contraction graph) will encompass the strong component on the lower level (the original graph), and this meets the first requirement. The resulting complex graph will show a region of the conceptual structure in which each concept is related to each other concept, and all of which will be encompassed by a sensory-motor idea identical to one that is also related to the other concepts. We have, therefore, a fully explicit model of the type of sensory-motor segments that have been proposed as the basis of syntagmata in previous chapters.

This model states the requirements that must be met in order for there to be semiotic extension; namely, we must know the identity of the concepts and their interrelations and the orientations of the relations that are involved in forming the strong component. Nothing else is involved, according to this model. All the information that is involved in the semiotic extension of a sensory-motor idea is incorporated into the graph representation. The empirical problems of discovering this information from utterances are considered in Chapter 8.

To give an example, *pour* and *coffee* can become part of the semiotic extension of the idea of an Action in forming the utterance fragment, *pours the coffee*. (The article cannot be explained with this graph.) The graph structure in Fig. 6.5 shows the interrelation of three concepts: Action$_1$, (Action$_2$ (pour)), and (Entity (Coffee)). These form a strong component when related with the orientations shown. The contraction of this strong component is labeled Action$_0$. Two of the concepts (Action$_2$ and Entity) are presumed to be part of the lexical retrievals of the words *pour* and *coffee*. Assuming that such sensory-motor ideas are parts of their lexical retrievals permits the interrelation of concepts to take place entirely at the level of Action$_1$, Action$_2$, and Entity. (It also provides a basis for explaining the programming of the articulation of individual words.)

The logical relations in Fig. 6.5 state the following: Action$_2$ *patients* Entity; Entity *is patiented by* Action$_1$; and Action$_1$ *is a result of* Action$_2$. These are oriented in the operative, receptive, and receptive directions, respectively.

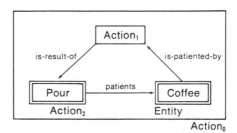

FIG. 6.5. Graph representation of *pours the coffee.*

The first two relations involve the same basic relation, *patients* (A, B) in opposite directions with the two concepts of action:

> *patients* (Action$_1$, Entity)
> *is-patiented-by* (Entity, Action$_2$).

The third involves a basic relation *results in* (A, B), which in its receptive orientation is:

> *is-result-of* (Action$_1$, Action$_2$).

This states that (Action$_2$ (Pour)) is the source of Action$_1$. There seems to be no felicitous expression which brings all of these relations to the surface, but if we force ourselves to produce the following sentence, the meaning follows the relations around and seems to describe a full circle (as predicted of a strong component):

> the action of pouring has as its patient the entity of coffee, which is the patient of an action which is the result of the action of pouring, etc.

In this representation, the transitivity of the verb *pour* has an effect on the entire structure of the strong component in the following way: The patient relation ties (Action$_2$ (Pour)) to Entity; Action$_1$ results from this (Action$_2$ (Pour)) as related to Entity; and the whole strong component contracts to produce the complex Action$_0$. The latter encompasses the transitive action. The assumption, that the lexical retrieval of *pour* brings up Action$_2$, provides a way for *pour* to have this effect on the conceptual structure, since (Action$_2$ (Pour)) can be specified in the lexicon as taking *patients* as its basic relation (in either orientation).

Transitive and Intransitive Events

Figure 6.6 shows the conceptual organization of an event with a transitive verb (*Luther pours the coffee*). It consists of the complex action shown in Fig. 6.5 combined with (Person (Luther)) and Event$_1$. Person is assumed to be part of the lexical retrieval of *Luther*. These concepts form a strong component, which contracts to Event$_0$. The relations inside Event$_0$ state the following: Person *performs* Action$_0$, Action$_0$ *results in* Event$_1$, Event$_1$ *is a result of* Person. (The orientations are operative, operative, and receptive, respectively.) The two results relations express the dependence of Event$_0$ on both the ideas of Person and Action.

This graph shows the type of Event in which a person performs an Action that produces a change of state in an Entity. The patient and agent

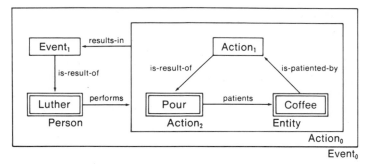

FIG. 6.6.   Graph representation of *Luther pours the coffee.*

(performer) cases are involved. Variations in this type of Event may have Person in the patient role and/or Entity in the performer role. Patient and performer belong to the category of cases that completes Events, and accordingly they appear as constituent parts of $Event_0$, and the relation of $Event_1$ to them both is that of a result. The patient case appears within the subconcept of $Action_0$, and this is the only channel provided for transitivity to affect the overall $Event_0$ structure.

In contrast to transitive structures, Fig. 6.7 shows the graph representation of a sentence with an intransitive verb, *Luther sits.* This conceptual structure is also a type of Event in which a person performs an Action but is different because here the performer equals the patient (cf. Goldin-Meadow, 1975). (This type of Event was used as the basis of the example of a syntagma in Chapter 4.) According to the representation, the performer of the intransitive Action of sitting also has the quality of being the patient; in this example, Luther both performs the act of sitting and is the one whose state changes as a consequence of this act. Other intransitive Actions can be represented in the same way provided that they include a performer.

The intransitive structure in Fig. 6.7 differs from the transitive structure in two respects. First is the simplicity of $Action_0$, which consists only of the Action concept retrieved along with the verb *sit.* Second, the concepts of Person and $Action_0$ are connected by two relations corresponding to the dual role of the person as the performer and the patient of the Action. These

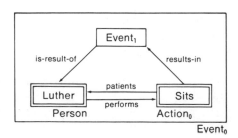

FIG. 6.7.   Graph representation of
Luther sits.

relations state: Person *performs* $Action_0$, and $Action_0$ *patients* Person; both of these relations are oriented operatively.

This operative patient relation has to be latent in intransitive sentences of English, because it cannot map onto the person–action concept sequence. This sequence conflicts wth the operative direction of the *patients* relation. Some intransitive verbs are paired in meaning and form with transitive verbs that take reflexive pronouns, and these may be examples of an explicit patient relation with $Action_0$, as in *Luther sits himself down.*

The intransitive structure in Fig. 6.7 is not the only one conceivable, but it seems to be the one with the fewest arguments against it. The main alternative is to reverse the orientation of the patient relation. However, such a move has two obstacles. First, the receptive orientation in this case would appear without the use of any orientation-changing syntactic devices, contradicting the definition of the basic logical relation as being *patients* ($Action_0$, Person). Second, in a graph representation, two lines running in the same direction (as would be the case if the relations were *is-patiented-by* and *performs*), between the same two points, are indistinguishable. Hence, we would be compelled to say that one line has both an operative and a receptive orientation, a contradiction.

Another possible representation would seem to be to find a new relation that simultaneously conveys both the performer and patient roles of Person. However, no such relation is known, and if the graph structure representation is correct, this alternative is not different from the one just rejected. A relation with two simultaneous functions is equivalent to a single line with two labels. Consequently, postulating such a relation would be the same as saying that a single line represents both an operative and a receptive orientation, which leads to the same contradition.

Thus, the least noxious solution seems to be to have the patient relation appear with an operative orientation, as in Fig. 6.7. This orientation avoids the contradictory assignments of relations to lines in the graph, because in this case there are two lines which run in opposite directions and hence cannot merge.

Segmentation

As hierarchical structures are constructed by the methods described above, different sensory-motor groupings can be created in the speech output. In the example of *Luther pours the coffee,* five segments are predicted:

$Event_0$	| Luther pours the coffee |
Person + $Action_0$	| Luther | pours the coffee |
$Event_0$ + Entity	| Luther pours | the coffee |

A given utterance should show one of these patterns. The last is perhaps the most interesting, because it demonstrates a grouping that would not be predicted from a grammatical description (it disrupts the verb phrase). The explanation is that the combination of Person and $Action_0$ into $Event_0$ is present even though the speech segment consists only of *Luther* and *pours*. The verb brings with it the idea of Action as part of the retrieval of *pour*, and this makes the strong component of $Event_0$ possible. The utterance segment is incomplete only inside the idea of Action. A speaker is this pattern can complete the conceptual structure (include every concept) by producing a final segment based on (Entity (Coffee)).

EXTENDING THE REPRESENTATION

In this section, the aim is to point out and elaborate upon applications of the basic methods described in the previous section for representing conceptual structures. Five topics are considered, in this order: (1) semantic focus; (2) effects of context; (3) utterance boundaries; (4) internal connectedness; (5) comprehension of utterances.

Semantic Focus

Semantic focus refers to a central idea in the conceptual structure, a concept or concepts to which the speaker tries to relate the rest of the conceptual structure as closely as possible. This focal idea is the motivation, informationally speaking, for the utterance's occurring. Often it is "new" information in the sense that the speaker offers it as a new focus of attention (Hornby, 1972), although it may actually be predictable in full or in part from the discourse or context. For example, in the sentence (in a context of gardening) *my roses are fine but weeds are everywhere,* the word *weeds* is unfortunately predictable but is "new" as far as the focus of attention is concerned.

There is a debate among linguists over the extent to which stress ("accent") is determined by the syntactic structure of sentences (e.g., Chomsky & Halle, 1968) or by the information structure (e.g., Bolinger, 1972). Bolinger writes, for example,

> The distribution of sentence accents is not determined by syntactic structure but by semantic and emotional highlighting. Syntax is relevant indirectly in that some structures are more likely to be highlighted than others. But a description along these lines can only be in statistical terms [p. 644].

The relevance of the present discussion to this debate is threefold. First, it provides a technique for determining the semantic focus of utterances based on their conceptual structures. Second, it counteracts what may be a tendency to see the debate in terms of a structural explanation of stress placement versus a nonstructural explanation. Insofar as semantic focus predicts stress placement, it can be said to obey a structural principle. The structure is not fundamentally syntactic in this case but conceptual, but still the speaker is constrained by it. Finally, it is possible that in many cases, stress placement is not completely predicted from semantic focus, although it is predicted within certain limits corresponding to an entire sensory-motor segment.

The ability to determine semantic focus is important also from the point of view of analyzing the conceptual structure of utterances. Very often speakers can report focal ideas, and sometimes they can report the order of semantic importance of several ideas. We can require that the predicted degree of focus should agree with the empirically reported order of semantic importance. The determination of focal values can place extremely strong empirical constraints on the analysis of the conceptual structures. Experience has shown an almost total pruning of alternative analyses once focal values are taken into account.

Moreover, the ability to calculate semantic focus offers a first step toward quantification in the psycholinguistic realm in which the variable quantified is an internal property of the utterance structure (as opposed to an external indicator, such as RT, or a statistical summary, such as word frequency).

"Focus" is conceived of as a variable. Each concept in a conceptual structure has a value of focus. The concept(s) with the highest focal value will be called the focal concept(s), those with the next highest value will be called the secondary focal concept(s), and so on. The basic definition is the following: A concept is focal to the extent that it can be reached from other concepts. To calculate the focal value of a concept, therefore, we should find the total length of all the incoming lines leading to the concept. The smaller this total, the greater the value of focus. The concept(s) with the smallest total will be the focal concept(s).

It is necessary to consider the notion of "distance" in the graph representation of the conceptual structure. Harary, Norman, and Cartwright (1965) define distance in terms of geodesics, as follows: "A *geodesic* from u to v is a path from u to v of minimum length. If there is a path from u to v in a digraph, then the *distance from u to v,* denoted $d(u,v)$, is the length of a geodesic from u to v [p. 32]."

Given a particular graph, one finds the distances (geodesics) between each pair of points. If a point cannot reach another point, the distance is considered to be infinite. All the distances in the graph may be organized into a distance matrix as shown by the example in Fig. 6.8 and the following matrix:

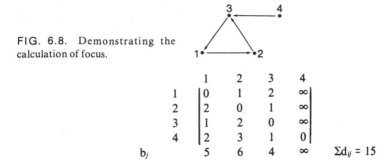

FIG. 6.8. Demonstrating the calculation of focus.

	1	2	3	4
1	0	1	2	∞
2	2	0	1	∞
3	1	2	0	∞
4	2	3	1	0
b_j	5	6	4	∞	$\Sigma d_{ij} = 15$

The sums of the columns, b_j, give the total distance *to* each point j *from* all the points of the graph. The total distance to point 1, for example, is 5 (= 0 + 2 + 1 + 2). The distance between pairs of points is not necessarily the same in both directions. In fact, none of the mutually reachable pairs in the graph above is reachable over the same distances. For example, from point 2 to point 3 the distance is 1, and from point 3 to point 1 the distance is 2.

The focal value of a point is found from the sum of all the incoming distances (including infinite distances) to the point, divided into the sum of the finite distances (Σd_{ij}) in the graph as a whole. That is,

$$F_j = \Sigma d_{ij} / b_j$$

Applying this to the distance matrix above, we have (F_j):

Point	F_j	RF_j
1	3.0	0.74
2	2.5	0.61
3	3.85	1.00
4	0	—

That is, point 3 is the focal point, an intuitively correct result, and point 1 is the secondary focal point, a result that is less obvious. Point 4, not reachable from any other point, is zero on focus.

A relative focal value can be found by dividing each focal value by the maximum focal value. Relative focus is useful for comparing the focal values of points in graphs of different sizes, because focal values may vary in magnitude as the number of points in the graph changes. The formula for relative focus, therefore, is:

$$RF_j = F_j / \max F_j$$

The results for the example in Fig. 6.8 are shown in the second (RF_j) column.

Applying these calculations to speech examples yields several results. The most important is that, in many cases, the focal concept is complex. That is, it is a higher-order idea that has not been individually lexicalized. The identification of stress with such a focal concept must necessarily be less than exact, a fact that limits any theory in which stress is predicted exclusively from the informational (i.e., conceptual) structure, but that leaves room for the determination of stress by other factors (cf. Chomsky & Halle, 1968).

For example, the focal concept in *Luther poured the coffee* is $Action_0$ (= *poured the coffee*). The following distance matrix is based on the conceptual structure given in Fig. 6.6:

	$Event_0$	$Event_1$	Person	Luther	$Action_0$	$Action_1$	$Action_2$	Pour	Entity	Coffee
$Event_0$	0	1	1	2	1	2	2	3	2	3
$Event_1$	1	0	1	2	2	3	3	4	3	4
Person	1	2	0	1	1	2	2	3	2	3
Luther	2	3	1	0	2	3	3	4	3	4
$Action_0$	1	1	2	3	0	1	1	2	1	2
$Action_1$	2	2	3	4	1	0	1	2	2	3
$Action_2$	2	2	3	4	1	2	0	1	1	2
Pour	3	3	4	5	2	3	1	0	2	3
Entity	2	2	3	4	1	1	2	3	0	1
Coffee	3	3	4	5	2	2	3	4	1	0
b_j	17	19	22	30	13	19	18	26	17	25

$$\Sigma d_{ij} = 206$$

Concept	F_j	RF_j
$Event_0$	12.1	.77
$Event_1$	10.8	.68
Person	9.4	.59
Luther	6.9	.44
$Action_0$	15.8	1.00
$Action_1$	10.8	.68
$Action_2$	11.4	.72
Pour	7.9	.50
Entity	12.1	.77
Coffee	8.2	.52

The secondary foci are also complex, although in different ways. $Event_0$ is the utterance as a whole, and Entity is retrieved with *coffee*. The lexicalized concepts are the least focal, but this is simply an artifact of the assumption that they are contained inside the sensory-motor ideas with which they are retrieved. In all other respects, however, it is clear that the semantic focus can be reflected only relatively imprecisely in the stress pattern of this utterance.

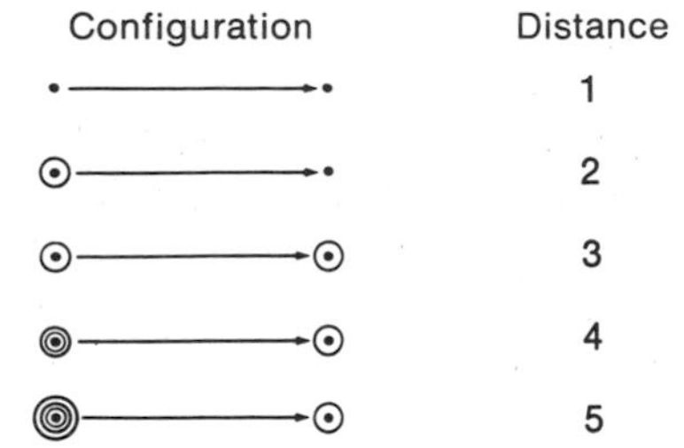

Configuration	Distance
•————————••	1
⊙————————•	2
⊙————————⊙	3
◎————————⊙	4
◉————————⊙	5

FIG. 6.9.   Illustrating vertical distances.

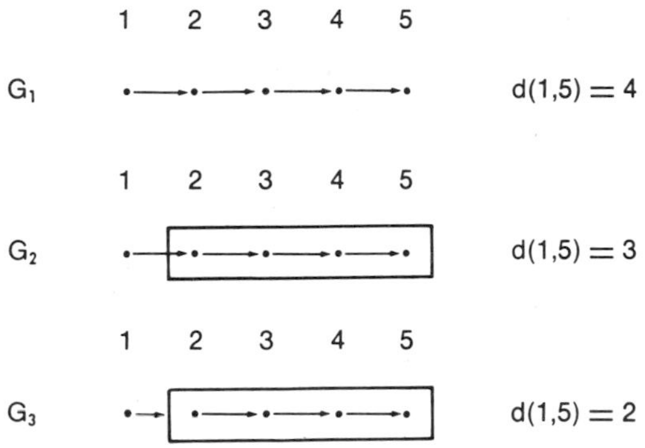

	1 2 3 4 5	
G_1	•——•—•—•——•	$d(1,5) = 4$
G_2	1 2 3 4 5 •—[•——•——•——•]	$d(1,5) = 3$
G_3	1 2 3 4 5 •—[•——•——•——•]	$d(1,5) = 2$

FIG. 6.10.   Illustrating geodesics containing vertical lines.

Note on Counting Distances in Hierarchical Graphs.   The existence of a vertical dimension in the graph structure does not alter the principle of basing distances on geodesics. The inclusion of one point by another is the equivalent of a reciprocal connection between the higher and lower points of one step. The configurations in Fig. 6.9 illustrate several different distances. The geodesic between two points often combines vertical and horizontal distances. For example, the geodesic between points 1 and 5 in G_1 of Fig. 6.10 is decreased by 1 step when the higher-level point is added to the graph (G_2). If point 1 connects directly to the higher-level point, the geodesic between 1 and 5 decreases another step (G_3).

Effects of Context

The approach to context described in this section is quite preliminary. It is meant merely as an illustration of one way in which context can affect conceptual structures and is by no means a general theory. The effect modeled is the shift in semantic focus that comes about when sentences are produced in different contexts. For example, the difference between *I walk on the beach* and *I walk on the beach* could correspond to a difference in context in which the latter version requires some contrast (e.g., a prior sentence, *he swims in icy lakes*).

In terms of a graphical representation of conceptual structures, it is a simple matter to extend the representation to include the context, both discourse and nonverbal, if we assume that the representation of the context can be expressed in the form of concepts and relations and that it becomes a part of the speaker's conceptual structure representation of each utterance. With a prior discourse context this additional conceptual structure is simply that part of the prior discourse that is contextually relevant. Thus, at any point, each utterance may be based on a richer conceptual representation than consideration of the utterance in isolation would show.

To analyze a particular case, I will use the example of *Í walk on the beach,* and show how it may be expanded by context. This example will have the further purpose of illustrating the conceptual structure of an utterance in the locative case. Thus, suppose that one says in an ironic spirit, *Í walk on the beach,* replying to the boast of an obnoxious hairshirt who said that he swims in icy lakes. The speaker's representation of the latter's utterance (the hairshirt's) becomes wholly or partly part of the conceptual structure of the former's utterance (the hero's). The conceptual structure of *Í walk on the beach* is more complex than appears from a superficial reconstruction, therefore, as it includes a contribution from the prior discourse. This contextual part is related to the Event of Ego walking at a specified Location. The stress marking of *Í* is a reflection of the incorporation of this context.

Utterances with Locatives.   This section discusses the conceptual structure of locative utterances. It is necessary to consider how to describe this conceptual structure before continuing with the example of contextual representation which is our main topic.

The locative is one of the cases in the category that extends Event structures. Accordingly, it is shown in the conceptual structure as a sensory-motor idea that is related to, but not part of, its Event. The intransitive verb *walk* induces an Event structure comparable to Fig. 6.7, and the locative case is connected with this event, as shown in Fig. 6.11.

This graph contains several points worth noting. First, the locative idea is not treated as part of $Event_0$, as noted, and this is accomplished by having

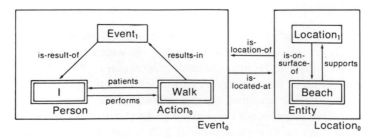

FIG. 6.11.   Graph representation of *I walk on the beach* (without context).

$Event_0$ and $Location_0$ relate only to each other, which they do bidirectionally. They jointly form a strong component, therefore, but because there is no other idea to which they both relate, there is no single sensory-motor idea that can be used to label the combination. The meaning of *I walk on the beach* is accordingly shown as "$Event_0$ at $Location_0$," rather than "$Event_0$," "$Location_0$," or some other single sensory-motor idea.

Second, the idea of a Location itself is semiotically extended to (Entity (Beach)). This latter concept interrelates with the idea of $Location_1$, and forms the strong component that is labeled $Location_0$. The relations inside this strong component are $Location_1$ *is-on-the-surface-of* (Entity (Beach)) and (Entity (Beach)) *is-the-surface-of* $Location_1$. The basic logical relation of location is taken to be *is-location-of* (A, B). This relation corresponds to the meaning of location in such examples as *the garden has a cottage, Chicago has the Cubs,* etc., which do not involve orientation-changing syntactic devices. The opposite orientation appears in *the cottage is in the garden, the Cubs are in Chicago,* etc., which make use of the copula, a verb strongly associated with receptive orientations (cf. Chapter 7). Accordingly, the orientation of $Location_1$ *is-on-the-surface-of* Entity is receptive, whereas that of Entity *is-the-surface-of* $Location_1$ is operative.

Third, the idea of $Location_0$ is related to $Event_0$ by the operative relation of $Location_0$ *is-location-of* $Event_0$ and the receptive relation of $Event_0$ *is-located-at* $Location_0$. The arguments for this assignment are parallel to those in the preceding paragraph.

Effect of Adding Representations of Context.   A distance matrix based on Fig. 6.11 (without context) gives the following values of focus F_j and relative focus RF_j (concepts whose focal value will be shifted after the context is added are in italics):

Concept	F_j	RF_j
Event_0	*14.5*	*1.00*
$Event_1$	10.4	.72
Person	*12.1*	*.83*
$Action_0$	11.5	.79
Ego	8.4	.58
Walk	8.1	.56
$Location_0$	12.8	.88
$Location_1$	9.5	.66
Entity	9.9	.68
Beach	7.3	.50

As with the earlier example, the most focal ideas appear as complex segments; $Event_0$ and $Location_0$ are first- and second-ranked, respectively (a result that seems to accord with intuition). The lexicalized concepts are the three least focal ideas, but again this is in part an artifact.

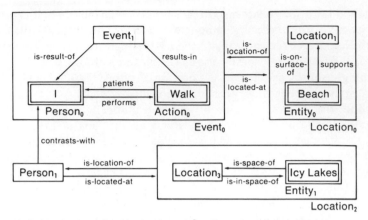

FIG. 6.12.   Graph representation of *I walk on the beach* (with context).

Figure 6.12 shows the conceptual structure of *I walk on the beach,* produced by adding to Fig. 6.11 a representation of the context. Less than the full prior utterance is included in this representation, however, and it contains only the ideas of $Person_1$ and $Location_2$, corresponding to the hairshirt and the icy lakes but not to the event of the hairshirt's swimming. This will illustrate that fragmentary representations of context also can affect the conceptual structure.

The addition of context increases the total length of incoming lines for all concepts in the Fig. 6.11 conceptual structure but increases them less for ($Person_0$ (Ego)) than for any other concept. This is because the context attaches directly to ($Person_0$ (Ego)). This arrangement corresponds to the hero's contrasting the hairshirt's person with his own (rather than other possible contrasts). It is possible to compute the minimum amount of context needed to shift the focus in any given conceptual structure. This is equal to one more than the difference, in the sum of incoming distances, between the original focal idea (which was $Event_0$ in the example) and the new focal idea. In the case of ($Person_0$ (Ego)), this difference was only three; therefore, a contextual representation which contains at least four concepts is sufficient to cause the focus to shift to ($Person_0$ (Ego)). The contextual representation in Fig. 6.12 contains five concepts. Even this partial representation of the prior discourse is more than enough to shift the focus of the utterance. Each context concept adds one more step to the total incoming distance of $Event_0$ than of ($Person_0$ (Ego)), because all of these concepts can reach the former only via the latter. The number of concepts in the context acts as a multiplier. No other concept apart from ($Person_0$ (Ego)) in the original conceptual structure will have a higher focal value than $Event_0$, and therefore all will be lower than ($Person_0$ (Ego)) for the same reason.

The following shows the focal values F_j and relative focal values RF_j computed from Fig. 6.12 (the concepts involved in the shift of focus are italicized):

Concept	F_j	RF_j
Event$_0$	*14.4*	*.94*
Event$_1$	10.8	.71
Person$_0$	*15.3*	*1.00*
Action	12.8	.84
Ego	10.8	.71
Walk	9.5	.62
Location$_0$	11.9	.78
Location$_1$	9.3	.61
Entity$_0$	9.5	.62
Beach	7.5	.49
Person$_1$	0	——
Location$_2$	0	——
Location$_3$	0	——
Entity$_1$	0	——
Icy lakes	0	——

The context itself has zero focal value in Fig. 6.12, as it cannot be reached by any concept in the original conceptual structure, giving the context infinite incoming distances.

The above example is, of course, artificial and highly simplified. Only a single relation from one contextual source is involved. In more realistic situations, the contextual associations would be far more complex.

The way in which context is represented in the present scheme is defective in one respect, namely, the lack of differentiation between types of context in terms of importance or appropriateness. Only bulk matters. A larger contextual contribution will have a larger effect. There are several alternatives by which this defect could be corrected. For example, more important contexts could be weighted more heavily or be given a larger number of relations to the conceptual structure; or only relevant relations could be included. Each of these modifications, which assume the ability to determine importance, would restrict the brute effects of sheer bulk on the conceptual structure.

Utterance Boundaries

The ability to expand the conceptual structure contextually creates the problem of defining the boundaries of utterances. I do not mean external boundaries for which such criteria as cessation of speech, pauses, exchanges of speaker turns, and so forth, are invoked. The problem involves the internal boundaries of utterances. It is, in principle, possible to trace relations to ideas outward in ever widening circles. Is everything that is traceable to count as part of the utterance? For example, *Í walk on the beach* presupposes the existence of someone else and implies that there is a beach, that it is sandy or pebbly, and so on. Should all of this information be included in the utterance? It seems that there should be a definition of the internal utterance boundary. The presupposition of a contrasting individual should be included in the example above, for example, but not the implication that the beach is sandy or pebbly. A flexible definition of the internal utterance boundary is that it is the maximum size of the conceptual structure at which incorporation of new information ceases to have any effect on the internal organization of the utterance. By this definition, therefore, all the information relevant to the internal organization is contained within each utterance boundary.

A convenient measure of the "size" of the conceptual structure is the sum of all the infinite distances between concepts, Σd_{ij}, divided by the number of concepts, n. For example, the "size" of the conceptual structure of *Luther pours the coffee* is 20.6; of *I walk on the beach* (without context) is 21.8; and of *Í walk on the beach* (with context) is 31.7. The measure of internal organization can be the change of relative focus discussed in the preceding section. Thus, a definition of the *utterance boundary* is the maximum relative sum of finite distances reached within the graph structure before changes in relative focus cease. This definition emphasizes that the boundary of an utterance is relative to the meaning of the utterance and its context and can expand or shrink according to these factors.

In the preceding section, it was pointed out that more extensive contexts should have a greater effect on relative focus. Yet the definition of an utterance boundary assumes that a point can be reached where further enlarging the context would cease to have an effect on relative focus. The resolution of this conflict depends on taking into account the concept to which the further context is connected. Any new context will shift the absolute focus of what is already in the cocneptual structure, and the size of this effect can be calculated. However, if the context attaches to the concept that is already highest in focus, the shift of focus will affect all concepts to exactly the same extent, and the relative focus will not change. Thus, utterance boundaries will tend to form when the context relates to the concept highest on focus. If further context attaches to $(Person_0 (Ego))$, for example, in *Í walk on the beach,* the shift of focus will be the same for every concept within the utterance and will not change the relative focus; therefore this further information from context will not be included within the utterance boundary.

Thus, the entire discourse is not incorporated into each utterance. Most of the time context relates to the most focal idea of an utterance and therefore is not included. This is the meaning of saying that utterances should "fit" their context. When an utterance is produced that does not relate to the prior discourse and the speaker does not intend for it to relate, it can be overtly marked ("this changes the subject, but. . . " or the equivalent). The necessity of this kind of marking can be easily understood in terms of the model of the utterance boundary. The new utterance boundary, if it were not marked, would expand enormously to include the whole discourse. Such expansion is the consequence when the context does not relate to any of the utterance's concepts. We have all had the experience, as listeners, in which an utterance out of the blue or an unannounced change of subject leaves us at sea, searching the entire context for a connection to the new utterance. In this situation, the utterance boundary apparently does attempt to expand to encompass the whole discourse, an effect which can be explained.

The properties of conceptual structure involved in determining the internal boundaries of utterances plausibly also exist in the consciousness of speakers. The semantic focus of concepts and distances of concepts within the conceptual structure seem to correspond to the speaker's own sense of the conceptual boundaries of speech.

Internal Connectedness

"Connectedness" refers to the extent to which the concepts in the conceptual structure are capable of reaching each other. Intuitively, it corresponds to the internal cohesion of an utterance. Different degrees of connectedness might reflect, in some utterances, stages of organizing the conceptual structure (cf. the last section of this chapter). Some utterances are relatively cohesive, in that every concept relates directly or indirectly to every other concept. For example, *I walk on the beach* and *Luther pours the coffee* are cohesive in this way. Other utterances are less cohesive, in that they contain some concepts that other concepts cannot reach, as in this example (actual utterance): *tell me what you were gonna tell me when I told you not to talk to me that other time.* Utterances that are still less cohesive involve a discontinuity of the utterance path, as in *I felt that was definitely her um a characteristic of her kind of a defensive response* (also an actual utterance). Still less cohesive are utterances in which there is a disconnection of part of the conceptual structure itself, such as in this constructed example: *she's really frightened that did you notice the door open?*

These differences in cohesion can be modeled within conceptual structure representations by means of a definition of "level of connectedness." Harary et al. (1965) distinguish four such levels, defined and exemplified as follows (disregarding a fifth level, a variant of the third):

Level 0.   In the lowest level of connectedness, at least one concept cannot reach, and cannot be reached by, any other concept. The graph representation

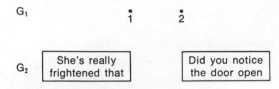

FIG. 6.13.   Level 0 of connectedness.

is said to be disconnected. Graph G_1 in Fig. 6.13, for example, is disconnected and is at Level 0 of connectedness. The last example, *she's really frightened that did you notice the door open,* has a similar overall conceptual structure (graph G_2). A Level 0 conceptual structure cannot possibly have an unbroken complete utterance path.

Level 1.   In a graph at this level of connectedness, at least one pair of concepts is mutually unreachable, although no concept is disconnected. For example, G_1 in Fig. 6.14 is at Level 1, since points 1 and 2 cannot reach each other. The example of a Level 1 conceptual structure, *I felt that was definitely her um a characteristic of her kind of a defensive response,* has the same overall organization (G_2). As at Level 0, there is not possibly an unbroken complete utterance path available through a Level 1 conceptual structure. Thus, Level 1, along with Level 0, is often associated with speech dysfluencies. The important property of Level 1 that distinguishes it from Level 0 lies in the conceptual organization rather than in the speech flow—at Level 1, even though there is a dysfluency, all the concepts are related to one concept or another. There is a general conception behind the utterance, but the parts are not consistently related. The relationship between *I felt that was definitely her* and   *a characteristic of her kind of* is of this loose kind, in which the connection is that both are related to *defensive response.*

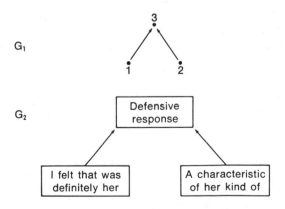

FIG. 6.14.   Level 1 of connectedness.

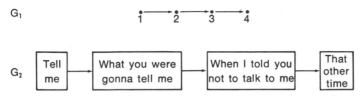

FIG. 6.15.   Level 2 of connecteness.

Level 2.   At this level of connectedness, at least one concept of each pair of concepts can reach the other. In such a conceptual structure, there is always at least one unbroken complete utterance path. For example, G_1 in Fig. 6.15 is connected at Level 2. The example at this level, *Tell me what you were gonna tell me when I told you not to talk to me that other time,* has the same overall structure (graph G_2). Such utterances have a purely cumulative form, and this apparently describes the process of producing them. The speaker moves from idea to idea with no attempt to provide an overall framework. The ideas build up successively into a larger conceptual structure, but there is no influence of later concepts on earlier concepts. Level 2 utterances lend themselves to speech that is associative rather than interlocking, in which utterances are permitted simply to extend outward. This type of utterance is more likely to occur in casual speech situations, therefore, and seems to predominate in the speech of some individuals more than others.

Level 3.   At the highest level of connectedness every concept can reach every other concept either directly or indirectly. There are always at least two complete utterance paths through a Level 3 conceptual structure. The graph in Fig. 6.16, for example, is connected at Level 3.

This pattern is familiar from the processes described earlier in forming strong components. The overall structure of *I walk on the beach* or *Luther pours the coffee* is of this kind and is connected at Level 3. On the other hand, *I walk on the beach,* with context, is connected at Level 2, because the context cannot be reached from the rest of the structure. Occasionally, alternate utterance paths through Level 3 conceptual structures can be found. An example would be, *sits Luther (on yon stump),* in which the sequence is $Action_0 \rightarrow Person$ rather than the reverse. In both sequences, however, there is the same strong component which contracts to $Event_0$.

Level 3 utterances are internally cohesive to a maximum degree, in the sense that every concept within them is related to every other concept, and

FIG. 6.16.   Level 3 of connectedness.

later concepts can influence earlier concepts. At any given point, the entire conceptual structure can be said to be brought to bear, therefore, including the parts not yet articulated.

This degree of connectedness does not depend on the speaker's choice of programming units; it is independent of this choice and depends only on the way in which the conceptual structure is arranged. An important observation, therefore, is that the level of connectedness is not reduced by choosing smaller programming units. This implication follows directly from the definitions of connectedness, and it means that the speaker can program an utterance in small chunks without affecting the level of connectedness.

Comprehension of Utterances

In comprehending speech, the listener interprets the sign structure of the speaker's utterances. The overt part of the utterance path consists of the sign vehicles of indexical signs that have sensory-motor content as their objects. It is necessary to interpret these sign vehicles correctly and to determine how they have been semiotically extended. Working out this extension means, for the listener, reconstructing the conceptual structure, and the speaker is able to influence the relative ease or difficulty of this process.

At least three mechanisms can be described in terms of conceptual structure which, if the speaker uses them, would have the effect of limiting the listener's errors of reconstruction: using "small" utterances (in terms of internal distances); using marked semantic focus (stress shifts); and using syntactic devices which impose overall patterns of conceptual structure.

"Small" Utterances. An utterance tends to be kept small in terms of internal distances if it is related to its context at the point in the conceptual structure that is (when the utterance is considered independently) already highest in focus. By definition, the context is not part of the utterance in this case. It is through this mechanism that we can explain the effects on comprehension of producing utterances which "fit" well into their contexts. Such utterances require of the listener the minimum in reconstruction. The context already predicts the point of highest focus, and the listener does not have to incorporate the context inside the boundaries of the utterance. Contextually fitting utterances may or may not be "small" in terms of physical length. The example mentioned earlier, *tell me what you were gonna tell me when I told you not to talk to me that other time,* although lengthy, arises from a conceptual structure that is small in terms of its relative internal distances.

Marked Focus. The converse principle to the use of "small" utterances is to enlarge the utterance by using a stress-marked shift of focus. The utterance is deliberately expanded in this case, incorporating part of the context. This aids the accuracy of the listener's reconstruction if he or she shares the same context as the speaker, because part of the (expanded) conceptual structure is available to the listener in advance. The first principle, which urges "small" utterances, and the second, which urges expansion of utterances, clearly cannot be followed simultaneously. Both methods presuppose a shared context of speech between speaker and hearer.

Syntactic Devices.   Some syntactic devices signal their presence within a few words and establish an overall plan of the conceptual structure. Very quickly, then, the speaker can forecast the general outline of the conceptual structure. An example of a syntactic device that permits this is the pseudocleft construction, from which the listener knows virtually immediately that the conceptual structure will consist of two equated sensory-motor ideas (cf. Chapter 7). Other syntactic devices, however, do not establish such an overall conceptual structure in this way or fail to signal their presence until relatively late in the speech input, and would not lend themselves to listener strategies of this kind. For example, gerundive nominalizations have an effect across smaller parts of utterances. Relative clauses are not signaled until the relative clause itself begins in the input. These devices should be less helpful to listeners than the pseudocleft. (Harris, 1977, has shown experimentally that the order in which information arrives in the speech input has an effect on speed of comprehension.)

The mechanisms described above obviously do not exhaust the means by which speakers can aid listeners. A most important mechanism not accounted for is the role of various deictic elements in speech. Nonetheless, it is obvious that communication is based on cooperation between the speaker and listener. The following section discusses a scheme for dividing responsibility for successful communication in general between the speaker and the listener.

Typology of Communication "Duties."   The speaker and listener can be viewed in terms of their respective "duties" with respect to communication. The following scheme for identifying and classifying these duties is based on the connectedness of graphs, and the role played by individual concepts in determining this connectedness. Some concepts strengthen the level of connectedness in that, if omitted, the level would go down. Some concepts are neutral in that, if omitted, the level of connectedness would not change. Some concepts have a weakening effect in that, if omitted, the level of connectedness would increase. (This typology and terminology are from Harary et al., 1965.)

It seems to be the special duty of the speaker to include strengthening concepts without fail, because otherwise the level of connectedness will suffer, and this cannot be adjusted by the listener. For example, *on the beach* is inadequate as an utterance because the strengthening concept of an Event, *I walk,* is omitted and cannot be supplied by the listener (assuming that it is not available from context). The category of strengthening concepts appears to correspond to the notion of nonredundant information, i.e., information that the speaker must provide.

Neutral concepts, by contrast, model redundant information. If they are omitted, the level of connectedness does not suffer. For example, *Tell me what you were gonna tell me* is connected as a whole at Level 2. Omitting *you* does not affect the possibility of reconstructing the overall Level 2 conceptual structure; e.g., *Tell me what were gonna tell me.* Such omissions are not unknown in speech, and they are expected not to adversely affect communication, even though they might reduce the grammaticality of the utterance. It would be of interest to have a large-scale statistical classification of word omissions from actual utterances. The prediction is that omitted words would more often correspond to neutral concepts than to strengthening concepts. From the point of view of "duties," neutral concepts are equally the responsibility of the listener and the speaker. Both share the communicative burden with such concepts. If the speaker fails to provide the concept, the listener can provide it instead.

Weakening concepts are the special responsibility of the listener. By omitting from his or her reconstruction of the conceptual structure any weakening concepts that the speaker has included, the listener is able to increase the level of connectedness. If a strengthening concept is nonredundant and a neutral concept is redundant, a weakening concept is extraneous. For example, *She's really frightened that did this mood mechanism will control her* (actual example) will go up from Level 1 to 3 if the listener simply does not process the word *did.*

Level 3 utterances cannot contain weakening concepts, as there is no way for them to be more strongly connected, and Level 0 utterances cannot contain strengthening concepts, as there is no way for them to be more weakly connected. For the other combinations of levels and types, there seems to be a correlation such that strengthening concepts are found generally at Level 3, neutral concepts at level 2, and weakening concepts at Levels 0 and 1.

The neutral concepts at Level 2 are one more reason why this level would tend to be the level of causal conversation. The strengthening concepts at Level 3 suggest, somewhat counterintuitively, that when communication is via noisy or otherwise difficult channels, all other things equal, the highest level of connectedness should be *avoided.* Something lost from the message could reduce the level of connectedness and might not be replaceable by the listener.

DERIVATION OF NEW RESULTS

The arguments presented below assume the general validity of interpreting graph structures as models of conceptual structures. I now will attempt to derive new results from deductions based on the theory of graphs and to check these against observations.

"Quantum" Restriction on New Information

At several points in this chapter, I have considered the effects of adding new information to conceptual structures. This information is usually regarded as coming from the context. It turns out that any single new relation and concept added to the conceptual structure can either shift the focus of this structure or change the connectedness but it cannot have both of these effects at the same time. There is a kind of "quantum" effect from adding new information, therefore, in which a single item of new information may have an effect on one or the other, focus or connectedness, but cannot have an effect on both. This quantum restriction supports a speech production strategy in which the speaker can select the focal point in advance, then add conceptual relations in order to build up the connectedness of the conceptual stucture; the focal point is required by the quantum restriction not to shift during this process and therefore it need not be processed more than once. Selecting different focal points leads to different utterances, as shown in the following examples:

1. Selecting *ring* as the focal point and adding information about location to build up the connectedness, the speaker produces,

the thing I like in the box is the ring

2. Selecting *in the box* as the focal point and adding *ring* to build up the connectedness, the speaker produces,

the thing I like is the ring in the bóx

3. Selecting both *in the box* and *ring* as focal points, the speaker produces two distinct phases of output, which may occur in either of two orders:

the thing I like is the ring; in the bóx

or

the thing I like in the bóx; the ring

In Example 3 each of the focal points has primary stress. According to the definition of a phonemic clause (Trager & Smith, 1951), successive primary stresses are separated by some form of terminal contour, and this is the case in the sentences in Example 3 (the terminal contours are marked ";"). The occurrence of these contours is predicted from the quantum restriction.

Neither *in the box* nor *ring* increases the level of connectedness because both are added as focal points. The level of connectedness is at most Level 1. (It cannot be greater than Level 1 because the two items of added information, in order for both to be focal, cannot be connected to each other.) The terminal contours therefore occur where there is a broken utterance path. In this way, we can see how the definition of a phonemic clause, a phonological unit, can be traced back to the organization of conceptual information. This combination of phonological and conceptual structure can be regarded as exemplifying the nature of syntagmata.

Analysis of the Quantum Restriction

The following discussion considers the quantum restriction in more detail. Apart from its intrinsic importance, this exercise illustrates the use of graph theory to derive new consequences for the description of mental structures. The following will be shown: adding a single relation and concept to any conceptual structure can change the minimum length of incoming lines in the graph representation or can increase the level of connectedness of the graph, but it cannot have both of these effects simultaneously. This argument will first be developed for the special case in which the points involved in the focus shift (or lack thereof) have finite incoming distances; then the results will be generalized to the case in which these points have infinite incoming distances. The argument will be developed for four cases: $C_1 \rightarrow C_2$ (connectedness Level 1 to 2); $C_1 \rightarrow C_3$; within C_2; and $C_2 \rightarrow C_3$.

In the discussion that follows it is necessary to bear in mind the relation between the connectedness of *graphs* and the connectedness of *points*. The connectedness of a graph can never be greater than the least connectedness of any pair of points within it. For example, a Level 2 graph may contain points that are connected at Level 3, and a Level 1 graph may contain points that are connected at Level 2 or 3. Table 6.1 summarizes the relationships of the two types of connectedness.

TABLE 6.1
Connectedness

Connectedness of any two points	Connectedness of the graph
1	1
2	1, 2
3	1, 2, 3
1, 2, 3	1
2, 3	2
3	3

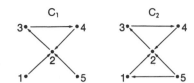

FIG. 6.17. Increasing connectedness to Level 2 from Level 1.

$C_1 \rightarrow C_2$. The argument has two steps:

1. Any points that are connected in a sequence in a Level 1 graph are themselves connected at Level 2. This is because, for each pair of points in a sequence, e.g., points 1 and 3 in the C_1 graph in Fig. 6.17, at least one point can reach the other. Therefore all geodesics (see p. 104) in a Level 1 graph are connected at Level 2.

2. Any new line that increases the connectedness of the graph to Level 2 must necessarily connect points that are connected at Level 1 in the Level 1 graph, i.e., are not part of any sequence in the graph. Therefore the new line cannot shorten any existing geodesic in the graph. These geodesics are already connected at Level 2. Hence, it is impossible for the new line to simultaneously increase the connectedness of the graph from level 1 to 2 and change the focus.

For example, the connectedness of points 1 and 5 in the C_1 graph of Fig. 6.17 is at Level 1. All other pairs of points are connected at Level 2. Therefore, to increase the connectedness of the graph to Level 2, it is necessary (and sufficient) to connect points 1 and 5. However, this cannot affect the incoming distances across geodesics at any of the points 2, 3, and 4.

$C_1 \rightarrow C_3$. A similar argument applies in this situation. Any new line that increases connectedness from Level 1 to Level 3 must connect two points at Level 3. These must be points that are already in a sequence that is connected at Level 1 or 2, but not at Level 3, in the Level 1 graph. Such a new line cannot shorten any existing geodesic, because it cannot be part of any existing sequence in the Level 1 graph and hence not part of a minimal sequence. Fig. 6.18 shows an example of a Level 1 graph converted to Level 3 by the addition of one line that is not part of any existing sequence. The line from 1 to 3 causes all pairs of points to become connected at Level 3, but the sum of incoming distances at point 1 (= 4) remains the same, and this is the lowest sum in both graphs.

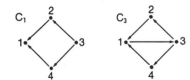

FIG. 6.18. Increasing connectedness to Level 3 from Level 1.

$$C_2 \quad \overset{1}{\bullet}\longrightarrow\overset{2}{\bullet}\longrightarrow\overset{3}{\bullet}\longrightarrow\overset{4}{\bullet}$$

$$C_2 \quad \overset{1}{\bullet}\longrightarrow\overset{2}{\bullet}\longrightarrow\overset{3}{\bullet}\longrightarrow\overset{4}{\bullet}$$

FIG. 6.19. Shifting focus within Level 2.

Within C_2. Adding a line to a C_2 graph can change the sum of incoming distances at a point without changing the connectedness of the graph. The possibility of these changes can be demonstrated by example (Fig. 6.19). Point 4 in the first graph has a sum of incoming distances of six; in the second graph this sum remains six, but point 3 has a sum of four, shifting focus to point 3. The additional line from point 4 to point 3 in the second graph does not increase the connectedness of these points or of the graph as a whole.

$C_2 \rightarrow C_3$. There are again two steps in the argument:

1. Only lines that increase the connectedness between pairs of points from Level 2 to 3 need to be considered. If the connectedness of two points is at Level 3, no additional line between them can improve the connectedness of the graph.

2. A new line between points connected at Level 2 cannot shorten any geodesic in the graph. For whichever line is added, it cannot be part of any existing sequence in the Level 2 graph and hence not part of any minimal sequence. Therefore, no line that increases the level of connectedness of the graph from 2 to 3 can cause a shift of focus.

For an example, see Fig. 6.20. The lowest sum of incoming lines is at point 3 (= 4). Adding a line that is not part of any existing sequence, from point 2 to point 4, increases the connectedness of the graph without changing the sums at any point or making the sum at point 4 lower.

Besides the four we have discussed, only two other cases exist, shifting focus within C_1 and within C_3, and in both it is possible to shift the focus by adding a single line, as within C_2.

Considering the six cases together, we can say that there is no change of focus when there is a change of connectedness for the graph as a whole ($C_1 \rightarrow C_2$, $C_1 \rightarrow C_3$, $C_2 \rightarrow C_3$), and there is no change of connectedness when there is a change of focus (within C_1, C_2, or C_3).

The Problem of Infinite Distances

The arguments I have discussed appear not to apply in one situation, namely, where a point in a graph is not reachable from some other (infinitely distant)

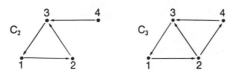

FIG. 6.20. Increasing connectedness to Level 3 from Level 2.

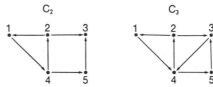

FIG. 6.21.   Illustrating potential
foci.

point. In this situation, it is possible for a single new line to be added to the
graph that makes the point reachable in such a way that the connectedness of
the graph increases *and* this point turns out to have the lowest sum of finite
incoming distances. That is, a single new line both increases the connectedness and shifts the focus. It is as if the formerly infinite distance had been
concealing a potential focal point. Figure 6.21 shows an example of this
phenomenon.[2] The following distance matricies refer to the C_2 and C_3 graphs
in this figure respectively:

$$C_2 = \begin{array}{c|ccccc} & 1 & 2 & 3 & 1 & 2 \\ \hline 1 & 0 & 2 & 3 & 1 & 2 \\ 2 & 1 & 0 & 1 & 2 & 3 \\ 3 & \infty & \infty & 0 & \infty & \infty \\ 4 & 2 & 1 & 2 & 0 & 1 \\ 5 & \infty & \infty & 1 & \infty & \infty \\ b_j & \infty & \infty & 7 & \infty & \infty \\ & F & F & & F & \end{array}$$

$$C_3 = \begin{array}{c|ccccc} & 1 & 2 & 3 & 1 & 2 \\ \hline 1 & 0 & 2 & 3 & 1 & 2 \\ 2 & 1 & 0 & 1 & 2 & 3 \\ 3 & 3 & 2 & 0 & 1 & 2 \\ 4 & 2 & 1 & 2 & 0 & 1 \\ 5 & 4 & 3 & 1 & 2 & 0 \\ b_j & 10 & 8 & 7 & 6 & 8 \end{array}$$

In the C_2 graph only point 3 is reachable from all the others. Points 3 and 4 are
connected at Level 2, and adding a line from point 3 and 4 increases their
connectedness, and the graph's connectedness, to level 3. This new line connot
affect the sum of incoming distances at point 3 (because of the quantum
restriction), but it eliminates all the infinite distances in the graph, and point 4
turns out to have the smallest finite sum of distances with this particular line
added.

The problem illustrated with this example arises because we have not
considered points with infinite incoming distances. In fact, it is possible to
generalize the quantum restriction to such points. In this generalization, finite
points are a special case.

If we look only at the finite entries in the C_2 distance matrix we can see that
several points (those marked "F": 1, 2, and 4) have the potential of being foci
in this graph. This is the case because where there are finite distances they

---
[2]I am grateful to Gary Kahn for discovering this example and raising the problem of infinite
distance.

have smaller sums of incoming distances than point 3 does. Thus, infinite entries do conceal potential focal points.

Generalization of the Quantum Restriction

Let us define a *potential focal set* in a graph as the set of all points in the graph such that each point in the set could be the focal point when some one line is added to the graph that increases the connectedness of the graph. This definition applies only to graphs with infinite entries, because only such graphs can have their connectedness increased. Each member of the potential focus set, apart from the focal point of a graph (which has finite incoming distances), must have at least one infinite incoming distance that conceals it as a potential focus point (if all the distances are finite, the distance at the point is known).

The quantum restriction can be phrased to apply to the potential focal set, which means that the restriction cannot be fully precise when this set has more than one member. For the C_2 graph in Fig. 6.21, for example, the quantum restriction can state only that an additional line that increases connectedness to Level 3 cannot at the same time shift the focus outside of the set of points marked with "F."

The quantum restriction, then, can be stated as a restriction on the potential focus set. In the special case where this set contains exactly one member all distances are finite and a line cannot be added to the graph that increases connectedness and shifts the focus from this one member of the set. When the set contains more than one member, there are infinite distances and an added line that increases the connectedness cannot shift the focus away from this set, meaning that one point of the set must be the focal point of the new, more strongly connected graph. On the other hand, a line can be found in some graphs which, when added to the graph, does not increase the connectedness and does shift the focus outside of the potential focus set. This generalization of the quantum restriction is important for interpreting the effects of adding new information in more realistic conceptual structures.

Point 3, the focus of the C_2 graph in Fig. 6.21, is *not* in the potential focus set of its graph, for the following reason: Comparing finite entries in the distance matrix, point 3 has a sum of incoming distances that is greater by three steps than the sum of incoming distances at any of the points, 1, 2, or 4 (Point 3 equals point 5). This difference means that adding a line that increases the connectedness of the graph must add more than three incoming lines to each of points 1, 2, and 4, in order for point 3 to be within the set of potential foci. However, there is no such single line, because no matter which line is added, if it increases the connectedness, it adds only three lines to the sum of incoming distances at one of the points 1, 2, or 4. This is because a line which increases the connectedness of the graph must join point 3 to one of points 1, 2, or 4. Whichever one of these is selected, it receives one line from point 3 and two lines from point 5, and no others.

The conceptual structure of the Level 1 example given earlier, *the thing I like is the ring; in the bóx*, is shown schematically in Fig. 6.22 (point 1 = *the thing I like*, 2 = *the ring*, 3 = Location$_0$, 4 = Location$_1$, 5 = Entity, and 6 = *the box*. The distance matrix for this graph is as follows:

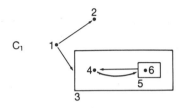

$$
\begin{array}{c|cccccc}
1 & 0 & 1 & 1 & 2 & 2 & 3 \\
2 & \infty & 0 & \infty & \infty & \infty & \infty \\
3 & \infty & \infty & 0 & 1 & 1 & 2 \\
4 & \infty & \infty & 1 & 0 & 1 & 2 \\
5 & \infty & \infty & 1 & 1 & 0 & 1 \\
6 & \infty & \infty & 2 & 2 & 1 & 0 \\
b_j & \infty & \infty & \infty & \infty & \infty & \infty \\
 & F & F & F & F & & \\
\end{array}
$$

FIG. 6.22. Conceptual structure of a Level 1 utterance.

The members of the potential focus set are {1, 2, 3, 4}, marked "F" in the distance matrix. (Point 4 equals point 3 if a line is added from point 2 to 4 directly.)

A line added from point 3 to point 2 increases the connectedness to Level 2 (corresponding to *the thing I like in the box is the ri̇ng*). According to the quantum restriction, this added line cannot move the focus outside of the potential focus set. Fig. 6.23 shows the resulting graph, and that the focal point is point 2 (the ring), one of the potential foci. The following is the distance matrix for this graph:

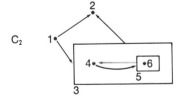

$$
\begin{array}{c|cccccc}
1 & 0 & 1 & 1 & 2 & 2 & 3 \\
2 & \infty & 0 & \infty & \infty & \infty & \infty \\
3 & \infty & 1 & 0 & 1 & 1 & 2 \\
4 & \infty & 2 & 1 & 0 & 1 & 2 \\
5 & \infty & 2 & 1 & 1 & 0 & 1 \\
6 & \infty & 3 & 2 & 2 & 1 & 0 \\
b_j & \infty & 9 & \infty & \infty & \infty & \infty \\
 & & & F & F & F & \\
\end{array}
$$

FIG. 6.23. Conceptual structure of a Level 2 utterance.

This graph also has a potential focus set, {3, 4, 5}, marked "F." The quantum restriction therefore predicts that no line can be added that increases the connectedness to Level 3 and also shifts the focus from this set, and this prediction also is correct. If the speaker of this conceptual structure increases the connectedness, the focal point must remain within the locative part of the utterance. Fig. 6.24 shows the only Level 3 conceptual structure that is possible (corresponding to *the thing I like in the bóx is the ring,* or *in the bóx is the ring which I like*), and the focal point is point 3, as seen in the distance matrix:

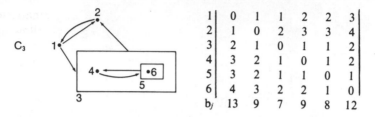

$$
C_3 \qquad
\begin{array}{c|cccccc}
 & 1 & 2 & 3 & 4 & 5 & 6 \\
\hline
1 & 0 & 1 & 1 & 2 & 2 & 3 \\
2 & 1 & 0 & 2 & 3 & 3 & 4 \\
3 & 2 & 1 & 0 & 1 & 1 & 2 \\
4 & 3 & 2 & 1 & 0 & 1 & 2 \\
5 & 3 & 2 & 1 & 1 & 0 & 1 \\
6 & 4 & 3 & 2 & 2 & 1 & 0 \\
b_j & 13 & 9 & 7 & 9 & 8 & 12
\end{array}
$$

FIG. 6.24.   Conceptual structure of a Level 3 utterance.

To show that one can add a line which shifts the focus in a Level 1 or 2 conceptual structure without changing the connectedness, it is necessary to use a more complex graph than examined hitherto. The examples in Fig. 6.25, like that in Fig. 6.23, are connected at Level 2. The first structure in Fig. 6.25 corresponds to *the thing I like in the box is the ring which belongs to the empress* (point 7 = Property, 8 = Event, 9 = *the empress,* 10 = Action,

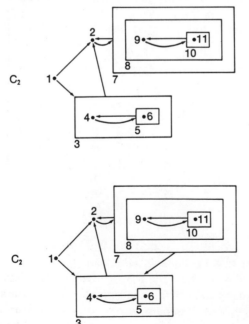

FIG. 6.25.   Illustrating shift of focus in a Level 2 conceptual structure. Compare to Fig. 6.23.

11 = *belongs*). The potential focus set contains only point 2, as we see when we increase the connectedness to Level 3 by adding a line from point 2 or point 7 (or any point inside of 7) to point 1, because these steps do not make point 1 into the focus. The second graph adds a line from point 7 to point 3, which does not affect the connectedness but which shifts the focus to point 3, outside of the potential focus set. The resulting conceptual structure corresponds to *the thing I like in the box is the ring which belongs to the empress,* in which stress has shifted over to *box* corresponding to point 3. The distance matricies for the first and second conceptual structures are, respectively, the following:

1	0	1	1	2	2	3	2	3	4	4	5
2	∞	0	∞	∞	∞	∞	1	2	3	3	4
3	∞	1	0	1	1	2	2	3	4	4	5
4	∞	2	1	0	1	2	3	4	5	5	6
5	∞	2	1	1	0	1	3	4	5	5	6
6	∞	3	2	2	1	0	4	5	6	6	7
7	∞	1	∞	∞	∞	∞	0	1	2	2	3
8	∞	2	∞	∞	∞	∞	1	0	1	1	2
9	∞	3	∞	∞	∞	∞	2	1	0	1	2
10	∞	3	∞	∞	∞	∞	2	1	1	0	1
11	∞	4	∞	∞	∞	∞	3	2	2	1	0
b_j	∞	22	∞	∞	∞	∞	23	26	33	32	41
		F									

1	0	1	1	2	2	3	2	3	4	4	5
2	∞	0	2	3	3	4	1	2	3	3	4
3	∞	1	0	1	1	2	2	3	4	4	5
4	∞	2	1	0	1	2	3	4	5	5	6
5	∞	2	1	1	0	1	3	4	5	5	6
6	∞	3	2	2	1	0	4	5	6	6	7
7	∞	1	1	2	2	3	0	1	2	2	3
8	∞	2	2	3	3	4	1	0	1	1	2
9	∞	3	3	4	4	5	2	1	0	1	2
10	∞	3	3	4	4	5	2	1	1	0	1
11	∞	4	4	5	5	6	3	2	2	1	0
b_j	∞	22	20	27	26	35	23	26	33	32	41

Some Interpretations

The notion of the potential focus set in a graph lends itself to an interpretation in terms of the changing processes within the speaker as he or she builds up a conceptual structure. In this interpretation, the potential focus set is the set of meanings to which, at any moment, the speaker is trying to relate all the other meanings of the utterance most closely. This set should eventually be reduced to one member. But before this stage is reached, the members of the potential focus set should presumably be related in meaning. To the extent that these concepts are not related in meaning, the potential focus set of the utterance is not only diffuse (because it has more than one member), but ambiguous (because the members are not related meaningfully). An empirical question is whether members of potential focus sets in real utterances are related in meaning, as we might expect, and under what conditions they are not related. In the Level 1 conceptual structure of Fig. 6.22, corresponding to *the thing I like is the ring; in the box,* the potential focus set contains some items that are not closely related: *the thing I like, the ring,* $Location_0$, and $Location_1$. By the time the connectedness level reaches 2, in Fig. 6.23, corresponding to *the thing I like in the box is the ring,* the potential focus set is entirely within the idea of location: $Location_0$, $Location_1$, and Entity. Thus, another empirical question is whether there is a correlation between the level of connectedness and the meaning relations of the potential focus set. At Level 3, this set contains only one element, the focal point. Some examples of potential focus sets in actual utterances are discussed in Chapter 8.

The quantum principle lends itself to another interpretation. This principle assures the speaker that he or she never has to keep track of more than one consequence (changing focus or increasing connectedness) of a given item of new information. The speaker can select a focal concept in advance, for example, and then incorporate further information from the context or from thinking, to build up the connectedness and form an utterance path. The quantum principle assures the speaker that the focus will not change during this process. This result thus corresponds to a strategy of speech production which consists of first finding the focal idea of an utterance, then building up the cohesion of the utterance, perhaps through several steps. How widespread such a strategy is, is another empirical matter, but my impression is that it dominates the speech processes of many individuals.

SUMMARY

This chapter has introduced the idea of a conceptual structure representation and presented a means for describing such a structure.

A conceptual structure is defined as a network of concepts and relations that conveys the speaker's meaning. It encompasses all the types of sign mentioned in previous chapters (indexical, iconic, symbolic) at a single level of representation. My intention is for the conceptual structure to be a model of the organization of concepts as speakers manipulate them. In respect to such psychological claims, a conceptual structure representation is distinguished from most representations designed for computer implementation and from transformational grammar representations.

Labeled directed graphs are introduced as a means for describing conceptual structures in formal terms, a goal toward which this chapter represents only the first step. In the interpretation of graphs proposed here, the points (nodes) of the graph are labeled with the names of concepts, and the lines (arcs) with the names of relations. The direction of the lines corresponds to the orientation of the relations involved and indicates the direction of the speech encoding sequence.

A large number of concepts from directed graph theory (Harary et al., 1965) apply to conceptual structure representations under this interpretation. Among the topics discussed are the following (in order of mention): definition of an utterance path; conceptual basis of syntagmata; model of semiotic extension; alternative segmentations of speech output (some of which disrupt grammatical segmentation); measures of the degree of semantic focus; the effects of context on semantic focus; definition of the internal (conceptual) boundaries of utterances; a measure of the degree of internal cohesion of utterances; the comprehension of utterances viewed as a reconstruction of conceptual structures, and some means that speakers might use to assist this process; and a "quantum" restriction on the effects of adding new information to conceptual structures, such that a new relation in a graph can either shift the point of focus or increase the level of connectedness, but not both at once. This last property of graphs allows speakers to choose the focus in advance and then to add new information that builds up cohesion without risking a change in focus.

7

Some Symbolic Signs

In this chapter I will continue the development of a means for representing the conceptual structure of utterances. The emphasis now shifts to what were termed symbols in Chapter 3. A symbol, according to Peirce (1931–1958), refers to its referent by means of a "law" or rule. The connection of a sign vehicle to the object of a symbolic sign is conventional. Within conceptual structures, such conventional signs can be seen in the output of the various syntactic and morphological devices that construct parts of the conceptual structure. These devices are conventional rules for relating concepts to each other. They are the productants in the case of symbolic signs. A syntactic device will be regarded as a collection of standardized steps that the speaker can take as a whole. Using a computer analogy, a syntactic device is like a subroutine, an action that may be labeled with a single name and that has a standardized effect on the conceptual structure.

Synactic devices play an essential part in establishing semiotic extension. This is because the sign vehicle produced by the syntactic device contains indexical and iconic elements. In addition to the method of semiotic extension based on the contraction of strong components, syntactic devices directly introduce sensory-motor concepts, and the devices themselves can be said to extend the sensory-motor content they introduce.

Semiotic extension achieved through the application of a syntactic device can be much more varied than semiotic extension that develops through contraction. The output of the device denotes whatever it conventionally denotes. The device can produce, by convention, the semiotic extension of sensory-motor ideas that are not (otherwise) directly related to concepts (thus avoiding constraints on contraction, which require labeled relations). The device for relative clauses, for example, can extend the idea of a Property to any conceptual structure that can be regarded as an Event.

At the same time, a symbolic sign can refer only as a whole. If one uses only a part of a symbolic sign (for example, just a relative pronoun), one does not convey a corresponding part of the idea of a Property. The total language uses a number of such specialized syntactic devices, each of which, functioning as a whole, conveys some particular meaning.

There is thus a reciprocal relationship between the two methods of semiotic extension. Contraction depends on there being labeled meaning relations between sensory-motor ideas and the ideas to which they extend, but this method can apply to any set of ideas that are so related. A syntactic device does not have to pay attention to labeled meaning relations between the sensory-motor idea and the ideas to which it extends, but it is limited in the identity of the sensory-motor ideas it can extend.

Syntactic devices resemble the "linguistic devices" described by Harrison (1972), who writes, for example:

> We must see language as an array of concrete and limited techniques for communication. . . [T]he machinery for this connection. . . will differ from one technique to another, depending on the peculiar functions and character of each [p. 101].

The term "syntactic device" should suggest a linkage to this conception of a linguistic device with its implications for specific, specialized operations carried out during communication. Unlike Harrison's proposal, however, the domain of syntactic devices will be restricted to symbolic signs.

The following sections discuss three syntactic devices of English: passive, restrictive relative clause, and pseudocleft. These devices correspond in name to transformations of the type which correlate with meaning differences, but syntactic devices do not function as transformations function. The single most important difference is that transformations do not have sign properties as syntactic devices do. For example, a passive transformation is sometimes said to relate passive structures to active structures; however, it is not correct to say that the passive sentence structure *denotes* the active sentence structure. The passive sentence structure, however, denotes various ideas of Event.

FORM OF REPRESENTATION

In order to represent the structure of syntactic devices, I will use a modification of the Augmented Transition Network (ATN) format (cf. Woods, 1970). The modified networks will be called PATNs (for *Parallel*

Augmented Transition Networks). An ATN is strictly "serial" in operation, whereas a PATN allows different steps to be taken at the same time.

To describe a PATN, the ATN format is relaxed in the following way: The organization of both an ATN and a PATN network is based on the logical dependencies between steps. In an ATN these dependencies are also taken to be a model of the temporal sequence of steps. In a PATN, we will distinguish between real-time increments and the dependencies of steps. Real-time increments will occur only when there is a logically unavoidable sequence of steps (e.g., a later step replaces something introduced at an earlier step). If two or more PATN steps interact according to the way the PATN is organized, and this interaction can take place whether the steps are simultaneous or sequential, they will be assumed to be simultaneous.

Increments of real time will be registered in a separate "T-count." PATN steps, although written sequentially down the page, will be regarded as representing logical dependencies exclusively. Unless there is an increment in the T-count, these dependencies will be assumed to be established and to interact all at the same (real) time. Such a schematism uses the ATN format to represent logical interrelations among steps and, independently, the T-count to represent temporal sequences.

We can think of each of the steps of a PATN as being carried out by a separate "computer" which is specialized for the step. The different computers representing the steps of the PATN are wired together in ways corresponding to the conditions stated in the overall PATN for taking the different steps. For example, a step that has another step as a condition has a wire that runs to it from the conditioning computer. All of the computers in the PATN at the same value of the T-count operate simultaneously, but a given computer will not produce an output until it receives a signal from the conditioning computer(s) connected to it. The mechanism operates as a "contingency network." For example, in Fig. 7.1, step 1 conditions step 2, and step 2 conditions step 3. These three steps may be taken in parallel, activated by a common trigger, but no step will have an output until signals arrive over its contingent wire. The trigger signal causes the step to be taken, and the conditioning signal causes it to send its output along with its output wire (thus (2) does not send its output to (3) until it has received a signal from (1), and so on). Problems of synchronization in this network can be handled in several ways. For example, the latency of each step may be zero; each step may have a memory that records the output of the step or the arrival of its conditioning

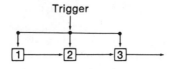

FIG. 7.1. Illustrating simultaneous activation of three PATN steps, two of which are contingent on other steps.

signal or both; a given computer may continue to generate its signal until it receives a conditioning signal and then output it. There may also be a lack of synchrony if the simultaneously operating computers have different running speeds. This should not cause difficulty for the overall PATN if the asynchronies that develop remain within limits. There may be, within these limits, degrees of parallelation in the sense that actions that are carried out in parallel take different amounts of time to execute.

Once started, a PATN will cause its output structure to emerge. The PATN does not build up a representation of this structure and put it in some other place (such as a memory store), because the device is called into action only in the context of a developing conceptual structure. It is part of the sign structure of its utterance. Therefore, whatever the PATN produces becomes directly a part of this conceptual structure. (This should not be taken to mean that the conceptual structure as a whole is not ever stored in memory.)

The PATN schematism could, in principle, be extended to represent procedures that are followed in forming indexical and iconic aspects of conceptual structures. Such a representation has not been attempted here, however, for the reason that the use of a PATN format demands assumptions, regarding the possible forms of conceptual structure and their limits, that seem quite premature. Syntactic devices have narrow domains of operation and relatively fixed effects; hence they are feasible targets of PATN descriptions. Syntactic devices, however, should be regarded as descriptively on a continuum with the rest of the conceptual structure, located at the most restricted, regular end.

All the same, the PATN descriptions in this chapter cannot be presented as complete in any sense. Each PATN captures some of the major functions of its construction, but certainly it does not capure all of them. One can assume, in fact, that it will be necessary to add a great deal of detail beyond that given.

Although the PATNs I describe are inspired by the ATN descriptions of Woods (1970) and others, they are not by any means based on operating computer systems or anything like them. An actual attempt to implement one of these devices no doubt would require various changes in the descriptions given, as well as vastly more detail.

Finally, it should be stated that I do not mean to imply that for each PATN step there is a corresponding psychological process. Such a claim cannot be sustained for either PATNs or ATNs. Rather, the PATN shows a mechanism that can be operated as a subsystem; this subsystem constructs a symbolic sign vehicle that denotes a certain object but has unknown psychological meaning internally. (Nonetheless, certain predictions derived from the PATNs I describe, particularly predictions of where errors in the construction process are likely to take place, are confirmed by observations of spontaneous use of the corresponding constructions; cf. Chapter 9.)

THE PASSIVE

Sign Structure of the Passive

A passive construction changes the idea of an Action into the idea of a Property, State, or Event that is produced as a corresponding simple sentence. The passive device accomplishes this effect by dividing the Action into two parts—the subject and the complement of a *subject-be-complement* sentence (for this reason, only Actions complex enough to have at least two parts can be passivized; what are regarded as intransitive Actions do not contain enough detail). The passive, moreover, correlates the ideas of Property, State, and Event with different "aspects— of the *be* relation. These are called the permanent, transitory, and emergent aspects, respectively.

Viewed as the productant of the passive symbolic sign, the passive PATN can be represented as follows:

Symbol:

$$P \mathrel{\rule[0.5ex]{3em}{0.5pt}} O \mathrel{\rule[0.5ex]{5em}{0.5pt}}\!\!\!\!\longrightarrow S$$

Passive   Action   Entity *be-evermore* Property
PATN   Entity *be-now* in State
                              Entity *be-come* part of Event

This shows that the PATN is capable of generating three different sign vehicles, each denoting Action, that differ in the aspect of *be* and the idea into which Action is changed.

The passive PATN requires a receptive orientation of the *patients* relation with the Action. This is because of orientation of this relation must be congruent with the *be* relation. Thus, the passive PATN becomes one of the major orientation-changing syntactic devices of English.

The analysis of the passive as a symbolic sign explains a number of the features of the passive construction that have not been accounted for hitherto (cf. R. Lakoff, 1971). In particular, the occurrence of the past participle inflection *-ed*, the use of a verb as the passivizer and specifically the use of *be* or *get* (in the emergent aspect only), and the conversion of the patient into a surface subject can be explained from the function of the syntactic device for changing the concept of an Action into that of a Property, State, or Event.

The organization of the passive conceptual structure is illustrated in Fig. 7.2, and it can be said to include the following:

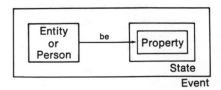

FIG. 7.2. Generalized conceptual structure of a passive sign vehicle. Only one of the ideas, State or Event, would appear in a given utterance (see text for explanation).

1. an initial concept of an Entity or Person, which may be complex and which functions as the grammatical subject;

2. a final concept of a Property of this Entity or Person, which is represented by an inflected past participle verb (this concept is present in each version of the passive);

3. a receptively oriented relation, which is represented by *be*, and which connects (1) and (2) as (1) *be* (2); this use of *be* reflects a receptively oriented *has-property* relation between (1) and (2);

4. different sensory-motor ideas (Event, State, Property) that are organized in relation to (1), (2), and (3). The content of this sensory-motor idea and the scope it has in the passive conceptual structure depend on the type of *be* relation.

The passive PATN generates conceptual structures with these characteristics, doing so in such a way that the passive, when called on as an autonomous subroutine by the speaker, can construct a passive conceptual structure without any further intervention.

The type of passive structure produced by the PATN is the "short passive," so called because it lacks an agentive ("by") phrase. In fact, short passives are far more common in speech (as opposed to in writing) than long passives, and agentless passives are the only passives in many languages (Lyons, 1968). Although no attempt is made here to analyze long passives, it would be only natural to regard the long passive as a case specification of the short passive (perhaps similar to the instrumental case). One advantage of this analysis is that the "agentive" phrase would not then itself require the passive PATN, and thus the short passive PATN described here could remain essentially unchanged.

Aspects of *Be*

The basic connecting relation of the passive is *be*. This relation is used for the introduction of the idea of a Property, but not always in the same way. The differences in the use of *be*, which are referred to as aspectual, correlate with different overall sensory-motor meanings, and these correlations can be introduced by the passive PATN.

1. *Permanent Aspect.* In *the door was closed (forever)* or *the castle was built of stone,* the *be* introduces a Property that is permanently true of the Entity. This meaning of a permanent Property is similar to the permanence conveyed in predicate adjectives, e.g., *the door is red, solid, etc.* The sensory-motor content associated with the permanent aspect is simply that of a Property.

2. *Transitory Aspect.* In *the door was closed (for the time being)* or *the peace was disturbed,* the *be* introduces a Property that is only temporally true

of the Entity or Person. Some predicate adjectives have this sense also, e.g., *the cat is hungry.* The transitory aspect is sometimes called the stative form of the passive (Curme, 1931), and the sensory-motor content associated with it is that of State. This concept can be brought out explicitly with an adverbial that describes the event of which the stative passive is the initial or terminal condition, e.g., *the peace was disturbed after the leader gave a provocative speech.*

3. *Emergent Aspect.* In *the door was (or got) closed* or *I was (or got) upset,* the *be* (or *get*) introduces a Property that is, at the time denoted by the utterance, just becoming true of the Entity or Person. This is sometimes called the actional passive (Curme, 1931). The sensory-motor content associated with the emergent aspect is that of Event, i.e., a change of state.

Scope of Sensory-Motor Content

In addition to being associated with its own aspect of *be*, each sensory-motor concept (Property, State, and Event) has a different scope in the passive conceptual structure. These differences can be seen to correspond to the definitions of the sensory-motor concepts given in Chapter 5. Evidence of differences in scope is obtained from use of pseudocleft sentences as probes (see Chapter 8 for further examples and discussion). The pseudocleft requires that the two clauses which are separated by *be* should have the same principal sensory-motor content. Becaue the pseudocleft device introduces an equality between these clauses (see the last section of this chapter), it can be used to probe the content of conceptual structures by attempting to combine different parts of utterances in pseudoclefts.

In the case of the actional passive, a pseudocleft corresponding to *I got upset* is,

what happened is (that) I got upset.

The entire passive structure appears in the second clause. Thus, we learn from this pseudocleft that the entire passive corresponds to the idea of a change of state (i.e., an Event). We do not find (*what happened is got upset* or *what happened is upset* in the intended meaning) although these forms of pseudocleft are possible with the different ideas of State and permanent Property.

To bring out the idea of a permanent Property in the pseudocleft, we can try,

What a property of the castle is is being built of stone.

The interesting aspect of this peculiar sentence is the occurrence of three instances of *be* in a row. The middle one belongs to the pseudocleft. The necessity of the third occurrence of *be* suggests that the *be* relation of the passive is not part of the idea of a Property but must be added to this idea in order to balance the occurrence of passive *be* in the first clause. (We do not have *what a property of the castle is is built of stone.*) This pseudocleft therefore suggests that the scope of the idea of a permanent Property includes the verb phrase *built of stone* but not the *be* relation itself.

Finally, a pseudocleft which brings out the idea of a State is,

What the state of the door is is closed,

in which there are two occurrences of *be*, the second belonging to the pseudocleft. This pseudocleft therefore suggests that closed, by itself, is sufficient to balance the occurrence of the *be* in the first clause, and that the idea of a State in the passive includes the *be* relation.

The organization of the passive conceptual structure in Fig. 7.2 and in the passive PATN below reflects the differences in scope shown with the pseudocleft between Event, Property, and State.

Receptive Orientation of the Passive

The receptive orientation of the passive means that the idea of Entity or Person must be the relatum of the logical relations involved in the conceptual structure. The receptive orientation coincides with the use of *be*, and the *patients* relation is also receptive in *the door was shut* and other passives. If this orientation were operative instead, the same word-order sequence *door–shut*) would be generated from opposite orientations—a conflict within the basic organization of the conceptual structure.

It is possibly due to such a conflict of orientation that the passive seems to be without meaning in sentences that involve measurement. For example,

it costs $20, *but**$20 are cost by it;
it lasts 20 minutes, *but* *20 minutes are lasted by it;
it extends 1 mile, *but* *1 mile is extended by it.

If we think that the nonpassive forms in these examples are receptive to begin with, we could say that trying to apply the passive makes them operative and that this leads to a conflict of orientation. The same word-order sequence has two incompatible meanings. The same argument can explain why these verbs also do not occur with nominalizations that reverse orientation,[1] for example,

[1]There is circumstantial evidence that "costs," "lasts," "extends," etc., represent receptive orientations. With this orientation the referent is the natural starting point of the relation, *measures* (x, y).

*the $20's costing;
*the 20 minutes' lasting;
*the 1 mile's extending.

PATN Model of the Passive Syntactic Device

The model herein follows the general approach of the ATN models (e.g., Woods, 1970), with two main exceptions: (1) The PATN distinguishes logical steps from temporal increments, with the former being simultaneous whenever possible; and (2) the PATN constructs a conceptual structure rather than a grammatical structure.

The number of temporal increments in the passive PATN is one, i.e., there are two times segments. That even one temproal increment is required is due to an operation of replacement carried out in the second time segment.

Memory is required for certain information, and this is entered into registers following actions at specified places in the PATN. The use of memory registers is due to the PATN operating through a time increment. Each item of stored information is assumed to be placed in a separate register, an assumption that is not known to have any particular psychological significance.

The chart in Fig. 7.3 summarizes the operation of the passive PATN. Processes that are parallel are organized together within the same time segment. The arrows show the interconnection of steps either for the flow of information or for conditions required by other steps (e.g., Step 1a is a condition for Step 3). The operations triggered at the start of the passive device establish the main concepts and a general *be-X* relation. Triggering

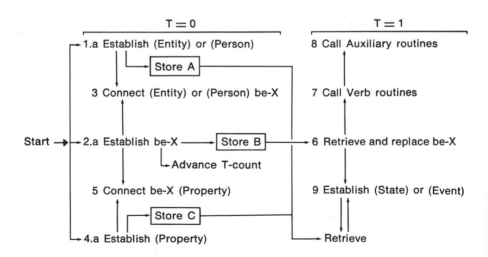

FIG. 7.3.   Flow chart of passive PATN.

these in parallel triggers other operations (also carried out in parallel). The basic structure of the passive emerges everywhere at once. The word order of the passive, as usual, is established by the directed arrows of the constructed graph structure. The temporal segmentation of this PATN does not, however, correspond to the word-order sequence. For example, Property, which is encoded last, is generated in the first temporal segment. The temporal segmentation, rather, separates an initial phase in which the general passive structure emerges from a final phase where the details of the verb morphology and the specific aspectual variant of *be* appear.

The detailed account of the PATN that follows presents, for each step of the device, the action taken and the condition(s) on taking it. Certain routing actions are included that are not shown in Fig. 7.3. The abbreviations "C1" and "C2" stand for "Concept 1" and "Concept 2," respectively, which refer to the literal conceptual content in the first and second positions of the passive. The meanings of "1" and "2" are probably best interpreted as referring to what the speaker is able to or wants to mention first ("Concept 1") and what he or she is not able to or does not want to mention first ("Concept 2"). Given this information, the passive device can impose all further tests and construct an appropriate passive structure.

T-count	PATN STEPS
0	1.a. Apply routines for Entity or Person to Concept 1 *Condition:* Event or Action

These routines include nominalizations and complements that introduce Entity or Person over Concept 1. When Concept 1 is already related to Entity or Person, Step 1a does not apply, although Step 1b, below, which stores the concept for later use, does apply. Step 1a thus accomplishes the same thing as an intrinsic Entity or Person but adds a nominalization or complement structure to the passive structure. The condition on this substep specifies Event or Action. These appear to be involved when Entity or Person is not intrinsically present, Action being limited to nominalizations. For example,

> *John's acting* was applauded
> (Entity (Event))

> *The acting* was applauded
> (Entity (Action))

> *That they endured it for so long* was noted
> (Entity (Event$_0$ (Event$_1$)—(Location)))

T-count	PATN STEPS

        b. Store Entity or Person in Store A
          Condition: Entity or Person

The action and condition are stated so as to accept both intrinsic and constructed (Entity) or (Person). The next substep sends this information to another step in the same temporal segment, where the concept is linked to the *be* relation.

        c. Send Entity or Person to Step 3
          Condition: Entity or Person

0   2.a. Establish *be-X*
          Condition: Concept 1 → Concept 2
                       Receptive

This step establishes a generic *be* relation without specifying the aspectual variant. Introducing the relation in generic form captures the similarity that exists among the *be-* and *get*-passives and the predicate adjectives. The only condition on Step 2a is that the *patients* relation between Concept 1 and Concept 2 should be receptively oriented, a condition that eliminates intransitive verbs from Concept 2. The next substep sends the generic *be-X* relation to Step 3 and Step 5, the first of which connects *be-X* with Entity or Person, and the second of which connects it with Property.

        b. Send *be-X* to Step 3 and Step 5
          Condition: *be-X*

The last substep stores *be-X* in a register from which it will be withdrawn when the processes introducing aspectual variation are carried out.

        c. Store *be-X* in Store B
          Condition: *be-X*
        d. Advance T-count
          Condition: Steps 1–5

0   3. Connect Entity or Person *be-X*
         Conditions: a. Entity or Person
                    b. *be-X*

The conditions here are met by the steps previously mentioned. This step builds up the utterance path of the passive by

T-count	PATN STEPS

attaching the initial concept of the *be* relation. The orientation is automatically receptive.

0   4.a. Apply Past Participle Routine to Concept 2
         Condition: $(C2 (Cv)) \longleftarrow (C1)$
                         $(Action)$

The Past Participle routine, which is not described in this PATN, creates the concept of a Property over Concept 2 when it is in the arrangement described in the condition, i.e., related to the idea of an Action and forming a strong component with it and (C1). For example, in *Max is pushed,* in Fig. 7.4, such a configuration is involved. Note that the orientation of the patient relation between *Max* and *push* must be receptive. Predicate adjectives, on the other hand, do not meet the condition, as they are intrinsically related to Property rather than to Action. Step 4a must apply only when Concept 2 is not a property. It creates the structure (Property (Concept 2)) and introduces the suffix *-ed.* The concept (Cv) is lexicalized as a verb, and Concept 2 may be the idea of an Action that is retrieved as part of the lexical retrieval of the verb. However, Concept 2 may also be more complex (as in the example, *the castle was built of stone*).

Adjectives, which retrieve the idea of a Property, are not subject to Step 4a, but an interesting question arises when we consider the effects of affixing the causative suffix, e.g., *brighten.* Should these modified adjectives be considered basically Properties or basically Actions? Apparently they are Actions, because if they were Properties there would be no mechanism for providing the past participle. A Property with an emergent sense appears without either the causative or past suffix in *the lights came to be bright.* The difference between this example and the passive lies in the existence of the concept of an Action. This idea seems to be associated with the

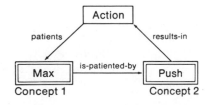

FIG. 7.4. Structure of Action with a receptive orientation.

T-count	PATN STEPS

causative suffix itself. The conceptual structure of causative adjectives, if they include Action, will therefore meet the condition specified for 4a, so the step will apply. The result will be (Property (Action (Property))), marked with the past participle, e.g., *brightened.*

      b. Store Property in Store C
        Condition: Property

Property is retrieved in the second temporal segment. Note that, in the case of this substep, the condition is also met by predicate adjectives. That is, any occurrence of Property is placed in Store C.

0   5. Connect *be-X* Property
        Conditions: a. Property
               b. *be-X*

This step completes the linking of the passive utterance path by attaching the final concept of the *be* relation.

1   6. Retrieve *be-X* from Store B
        Condition: a. $T = 1$
              b. *be-X* in store B

This step occurs when the T-count advances to 1. It bridges the temporal gap by retrieving the generic *be* relation from a designated store. The following substeps introduce the aspectual variant.

      a. Replace *be-X* by *be-evermore*
        Condition: Permanent Property
      b. Replace *be-X* by *be-now*
        Condition: Transitory Property
      c. Replace *be-X* by *be-come*
        Condition: Emergent Property

These conditions are met by the speaker's knowledge, the temporal frame, and other factors indirectly reflected in the conceptual structure as aspectual variation. Causative adjectives are classified as emergent and hence are linked with *become.*

T-count	PATN STEPS

1

    7.a. Apply the *be* verb routine
         Conditions: a. Step 6a, b, or c
                b. Step 7b not taken
      b. Apply the *get* verb routine
         Conditions: a. Step 6c
                b. Step 7a not taken

These steps introduce the appropriate morphological root corresponding to the aspectual variant established in Step 6. The conditions are such that *be* may be used with any aspect, but *get* may be used only with *be-come.* The steps are mutually exclusive, and they each have the negation of the other as one condition.

1

    8. Apply Modal, Tense, Aspect, and Number routines to *be* or *get.*
      Condition: Step 7

The true main verb of the passive is the so-called passivizer; this verb (*be* or *get*) carries the morphological burden of modal, tense, aspect (i.e., nonpassive aspect), and number specification.

1

    9.a.(1) Retrieve Property from Store C
         Condition: Property in Store C
      (2) Establish State over Property
         Condition: be-now

This substep establishes the concept of State associated with the transitory aspect, with a scope that includes Property and hence also includes the relations with this concept, namely, *be-now* and the *patients* relation between Concept 1 and Concept 2.

      b.(1)(a) Retrieve property from Store C
            Condition: Property in Store C
         (b) Retrieve Entity or Person from Store A
            Condition: Entity or Person in Store A
       (2)   Establish Event over Entity or Person and Property
           Condition: be-come

T-count	PATN STEPS

This substep completes the aspectual differentiation by establishing Event over both Property and Entity or Person. There is no substep of Step 9 for the *be-evermore* aspect, since a Property with the required scope for this aspect is provided at Step 4. The permanent aspect, therefore, does not rely on any special step.

THE RESTRICTIVE RELATIVE CLAUSE

The term "restrictive relative clause" is understood to refer to the type of relative clause which modifies or "restricts" the domain of reference of the main clause. For example, in *islanders who find treasure get rich,* the relative clause limits the reference domain of the main clause, *islanders get rich,* to islanders who find treasure. In contrast, a nonrestrictive relative clause, such as *islanders, who are surrounded by the sea, usually have a fish diet,* does not limit the domain of reference of the main clause, *islanders usually have a fish diet,* in any way. Rather, the relative clause provides additional information, somewhat like a conjoined clause. The discussion in this section is confined to restrictive relative clauses.

Sign Structure of the Relative Clause

Such clauses are a way of constructing complex modifiers and this is achieved by intersecting two ideas of an Event. For example, *islanders get rich* intersects with *islanders find treasure.* The relative clause device does this provided that the Events have a point in common (the modified head noun, *islanders*). The intersection is accomplished by making one Event into a Property of the point that the two Events have in common. This extension of Property to Event is the principal semiotic extension of the relative clause syntactic device.

Although the reference domain of the main clause is restricted by the relative clause, it is important to note that the Event in the relative clause is made into the Property of the Person or Entity in common with the main clause, not the property of the main clause Event as a whole. That is, we can reformulate the example above as *x gets rich, and x finds treasure,* where *x* is *islander* (cf. the discussion of properties in Chapter 5). As a consequence of being limited to Person or Entity modification, the relative clause device must include a subdevice that extends the idea of Entity or Person to the common point between the two Events when this is not already an Entity or Person. This subextension occurs, for example, in *treasure finding which involves underwater exploration is a specialty of these islanders.*

Sign Structure of the Relative Clause

Viewed as the productant of a symbolic sign, the relative clause device constructs a sign vehicle in which the common point in the two Events is marked by *wh* and this sign vehicle denotes as the object of the sign the intersection of events and that one of the Events limits the common point.
Symbol:

$$P \text{———————} O \text{———————} \rightarrow S$$

Relative	Intersecting	common point and
Clause	Events, one	and limiting Event
PATN	limiting	marked *wh*
	common point	

Functions of the Relative clause

An important aspect of relative clause functioning is that it includes two kinds of indexes. These are combined in the relative pronoun. The relative pronoun indicates the point of intersection of the two Events and it indicates which Event is the Property. This dual function can be related to the functions proposed by Ehlich (1978) for anaphora and deixis. According to him, anaphora instructs the listener to keep in the focus of attention that which is already in focus, and deixis instructs the listener to shift the focus of attention. Relative pronouns seem to fulfill both functions simultaneously. In this way they achieve the desired modification of the common point. In *Islanders who find treasure get rich,* for example, the anaphoric function keeps in the focus of attention *islanders* and the deictic function brings into the focus of attention *find tresaure.* Neither function alone is sufficient to explain the effect of the relative clause modification.

Silverstein (1976) discusses a theory in which the use of deictic words indicates and presupposes the existence of what the word points to (rather than symbolizes it). This provides a second sense in which relative pronouns involve deixis. For example, a tense marker on a verb has a deictic use that indicates and presupposes a moment of speaking. *This table* in a deictic sense indicates and presupposes the existence of a referent of *table.* Relative pronouns are similar to these other deictic uses in that they indicate and presuppose the existence of something, namely the common point between two events and the idea of a Property that includes one Event.

The organization of a relative clause from this point of view is suggested by the diagram in Fig. 7.5. The labels on the lines in the figure connecting *who* with the main and relative clauses are meant to distinguish the two functions of the relative pronoun mentioned above. This particle indeed behaves as a sign post (as Peirce, 1931–1958, described it), in fact, as a rather complex, multipurpose one.

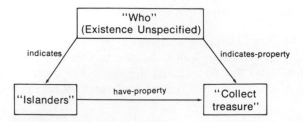

FIG. 7.5. Organization of anaphoric and deictic functions in a restrictive relative clause (see text for explanation).

The conceptual content of the relative pronoun is represented as supporting these functions. It has both the meaning of Existence and of Unspecified. Unspecified supports the anaphoric function of keeping in the focus of attention that which is already in focus (it is indicated as being "unspecified"), and Existence supports the deictic function of bringing into the focus of attention something new (it is indicated as "existing"). The relative clause device introduces the concept of Existence Unspecified into the conceptual structure along with relations labeled *indicates* and *indicates property*.

Other Comparable Systems

The association of relative pronouns with a deictic function appears in the emerging relative pronoun system of Tok Pisin, a forming creole of New Guinea (Sankoff & Brown, 1976). In this system, a relative clause marker, "ia," is used before and also occasionally after relative clauses. This form apparently has derived from the deictic term *here* in the partially English-based pidgin from which the creole is evolving.

In American Sign Language, used by deaf persons, relative clauses are produced in a different part of the signing space from the main clause, and they are accompanied by various deictic gestures of the head, eyebrows, and so forth, which seem analogous to relative pronouns in function.[2] In these two unusual linguistic systems, therefore, as in spoken English, there is a deictic function involved in relative clauses.

PATN Model of a Restrictive Relative Clause Device

The flow charts in Figs. 7.6 and 7.7 summarize the operation the relative clause PATN. Two charts are given, because the temporal segmentation of steps is not the same in right-branching and center-embedded relative clauses; the right-branching PATN appears in Fig. 7.6 and the center-embedded one

---

[2]The formation of relative clauses was demonstrated to me by Ted Supalla.

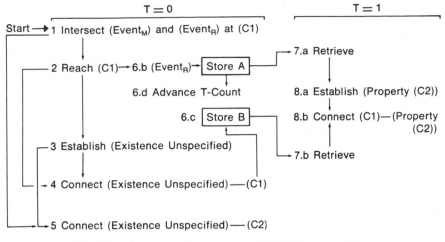

FIG. 7.6.   Flow chart of relative clause PATN (right-branching).

in Fig. 7.7. In both of these types, when the device is triggered, there is an action that intersects two events around a shared concept. This shared concept is eventually indicated with a relative pronoun.

The temporal segmentation into T = O and T = 1 of the relative clause PATN generally corresponds to the word-order sequence within the

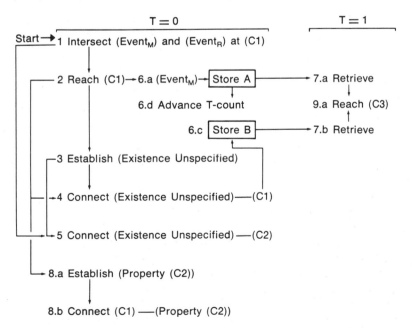

FIG. 7.7.   Flow chart of relative clause PATN (center-embedded).

utterance. In a right-branching structure, the first time segment develops $Event_M$ and stores $Event_R$, which is then developed in the second time segment. In a center-embedded structure, this order is reversed. In both types, the first segment precedes the relative pronoun, but the idea of a Property for the relative clause is built up in the second time segment in a right-branching clause and in the first segment in a center-embedded clause.

In the notation of this PATN, (C1) is the overlapped concept in both events; (C2) is the rest of the relative clause $Event_R$; and (C3) is the rest of the main clause $Event_M$. These are distinct concepts that are defined by the PATN structure and by the speaker's choice of $Event_R$ and $Event_M$. The meaning of the symbol $Event_M$ is probably best interpreted as the event that the speaker regards as primary, and $Event_R$ is the event that he or she regards as secondary. Other pragmatic interpretations may be possible.

T-count	PATN STEPS

0
    1. Intersect $Event_M$ and $Event_R$ at (C1)
      Condition: (C1) is in both $Event_M$ and $Event_R$

This step takes place entirely on the conceptual level. It produces the structure shown in Fig. 7.8 from the two Events mentioned in the condition.

0
    2. Reach Concept 1
      Condition: ($Event_M$ (C1) ———— (C2))

This action carries the utterance path from wherever it currently is (required to be in $Event_M$) to (C1). The condition does not specify the direction of the relation between C1 and C2 or C3, because if the structure is right-branching, C3 will be on the utterance path before C1 is reached, whereas if the structure is center-embedded, C1 will be on the utterance path before C3.

0
    3. Establish Existence Unspecified
      Condition: Step 2

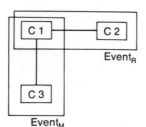

FIG. 7.8.   Overlapping Events at Concept 1.

T-count	PATN STEPS

0

    4. Connect Existence Unspecified → C2
                                     indicates
        Conditions: a. Step 2
                   b. Step 3
    5. Connect Existence Unspecified → C2
                              indicates property
        Conditions: a. Step 3
                   b. Step 1

$C2$ is in Event$_R$, which is still available at this stage. Steps 3, 4, and 5 create the configuration shown in Fig. 7.9. There is not yet any distinction between center-embedded and right-branching structures.

0

    6.a. Store Event$_M$ in Store A
         Conditions: a. C1 → C3
                   b. Step 2

Condition a arises only in center-embedded structures. In a right-branching structure, the orientation of the relation is reversed, $C3 \to C2$. Hence, the two types of relative clause can be distinguished by the structure of Event$_M$. For example, in the center-embedded sentence that follows, the Event$_M$ order is C1—C3, whereas in the right-branching sentence it is C3—C1:

The pen that	I wrote with	belongs to Bronson
C1	C2	C3
		(center-embedded)

Bronson owns	the pen that	I wrote with
C3	C1	C2
		(right-branching)

    b. Store Event$_R$ in Store A
        Conditions: a. C3 → C1
                  b. Step 2

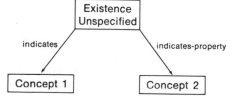

FIG. 7.9. Intermediate stage in constructing relative clauses.

T-count	PATN STEPS

This step accomplishes the same thing for right-branching structures.

    c. Store C1 in Store B
       Condition: Step 2

This last substep is necessary for later (T = 1) steps in both the right-branching and center-embedded structures.

    d. Advance T-count
       Condition: Steps 1–6

Step 6c concludes all the operations in the first time segment, with the exception of one step given below that is involved with center-embedded relative clauses.

1   7.a. Retrieve contents of Store A
              Condition: T = 1
        b. Retrieve C1 from Store B
              Condition: T = 1

This concept is used in Step 8.

0 or 1   8.a. Establish (Property (C2))
              Conditions: a. T = 0 and C1 → C3
                   or b. T = 1 and C3 → C1

This step is taken in all relative clauses, but only once in each. If the structure is center-embedded, it occurs in the T = 0 segment as specified in Condition a. If it is right-branching, it occurs in the T = 1 segment. In both situations, the PATN extends the idea of Property to C2.

        b. Connect C1 → Property
           has-property
        Conditions: a. Step 2
                   b. Step 7.b
                   c. Step 8.a

By the end of Step 8, the PATN has constructed the configuration shown in Fig. 7.10. This exists in both center-

T-count	PATN STEPS

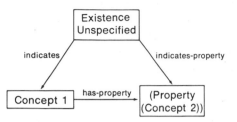

FIG. 7.10. Final stage in constructing relative clauses.

embedded and right-branching relative clauses. In the right-branching case, Step 8 is the last of the PATN, but in the center-embedded case one further step is taken to return the utterance path to the main clause.

1   9. Reach C1
            Conditions: a. T = 1
                             b. C1 → C3

Concept 1 is expressed in speech only once. Because this occurs in Step 2 in both right-branching and center-embedded relative clauses, it does not occur again in Step 8 or 9. The effect is the characteristic omission of the overlapped concept from the relative clause itself.

Concords in Relative Clauses

There are two distinct systems of concord involved in relative clauses, and these can be explained in terms of the relative clause PATN. There is also a lack of concord at one place where it might be expected.

1. The relative clause can be embedded entirely within the main clause, but regardless of the complexity of this embedding or the number of embeddings, number and person concords cross the embedding(s) and always hold. This fact was one of the strongest arguments against a simple finite state grammar in Chomsky (1957).

These concords around center-embedded relative clauses arise from the conceptual structure of Event$_M$. This structure is always intact in the PATN, and there is nothing in the PATN that should disrupt concords that occur within it.

2. Number and person concords also exist between the head noun phrase and the relative clause verb when the noun phrase is the subject of the verb—for example, *a teacher who confuses/*confuse*. These concords arise with in Event$_R$, which also is always intact in the PATN.

3. The relative pronoun does *not* participate in any concords, despite the availability of number inflection with one form—for example, *cars that/*those fall into pot holes*. The explanation is that the relative pronoun arises from a completely different set of relations from those involved in concords, namely, *indicates* and *indicates property*. These relations reflect the anaphoric and deictic functions of the relative pronoun, and it is this participation in a separate system that protects it from the necessity of concord.

A Reason Why Multiple Center-Embedded Relative Clauses are Difficult to Understand.

In terms of memory load and temporal segmentation, center-embedded relative clauses do not seem to differ radically from right-branching relative clauses. However, the content of what is stored and used in the second time segment does differ between the two types of relative clause, and it differs in a way that could lead to dramatically different consequences of multiple embeddings. In a right-branching structure, what is stored at Step 6 consists of $Event_R$, whereas in a center-embedded structure the storage consists of $Event_M$. Multiple embeddings always take place within $Event_R$ in both types. Thus, for a right-branching structure, there is never more than one $Event_R$ stored, no matter how many embeddings there are. This is because each earlier $Event_R$ is completed before the next $Event_R$ occurs. With center embeddings, the situation is the reverse. Successive embeddings occur in $Event_R$; therefore $Event_M$ is not completed, and the number of distinct $Events_R$ in storage must increase with each additional embedding. The difficulty of multiple center embeddings, according to this interpretation, is due to the ample opportunities for blending, confusing, and forgetting parts of the different $Events_R$ that are stored in the same place.

THE PSEUDOCLEFT

The pseudocleft structure is very useful as a probe of other conceputal structures. A device that produces pseudocleft utterances takes the following steps:

1. it selects an appropriate sensory-motor idea;
2. it introduces the same sensory-motor idea on both sides of the pseudocleft *be*;
3. it introduces (Existence Unspecified) above the first of these sensory-motor ideas;
4. it introduces a relation of identity represented in *be*;

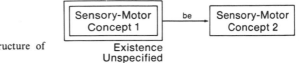

FIG. 7.11.   General structure of
the pseudocleft.

5. it arranges the conceputal structure within each of the sensory-motor ideas into a cohesive network.

Fig. 7.11 shows the general organization of the pseudocleft according to the pseudocleft PATN.

Sign Structure of the Pseudocleft

Viewed as the productant of a symbolic sign, the pseudocleft device constructs a sign vehicle that is equivalent to such indicating sentences as *this is x*. It introduces a *wh*-term and promotes some sensory-motor idea to an equal position with this *wh*-term; it introduces a form of *be*; and then it replicates the first sensory-motor idea in the second clause. This construction is the sign vehicle that refers to the object of the symbolic sign. This object, viewed as part of a sign, seems to be the conceptual content that is presented twice in the two clauses. For example, in *What I walk on is the beach*, the object of the sign are the concepts of the Entity and Beach. Using the standard representation, the pseudocleft can be viewed as follows:

Symbol:

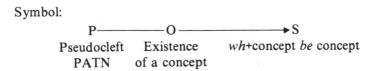

Use of the Pseudocleft

Unlike the passive and relative clause devices, the pseudocleft device makes no independent contribution to the semiotic extension of the utterances in which it is used. It manipulates and rearranges the sensory-motor content, which would be in the conceptual structure in any case without the pseudocleft. Its principal function, instead of semiotic extension, seems to be comprehensible in pragmatic terms rather than conceptual. The pseudocleft constructs an expression out of a conceptual structure, providing a method for expanding and differentiating, in terms of meaning, a *wh*-term such that the speaker may indicate concepts as well as objects. It does, with respect to conceptual structures, in other words, what the deictic referring words such as *this,* and *that* do with respect to objects.

The following examples show schematically what appear to be the meanings of various pseudoclefts (the use of the concept Existence Unspecified will be discussed in the next section):

> *Existence Unspecified of Entity₁ is Entity₂*
> What I walk on is the beach

The meaning of both halves of this example is Entity, and the second half specifies what it is that is indicated in the first half.

> *Existence Unspecified of Location₁ is Location₂*
> Where I walk is on the beach

The meaning of both halves is now Location, with the second specifying the first.

> *Existence Unspecified of Event₁ is Event₂*
> What happened is (that) I gave the wrong lecture

Here the meaning of the two halves is Event, with the second specifying the first.

> *Existence Unspecified of Action₁ is Action₂*
> What I did was sing a song

The second half is Action, but the first half is Event. Nonetheless, there is a pro-verb *do*, which focuses on the second Action specifically, and this specifies the first half *do*.

Topicalization in the Pseudocleft

If the use of the *wh*-term of the pseudocleft parallels that of the *wh*-term of the relative clause, the pseudocleft can be said to use the concepts of Unspecified and Existence to perform phoric and deictic functions. The phoric function of the pseudocleft is cataphoric but functionally could be the same as the anaphoric function it has in the relative clause. It instructs the listener (Ehlich, 1978) to hold in attention that which follows, which is the first half of the pseudocleft (Unspecified supports this function). The *wh*-term also deictically indicates the second half of the pseudocleft, i.e., instructs the listener to bring the information it contains into the focus of attention (Existence supports this function). The pseudocleft thus becomes the device par excellence for isolating topics and introducing comments on them. For example, *what I did was sing a song* creates a topic (by telling the listener to keep in attention the

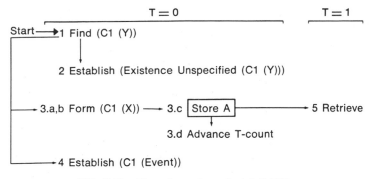

FIG. 7.12.   Flow chart of pseudocleft PATN.

first clause) and delivers a comment on it (by telling him or her to bring into attention the second clause).[3]

PATN Model of a Pseudocleft Device

Figure 7.12 shows the flow of information, including conditions, within the pseudocleft PATN. The T = 0 time segment is the site of most of the activity of this PATN; the T = 1 time segment simply plays out what the first segment has written and stored in memory. Thus, the full pseudocleft emerges everywhere at once. (Note that Fig. 7.12 is incomplete; it omits Steps 5, 6, 7, and 10 below, and numbers Step 9 as 5.)

T-count	PATN STEPS
0	1. Find Concept 1 *Conditions:* a. (Event (Concept 1)) b. (Concept 1 (Y))

The first condition states that the concept labeled "1" must be part of an Event; and the second condition states that it must be at least complex enough to contain one other concept. This is to guarantee that the first clause of the pseudocleft will have content.

0	2. Establish (Existence Unspecified (Concept 1 (Y)) *Condition:* Step 1

This introduces the cataphoric and deictic elements of the

---

[3]I am grateful to Ilene Lanin for discussing these points with me.

T-count	PATN STEPS

pseudocleft. Because Existence Unspecified encompasses Concept 1 (and whatever Concept 1 encompasses), it is not necessary to separately introduce relations between Existence Unspecified and Concept 1.

0   3.a. Duplicate Concept 1
        Condition: Step 1
     b. Establish (Concept 1 (X))
        Conditions: Step 3a
     c. Store (Concept 1 (X)) in Store A
        Condition: Step 3b
     d. Advance T-count
        Condition: Step 3c

This complex step accomplishes the following: it duplicates the sensory-motor content of Concept 1 (but does not duplicate Y, which is kept in the first clause); it inserts the focal part (X) which is judged to be the new or comment information; and it stores the new (Concept 1 (X)) for use in the T = 1 segment.

0   4. Establish (Concept 1 (Event))
       Condition: Step 1

The step places whatever is Concept 1 above its own Event. Note that it is only Concept 1 that is elevated in this way, not (Concept 1 (Y)). This operation is crucial for the pseudocleft construction as represented here, in two ways. First, it provides that the meaning of the first half will be equated to that of the second half (Concept 1 in both), while each half incorporates different detailed information. Second, it rearranges the first half in such a way as to ensure that the level of connectedness of the event is not disrupted. This is accomplished without any part of the Event's conceptual structure being changed, except for one of its concepts being, so to speak, wrapped around the outside; all the other concepts and relations are left intact. The wrapped-around concept dominates the rest, which means that this concept cannot reduce the level of connectedness.

0   5. Establish *be*
       Condition: (Extistence Unspecified (Concept 1 (Event)))

T-count	PATN STEPS
0	6. Connect (Existence Unspecified (Concept 1 (Event))) *be* *Condition:* Step 5
0	7. Apply *be* verb routines *Condition:*Step 5
0	8. Apply Modal, Tense, Aspect, and Number routines to *be* *Condition:* Step 7

These steps select the root verb *be* and appropriately inflect it on the basis of the content of the first clause.

| 1 | 9. Retrieve contents of Store A
Condition: T = 1 |
| 1 | 10. Connect *be* (Concept 1 (X))
Condition: Step 9 |

These final steps carry the utterance paths to the second clause of the psuedocleft. (Note that Step 9 is numbered Step 5 in Fig. 7.12)

SUMMARY

Syntactic devices are regarded as contributing symbolic signs to the conceptual structure and as enriching the ability of the speaker to accomplish semiotic extension. Each device constructs a particular portion of the conceptual structure of the utterances it appears in and functions as a whole. The three syntactic devices analyzed in this chapter are the passive, restrictive relative clause, and pseudocleft constructions. The use of *wh*-terms in the second and third of these is analyzed in terms of anaphoric or cataphoric and deictic functions.

The syntactic devices are represented in the form of PATNs (Parallel Augmented Transition Networks), which permit different steps to be taken at the same time. This is achieved by drawing a distinction between the logical dependencies of the PATN steps and the increments of operating time (in an ATN these are merged). A PATN, once started, causes the corresponding part of the conceptual structure to emerge. The passive PATN is the most complex, but it accounts for three different passive senses and two different "passivizers" without recourse to permutation. The restrictive relative clause device distinguishes right-branching and center-embedded relative clauses; it also provides an explanation for the greater difficulty of multiple occurrences of the latter. The pseudocleft device accounts for various types of pseudocleft sentences without positing an underlying structure of separate clauses (cf. Peters & Bach, 1971).

 DATA

8

Analyses of
Conceptual Structure

This chapter consists of two parts. The first is a description of various methods I have used for investigating conceptual structures. The second presents certain findings relating to the analysis of conceptual structures, including reliabilities of classifying sensory-motor content and extended analyses of examples taken from spontaneous speech.

METHODS

Distinction Between Concepts and Relations

This distinction is fundamental to the interpretation of graphs as conceptual structures, and it can itself be investigated by means of tests based on properties of points and lines in graphs.

According to an intuitive definition, concepts are fixed ideas in conceptual structures, and relations are transitions or dynamic ideas between pairs of fixed ideas. Sometimes there is a sense of "movement" associated with relations that is lacking in concepts. For example, in *John's boat*, the words *John* and *boat* correspond to fixed ideas, whereas the relation of possession appears to be a transition or conceptual movement from *John* to *boat*. This intuition of movement, however, is elusive and unreliable. It can be entirely replaced by the following test.

In terms of graphs, it is possible to determine whether a given meaning element of the conceptual structure should be represented as a point or line by making use of a unique property of points in graphs. One learns from graph theory that weakening points can be subtracted from graphs and the level of connectedness of the graph thereby increased. If a point disconnects a graph, then removing it will increase the level of connectedness from Level 0 to some higher level. Thus, if a given logical conception functions as a concept, it will be possible to find a conceptual structure whose level of connectedness increases when the concept in question is removed.

The mechanism of the test is to create such a conceptual structure through substitution, and it includes two parts, the test item and substitute item. We begin with a Level 1, 2, or 3 conceptual structure. We add the substitute item and try to disconnect the structure in such a way that the *test* item has become the weakening point while at the same time the substitute item has become connected to the rest of the conceptual structure. The empirical question is whether it is possible to make this kind of a substitution. If the test item does, in fact, function as a point, it should be possible to make it into weakening point by inserting an appropriate substitute item. However, if it functions as a relation, this will be impossible. The proof of the substitution will be that the connectedness does increase when the test item is removed from the conceptual structure.

The following example demonstrates a concept using this method. We start with an utterance, for example, *we buy cars from Sweden because they last 11 years.* The connectedness of this structure clearly is greater than zero. We establish a test of the status of *cars from Sweden,* which intuitively is a concept, by adding a substitute item and forming a Level 0 utterance corresponding to a disconnected graph structure, e.g., *we buy cars from Sweden watches from Switzerland.* The connectedness of this test string clearly increases when we remove *cars from Sweden,* for we get *we buy watches from Switzerland.* From this we can conclude that *cars from Sweden* acts as a single point in the conceptual structure; i.e., it functions as a concept.

This test is definitive. Although at first glance it may seem to be a simple matter to arrange a context in which a given constituent disconnects the corresponding graph and to then reconnect the graph by removing the constituent, in fact this is possible only with concepts. Lines, in contrast to points, cannot be weakening. Harary et al. (1965) give the following theorem:

> Theorem 7.10. There are no lines in any digraph whose removal increases its category [of connectedness, i.e., level].
>
> This assertion can be easily verified. For if x is any line of D [a digraph], any path or strict semipath [a sequence in which the lines are not consistent] in $D-x$ is already in D. Hence, the category of $D-x$ is at most that of D [p. 205].

The test we have described is therefore bound to fail for any meaning that functions as a relation. For example, we can test *from* in the aforementioned utterance as follows: First we form a disconnected utterance by adding another item: *we buy cars from Sweden from Switzerland.* Then, we omit *from* to obtain, *we buy cars Sweden from Switzerland.* Clearly this structure is still disconnected. Thus, we have not been able to find a substitution and thereby show that *from* functions as a concept.

A limitation on this test, suggested by this guarded phrasing, is that contexts can be found in which concepts are not weakening. Hence omitting them cannot increase the level of connectedness. This possibility makes the test for a relation tentative, but it does not affect the test for a concept. Also, the logical conceptualization under test must be lexicalized, and this is usually possible.

More crucial limitations on this test are that the test item must appear in the disconnected context in exactly the same way as it appears in the original utterance. Also the substitute item must be an appropriate replacement, although there is no requirement that it should be used in the same way as the test item. These steps must be taken, for otherwise there is no basis for the discrimination of points from lines. It is easy to make a relation look like a weakening point by using the relation arbitrarily; *we buy cars from from Sweden,* a level 0 structure, for example, is increased to level 3 simply by omitting one occurrence of *from.* But neither occurrence of *from* in the disconnected test structure is used in the original way.

Thus, *cars from Sweden* was used in the test as the object of the verb *buy* and *from* was used in the test in the appropriate case relation between *cars* and *Sweden.* The substitution item was, in turn, used appropriately. Thus, we used *watches from Switzerland* and *from Switzerland,* respectively.

The mechanism of this test corresponds to, and thus can replace, the intuitive definitions of concepts and relations given earlier. Because a relation corresponds to a transition between concepts, it cannot appear without the concepts that it relates. Removing it alone, therefore, cannot increase the connectedness of these concepts and might, in fact, reduce it. A concept, on the other hand, because it is a fixed point, can be isolated in a graph. Removing it will then increase the connectedness of the graph.

This test can be used to classify some grammatical categories as either reflecting relation or concept uses. As seen above, noun phrases, such as *cars from Sweden,* function as concepts, and prepositions with noun phrase objects, such as *from,* function as relations. Common nouns also function as concepts:

Original (Level 3): paints the *wall*
Disconnect (Level 0): paints the *wall* picture
Omit *wall* (Level 3): paints the picture

The article in this phrase, on the other hand, seems to function as a relation:

Original (Level 3): paints *the* wall
Disconnect (Level 0): paints *the* wall a picture
Omit *the* (Level 0): paints wall a picture

The disconnected version of this sentence could be *paints a the wall,* which is re-connected by omitting *the.* However, this is not a legitimate test, as *the* is not used in the original way in the test sentence.

Verbs function as concepts, as shown in two tests, one for a transitive verb and the other for an intransitive verb:

Original (Level 3): *paints* the picture
Disconnect (Level 0): sells *paints* the picture
Omit *paint* (Level 3): sells the picture

Original (Level 3): Max *sits*
Disconnect (Level 0): Max *sits* walks
Omit *sit* (Level 3): Max walks

In cases where intuitive classifications are obscure, this test can lead to a classification; in other cases, where one has stronger intuitions, it confirms the obvious. Perhaps it is not completely obvious in advance that articles function like relations (although we must remember that classifying anything as a relation is tentative). Another unobvious classification is that auxiliary verbs also apparently function as relations:

Original (Level 3): Max *was* sitting
Disconnect (Level 0): Max has *was* sitting
Omit *was* (Level 0): Max has sitting

On the other hand, modal verbs are definitely concepts:

Original (Level 3): Max *must* be sitting
Disconnect (Level 0): Max should *must* be sitting
Omit *must* (Level 3): Max should be sitting

Use of the Pseudocleft Construction

According to the PATN representation of pseudoclefts in the preceding chapter, these sentences consist of two parts that are equated in sensory-motor content. Each part is required, in addition, to be coherently organized internally. Therefore, it is possible to use the pseudocleft structure to test structures for sensory-motor content by comparing them to other structures with known sensory-motor content.

The requirement of forming a coherent conceptual structure in each half of the pseudocleft can be shown in the following examples:

?where I walk on is the beach
*what I walk is on the beach

?when I walk at is five P.M.
*how I walk on is stilts ("on" in the sense of support)

In each case an unassimilable concept occurs in one or the other half of the pseudocleft. This concept breaks up the conceptual organization. We see, for example, that the preposition *on* does not like to appear within a structure directly dominated by Entity (second example); however, it does not mind appearing in a structure directly dominated by Location (*where I walk is on the beach*). Thus we can infer, regarding the conceptual structure of *I walk on the beach,* that *on* is not directly dominated by Entity, but that there is some other idea present (i.e., Location).

The graph structure in Fig. 8.1 is a representation of the conceptual organization of *I walk on the beach* (this figure repeats Fig. 6.11). Several constituents of this structure can be demonstrated by appropriate pseudo-clefts.

The simplest constituent to demonstrate is $Event_0$ with the pseudocleft *what happens is (that) I walk.* This sentence shows that *I walk* alone is sufficient to form the idea of an Event (supporting the treatment of Location as a case-like extension of the idea of an Event). The different parts of the above sentence are interrelated as follows: the second half consists of Person and $Action_0$ joining with $Event_1$ to form $Event_0$, and all of this equated to another occurrence of $Event_0$ in the first half that also includes an Action (*happens*).

An interesting contrast appears between the pseudoclefts that demonstrate Entity and $Location_0$. Entity is shown in *what I walk on is the beach,* in which the Entity in the first half is equated with another occurrence of Entity in the second half. $Location_0$ is shown in *where I walk is on the beach*, in which $Location_0$ in the first half is equated with $Location_0$ in the second half. The position of *on* is different in the Entity and $Location_0$ pseudoclefts, therefore, in accordance with the conceptual content of each pseudocleft's second half. This effect can be understood in terms of the organization of $Location_0$ in Fig. 8.1 for which, in fact, it provides evidence.

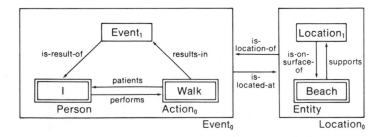

FIG. 8.1 Conceptual structure of *I walked on the beach* (repeats Fig. 6.11).

The use of pseudoclefts as probes has played a part in determining various of the conceptual structure representations in this book. An important example is the analysis of transitive and intransitive verbs. The subjects of intransitive verbs function both as performers and as patients of actions as shown in the following examples:

what Luther did was sit
what Luther did with himself was sit

In the first example, *sit* is equated with an Event that specifies only the performer, and in the second *sit* is equated with an Event that specifies the patient as well. This dual relationship contrasts with the single relationship of subjects to transitive verbs. The following examples show that the subject is exclusively the performer of the action with such verbs (as is, of course, obvious):

what Luther did was pour the coffee
what Luther did with the coffee was pour

In the first example, *pour the coffee* is equated with an Event that specifies the performer and itself includes the patient. In the second example *pour* is equated with an Event that also specifies the patient. The subject, in other words, does not have the property of being a patient.

Hierarchical Clustering Procedures

"Heirarchical clustering" refers both to a procedure for collecting proximity or relatedness judgments and to an algorithm, due to Johnson (1967), for forming clusters based on these judgments. The method and Johnson's algorithm were used by Miller (1969) to estimate the semantic relations among individual words, but the first application of the procedure to words in sentences seems to have been by Levelt (1970b) and Martin (1970). It is the latter application that is of interest here, particularly to the exploration of the effects of syntactic devices on conceptual structure.

Relatedness judgments of words in sentences can be collected in various ways (Levelt, 1970a). One simple method is to provide a seven-point rating scale ranging from "less related" to "more related," and to ask subjects to judge pairs of words for relatedness as they are used in sentences. For example,

Luther pours the coffee
pours—coffee

less   ____ ____ ____ ____ ____ ____ ____   more
related   related

Subjects typically rate such verb–object pairs near the "more related" end of the scale and other pairs such as *Luther* and *the* near the "less related" end (Levelt, 1970b).

In the use of hierarchical clustering, subjects must rate all $n(n-1)/2$ pairs of words from sentences n words long, one pair at a time. The data from this procedure form half of a $n \times n$ matrix of relatedness values, and the clustering algorithm constructs a tree based on this matrix.

An example of such a matrix contains data that I have collected for the sentence *the door got closed* (these data are typical of Levelt's with similar sentences):

	the	door	got	closed
the	—			
door	6.3	—		
got	1.2	4.6	—	
closed	1.1	5.6	6.1	—

The ratings summarized in this matrix were collected from 20 subjects. Their instructions said to judge how "related" the words of each pair are in the context of the sentence without further explaining the ambiguous word "related" (and no subject asked for an explanation). Each word pair was presented on a separate rating sheet on which the sentence appeared as well. In all other respects, the method approximated that of Levelt (1970b). The "more related" end of the scale was defined as seven on the seven-point scale.[1]

The Johnson algorithm exists in several forms. For reasons that will become clear, only the "maximum" ("connectedness") method is appropriate in this study, and this method will be demonstrated with the use of the data above. It is important to make clear the operation of this algorithm in order to present an argument I wish to discuss later. (For details regarding all versions of the Johnson algorithm, see Levelt, 1970a).

The algorithm operates as follows: Begin with the individual words of the sentence, which are, by definition, related to themselves to the maximum degree; each individual word is therefore defined as one cluster. Next seek the highest relatedness value in the matrix, which in the example is 6.3 between *the* and *door,* and form a cluster from these words. Next find the second highest relatedness value, which is *got* and *closed* at 6.1, and form another cluster from this pair.

At this point, two clusters have been formed beyond the level of individual words. In terms of conceptual organization, these correspond to the Entity (*the door*) and the emergent Property (*got closed*) of the passive. The algorithm continues to form clusters by seeking the highest relatedness

---

[1]This research was carried out with the help of Karen Lindig.

values. The next highest value is 5.6 between *door* and *closed,* and so a cluster is also formed here. However, *door* has already been clustered with *the,* and *closed* with *got.* The algorithm considers each of these clusters to be a single point in the relatedness matrix. It therefore forms a new cluster of *the door* and *got closed,* even though the relatedness of *the* and *closed* is the weakest in the matrix. (It is for this reason that this method is called the "maximum method," because new clusters are formed on the basis of the strongest relationships.) The algorithm has now formed a structure that corresponds to an Event in terms of a conceptual structure representation of the passive, and the reconstruction is complete. (No further clusters can be formed.) The resulting tree is shown in Fig. 8.2.

However, before we can conclude that this tree conforms or does not conform to a conceptual structure representation, it is necessary to examine the meaning of the relatedness value (5.6) assigned to the cluster formed from *the door* and *got closed.* This value was actually determined in a different way, by presenting subjects with *closed* and *door,* and it is *these words* that they rated at an average value of 5.6. Two assumptions have to be made. The clustering algorithm assumes that no third word that is related to the first two words could be related more strongly than these two are to each other (this is the ultrametric inequality; cf. Levelt, 1970a). This assumption appears to be valid for the data in the matrix above.

The second assumption is different and is not valid. It is that the relatedness between a *cluster* and another cluster, or that between a *cluster* and a single word, cannot be stronger than the strongest relation between any of the *words* in the two clusters, or between any of the *words* of the cluster and the single word. This assumption is not the ultrametric inequality assumption, and the psychometric validity of the latter cannot guarantee the validity of this assumption. In fact, it is an empirical question that can be answered only by experiment. We must directly test the relatedness of constituents to see whether it is true that the strength of relatedness between *the door* and *got closed* is not greater than that between *door* and *closed.*

Accordingly, in our studies of the strength of relatedness, we have included pairs of constituents as well as pairs of words. Subjects rate these constituents

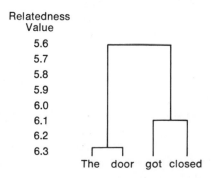

Relatedness
Value

5.6
5.7
5.8
5.9
6.0
6.1
6.2
6.3

The   door   got   closed

FIG. 8.2   Tree built up for *the door got closed.*

on the same seven-point scale. (The constituent pairs and word pairs are presented as part of a single response booklet.) The finding from this procedure is that, consistently, the relatedness of constituents is greater than the strongest relatedness of the words within these constituents. This result suggests that the clustering algorithm can be misleading unless direct relatedness ratings of constituents are taken into account. It makes a difference whether the subject rates pairs of words or pairs of constituents, because the structure that is present in the constituent apparently can add to the degree of perceived relatedness. Actually presenting the structures to subjects will change their judgments of the relatedness. This form of relatedness cannot be reconstructed by the clustering algorithm, because it uses only the relatedness of pairs of words. In the specific case of *the door got closed,* for example, the direct relatedness of *the door* and *got closed* is 6.8, compared to 5.7 (the relatedness of *door* and *closed* alone).

An important insight into the source of this difference comes from a 1975 study of word-to-word relatedness by Terbeek, Fenwick, and Grossman (in preparation). They compared two methods of presenting word pairs. In one (similar to Levelt's method), all pairs of words from a given sentence appeared on a single sheet of paper, and the sentence was identified at the top of this sheet; 15 other sentences appeared on their own different sheets and were also identified. In this situation, it was possible for the subjects to take into account the sentence structure in which each word pair occurred. In the other situation, the same word pairs from these 16 sentences were presented in a thoroughly mixed order, and no sentence was identified for the subjects. In this case, the subjects could not know the use of the word pairs in the sentences.

Terbeek et al. could find *no systematic differences of any kind* between the relatedness ratings produced with these two methods. Thus, it made no systematic difference whether, for example, *door* and *closed* were rated as an isolated pair of words, or as a pair of words in a sentence, *the door was closed.* This surprising result supports our own result by also showing that the word-pair ratings do not necessarily reflect the effects of sentence structure. And it adds to this conclusion the further insight that the word-pair ratings are mainly sensitive to lexical relationships. Given a verb and noun, for example, there seems to be a certain degree of relatedness apart from the specific role these words may play in given sentence structures. When several of word pairs are combined mathematically, a tree such as Fig. 8.6 can result. This form of tree structure may have little or nothing to do with sentence organization apart from lexical organization, however, contrary to the conclusions of Levelt (1970b) and Martin (1970).

If we attempt to incorporate the two types of relatedness information (words and constituents) into a single representation, it seems that a more nearly complete picture of the sentence structure should result. In fact, doing this with *the door got closed* produces a combined representation that closely

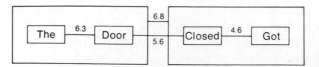

FIG. 8.3   Reconstructed conceptual structure of *the door got closed.*

resembles the conceputal structure representation of this sentence as generated by the passive syntactic device. This is shown in Fig. 8.3 (compare to Fig. 7.2).

It seems to be the case, therefore, that ratings of pairs of constituents and pairs of words must both be taken into account in reconstructing the conceptual structure. I have collected such data for a variety of sentence types, including passives (all three types), relative clauses, and pseudoclefts. In all of these cases, a reconstruction based on word pairs alone underestimates the strength of the relatedness of the constituents that are introduced by syntactic devices. Figs. 8.4 and 8.5 show reconstructed conceptual structures of the relative clause and pseudocleft types, respectively (compare to Figs. 7.8 and 7.11).

These structures approximate those predicted by the relative clause and pseudocleft PATNs. Fig. 8.4 shows the effects of treating *Ralph borrowed the wok* as a property of *wok* in the strength of the line (6.0) between the relative clause and *wok*, which is greater that that between *borrowed* alone and *wok* alone (5.2). The value of 6.0 is the direct rating of *the wok* and *that Ralph borrowed.* Also, the strength of the connection between the entire main clause and the entire relative clause (6.5) is greater than that of any pair of words between the two clauses, corresponding to the relation of the relative and main clauses as wholes. This value is the direct rating of *Max owns the wok* and *that Ralph borrowed.* (The graph does not show the specific role of the relative pronoun, as this was not rated separately from the relative clause.)

Fig. 8.9 shows a reconstructed pseudocleft structure. This structure shows that the strongest relationship is between the two halves of the pseudocleft that are equated for sensory-motor content (Entity).

The word-by-word reconstruction of these same sentences shows a similarity of form but reverses the relative strengths of the relationships. The

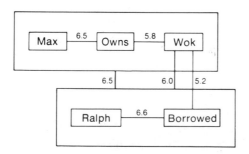

FIG. 8.4   Reconstructed conceptual structure of *Max owns the wok that Ralph borrowed.*

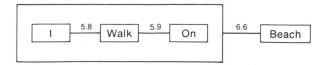

FIG. 8.5   Reconstructed conceptual structure of *What I walk on is the beach.*

weakest relationship in the relative clause structure according to the word-by-word method is that between the main and relative clauses. Similarly, the relationship between the two halves of the pseudocleft turns out to be the weakest according to this method. Thus, it appears, once again, that the word-by-word method does not register the higher constituent structure generated by syntactic devices.

The purpose of this brief exposition has been to demonstrate the use of the hierarchical clustering method (as supplemented) to investigate conceptual structures. In addition, however I have tried to show that Levelt's and Martin's interpretation of word-to-word relatedness ratings as recovering *sentence* structures is inadequate and that we must consider constituent-to-constituent or constituent-to-word ratings.

Labeling Concepts and Relations

The methods discussed thus far identify the parts of conceptual structures that should be regarded as concepts and with a lesser degree of confidence, the parts that should be regarded as relations. However, these methods do not yield the labels of concepts or relations. This step remains the most problematical of any in the analysis of conceptual structure. In general, intuition is still the best guide. For example, we can recognize the patient relation in *the ball was carried,* because the logical formula, *patients* (Carry, Ball), appears to correspond to the meaning of the sentence (apart from orientation).

The problem of labeling is less difficult with concepts than relations. First of all, sensory-motor concepts have been defined in Chapter 5, and there is usually sufficient information from an utterance and its context to recognize which of these definitions applies. Second, non–sensory-motor concepts are generally lexicalized or zeroed according to well-known processes, and it is thus possible to use the lexical items themselves as the labels of non–sensory-motor concepts in many cases. (Concepts are not lexical items, of course.) Very often this requires changing the form class of verbs to noun, but because concepts have no form classes of any kind, this shift is purely cosmetic. An example would be *sitting* in (John)*performs* (Sitting), which is the content of *John sits.*

The difficult problem arises in labeling relations. For example, *from* was shown to probably correspond to a relation in *cars from Sweden,* but how should this relation be labeled in a graph representation? Because there is a lexical item, we should try to make use of it, but this word has a multiplicity of senses and is unusable as a label without modification. In the phrase *cars from Sweden,* the meaning of *from* appears to have something to do with the idea of a source, and we can try to incorporate this into the meaning. For example, we can label the relation *from-source.* Paraphrasing with this label gives *cars from the source, Sweden,* which apart from the comma is not too far off. We can check with other examples; for instance, *money from home* becomes *money from the source, home*, and there are others of a similar kind.

However, we encounter a problem when the term referring to the object being transferred from the source is not specific. For example, *trouble from the economy* clearly involves the idea of a source but is not paraphrased by *trouble from the source, the economy* except in an ironic sense that contrasts with the sense we want. If we change the label to *originates-from,* we avoid this problem; for example, *trouble originates from the economy; money originates from home;* and *cars originate from Sweden.* Thus, tentatively, we can label this relation *originates-from.*

The basic form of this relation, however, will be said to be *originates* (A, B), and the version we have labeled *originates-from* (B, A) will be said to be the receptive orientation. In the case of this relation, meaning offers a guide to the orientation. The receptive orientation would seem to be the one in which the thing being received from the source is the first argument to be mentioned; hence *originates-from* (B, A) should be called the receptive orientation.

Table 8.1 gives several examples of the more important relations in their operative and receptive orientations. These are discussed in the paragraphs that follow.

The first three examples involve forms of the locative relation. The distinction between location in a container (two- or three-dimensional), location on a surface, and location at a point (strictly speaking, at the region of a point; Miller & Johnson-Laird, 1976) corresponds to the prepositions *in, on,* and *at.* Whenever possible, lexicalizations are incorporated into the label of the relation. The labels of the operative orientation include these prepositions and are based on Bennett (1972); those of the receptive orientation do not include them and are based on Leech (1969). In each pair of relations, because there are no orientation-changing syntactic devices, the direction of the orientation has been decided by the meaning. The receptive orientation would seem to occur in phrases where the location is mentioned first and the thing being located there second. In these cases, the location "receives" the object. In the operative orientation, the object mentioned first moves to its location. These intuitions are obvious and iconic when the object is actually mobile. Immobile objects like houses are assumed to be consistent with the model of mobile objects.

The performer and patient relations, which appear within Events and relate to Actions, have orientations decided by the criterion for a "basic" relation

TABLE 8.1
Examples of Conceptual Relations

Relation	Example
O located-in (A, B)	a cottage in the garden
R contains (B, A)	the garden has a cottage
O located-on (A, B)	I walk on the beach
R supports (B, A)	the beach where I walk
O located-at (A, B)	the house at the corner
R contiguous-to (B, A)	the corner contiguous to the house
O performs (A, B)	Max plays
R performed-by (B, A)	the playing of Max
O patients (A, B)	plays the Sousaphone
R patiented-by (B, A)	the Sousaphone is playable
O state-of (A, B)	after starting (A) the cars (B)
R in-state-of (B, A)	before the cars (B) were started (A)
O processes (A, B)	baking a cake
R in-process-of	the cake is baking
O property-of (A, B)	strong will
R has-property-of (B, A)	the sunset was colorful
O originates (A, B)	Max sells Mary a book
R originates-from (B, A)	Mary buys a book from Mary
O sent-to (A, B)	Max sells a book to Mary
R receives (B, A)	Max sells Mary a book
O causes-part (A, B)	the disease caused the symptom
R part-of-cause (B, A)	the symptoms of a disease
O causes-reaction (A, B)	the sound made him drop the tray
R reaction-from-cause (B, A)	he dropped the tray from the sound
O causes-whole (A, B)	running caused his fright
R whole-from-cause (B, A)	his fright was from running
O results-in (A, B)	$Action_0$ results in $Event_1$
R is-result-of (B, A)	$Event_1$ is the result of Person

(cf. Chapter 3). The basic relation is defined as one that can correspond to speech without the use of any orientation-changing syntactic devices. On this criterion, *performs* (A, B) and *patients* (A, B) are basic relations and underlie the operative orientation.

The relation of *state-of* (A, B) and *in-state-of* (B, A) appear when the sensory-motor content is the idea of a State, and they replace what would be, in a nonstate, the patient or performer relation. The B argument is the thing that is in the state represented by the A argument. The receptive orientation mentions the object or person (B) that is in the state first. Thus, *before the cars were started* is receptive, and *after starting the cars* is operative. Each of the receptive and operative orientations can appear with either an initial or a final state of an event (e.g., *after the cars were started* is still receptive, and *before starting the cars* is still operative). The conjunctions *before* and *after*, together with other forms such as the subjunctive mood, have the effect of specifying that there is no change of state (cf. Chapter 5), and this corresponds to the conceptual relations of *in-state-of* and *is-state-of*.

The process relations are parallel to the state relations, in accord with the definition of processes as the temporal continuations of states. In the receptive orientation, therefore, the thing that is being processed is mentioned first, and in the operative orientation the process is mentioned first.

The property relations in Table 8.1 are for Person or Entity Properties, which are defined as conditions on the existence of their Persons or Entities. From the point of view of this definition, the receptive orientation occurs when the Entity whose existence is being conditioned is mentioned first. It is this thing that "receives" the condition of its existence. Thus, passives, restrictive relative clauses, and predicate adjectives, for example, make use of the receptive orientation, *has-property-of*. The verb *be* seems to specialize in expressing this orientation. Apposition of adjectives to nouns, where the condition is mentioned before the Entity being conditioned, in contrast, makes use of the operative orientation, *is-property-of*.

The relations involving sources have already been discussed. However, now they can be compared to the converse relations that involve destinations. The operative source relation was said to be *originates* (A, B) because of the meaning of the relation, in which the thing transferred starts from the referent A. The same argument leads us to classify *send-to* (A, B) as operatively oriented and *received* (B, A) as receptively oriented. The four examples of source relations listed in Table 8.1 involve different orientations of these relations. Considering the cited relations, we have the following:

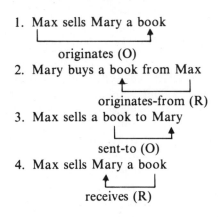

1. Max sells Mary a book

   originates (O)
2. Mary buys a book from Max

   originates-from (R)
3. Max sells a book to Mary

   sent-to (O)
4. Max sells Mary a book

   receives (R)

In addition to these relations, each sentence involves the other relation in one of its orientations. Thus, (1) and (2) involve Mary *receives* book; and (3) and (4) involve Max *originates* book.

The three relations based on causation correspond to the varieties of causes distinguished, for other purposes, in Chapter 3. This is not an exhaustive list by any means, but suggests a rationale for introducing distinctions in this domain. The orientation in each case has been decided from the meaning. The receptive orientation would seem to exist when the first-mentioned argument is the result: it "receives" the causal effect, whatever it may be. Wason and Johnson-Laird (1972) found a strong tendency among college students to regard temporal sequences as cause-effect sequences, and that could underlie the operative orientation of causal relations.

The final relation in Table 8.1 is different from all the others in having no lexical manifestations. This relation in both its orientations appears in the model of semiotic extension presented in Chapter 6, where it makes possible the completion of certain strong components (Event, State). For example, Person *performs* Action is not a strong component until it is related to Event by *results-in* and *results-from*. The orientation of these relations is such that the receptive version, Event *results-from* Person, signifies that the Event is caused by the Person, and the operative version, Action *results-in* Event, signifies that he or she causes the Event by performing the Action. In the case of a receptive orientation of the performer relation, *performed-by* (Action, Person), the same relations with Event are involved but with the orientations to Person and Action reversed. The decision that the orientation of *results-from* is receptive is based on its meaning, because the first concept is a consequence of the second. The two results relations are also involved in the sensory-motor idea of State, when this concept replaces that of an Event (e.g., *the men would have started their cars,* etc.)

Orientation in Different Languages

It is possible to speak of entire languages as having an orientation tending to be operative or receptive. English, for example, is generally oriented operatively, whereas Japanese is generally oriented receptively. English and Japanese are oriented in opposite directions in the sense that where a syntactic device is needed in one language to achieve a certain orientation, in the other language no syntactic device is used for the same orientation. For example, where in English a receptive relation is produced through a syntactic device, in Japanese the equivalent receptive orientation is acheived in a simple sentence. Conversely, Japanese has to use syntactic devices to create operative orientations that in English would occur in simple sentences. This difference in orientation appears in particular with the patient relation.

The syntactically simple form of English verb phrases, such as *writes letters,* can be matched to syntactically simple Japanese verb phrases, *tegami-o kaku* (where *tegami = letter, o =* object marker, and *kaku = writes*). In both of these verb phrases, the appropriate label for the logical relation is *patients* (A, B), and this is the basic form that does not use any orientation-changing syntactic devices. Therefore, we have the following classifications based on this formula:

English: *writes the letter* = referent–relatum = operative
Japanese: *tagami-o kaku* = relatum–referent = receptive

For the same logical meaning, the verb phrase in English is operative and in Japanese is receptive. Conversely, the passive in English creates a receptive orientation,

English: *the letter was written* =   relatum–referent = receptive

whereas in Japanese an adjectival complement is used to create a corresponding operative orientation,

Japanese: *kaita tegami* = referent–relatum = operative

(the verb *kaku* is inflected as a past participle, *kaita,* a device for making a modifier, not unlike the English use of the past participle). Once again, the same logical meaning, *patiented-by* (Letter, Writing), has opposite orientations in the two languages, receptive for English and operative for Japanese. This difference is such that the basic logical form is always operative in English and always receptive in Japanese, and in this sense the languages can be said to be oriented in opposite directions.

This difference in orientation conditions other differences. A particularly clear case is the use of prepositions in English in contrast to the use of postpositions in Japanese. Both languages insert particles between the arguments of logical functions. In a graph structure representation, this corresponds to the position of the relation between two concepts. When in English a preposition is used with the patient relation, e.g., *push on the horse,* the preposition marks the relation in the conceptual structure, push *patients* horse. Japanese achieves the equivalent marking in a receptive orientation, and this means the participle has to be a postposition. The logical form is *patients* (Push, Horse), and the receptively oriented conceptual structure is horse *patients* push. Therefore, the particle marking the relation appears after the noun and is a postposition.

A variety of other relations involves the same use of particles and leads to prepositions or postpositions depending on the orientation of the language. Some examples of matched English–Japanese pairs are the following:

O   *sent-to* (Gift, John)   gift *sent-to* John   *a gift for John*
R   *sent-to* (Omiyage, John)   John *sent-to* omiyage   *John e* (= to) *no* (= adj. ending) *omiyage*

R   *possess* (John, Book)   book *possessed-by* John   *a book of John's*
O   *possess* (John, Hon)   John *possess* hon   *John-no* (= poss.) *hon*

O *located-in* (Shed, Garden) shed *located-in* garden *a shed in the garden*

R *located-in* (Koya, Niwa) niwa *located-in* koya *niwa-ni* (= loc.) *aru* (= participle) *koya*

O *performs* (John, Pushing) John *performs* pushing *John pushed*

O *performs* (John, Osu) John *performs* osu *John-ga* (= subj.) *osu*

In each of these examples, except for the last, both languages insert a particle that corresponds to the relation between two arguments. Since the languages are oriented in opposite directions, the equivalent particles in these cases are prepositions and postpositions. The genitive example, where English is receptive and Japanese operative, shows that the specific orientation of a relation is not the important factor for predicting whether this particle is a preposition or postposition. What is crucial is the orientation of the basic relation in the two types of language. In the one situation where the orientations are the same, subject and verb, Japanese, being a language with postpositions, is permitted to have a marker as predicted. English has no particle, however, which means that a strong test of the prediction that Japanese and English should be the same in this relation is out of the question. Nonetheless, because English should also have a postposition in this case, the absence of such a particle is at least predictable.

The primary definition of a basic relation depends on whether orientation-changing syntactic devices must apply in order to achieve the opposite orientation of the basic relation. This connection with syntactic devices priedicts other grammatical features. Languages, insofar as they are internally consistent, may align themselves along the axis of overall orientation.

According to Greenberg (1963), a number of grammatical characteristics do coincide with the OV and VO patterns:

> ... certain languages tend consistently to put modifying or limiting elements before those modified or limited, while others just as consistently do the opposite. Turkish, an example of the former type, puts adjectives before the nouns they modify, places the object of the verb before the verb, the dependent genitive before the governing noun, adverbs before adjectives which they modify, etc. Such languages, moreover, tend to have postpositions for concepts expressed by prepositions in English. A language of the opposite type is Thai, in which adjectives follow the noun, the object follows the verb, the genitive follows the governing noun, and there are prepositions [p. 76].

The common feature that Greenberg mentions, whether "modifying or limiting elements" appear before or after the elements that they modify, clearly corresponds to a difference in orientation, and this would suggest that the variety of grammatical characteristics he mentions is conditioned by a single system influenced by orientation.

FINDINGS

It has not been possible to keep "findings" out of the first part of this chapter. The distinction between "methods" and "findings" is further eroded by the description under "findings" of yet another method (temporal measurement). Nonetheless, in this case the results are the main interest. The topics included in this second part of the chapter are: (1) reliability of sensory-motor classifications: (2) temporal stability of sensory-motor segments in speech output; and (3) examples of conceptual structures in spontaneous discourse.

Reliability of Sensory-Motor Classifciations

Two reliability measures are of interest; these might be called the "maximal" and "minimal" reliabilities of sensory-motor classifications. The "maximal" reliability is obtained when utterances are classified into sensory-motor segments by experienced judges. For this purpose, I have compared my own classifications with those of K. Lindig regarding the segmentation of two passages ("Oscar" and "Diana") from Terkel (1970). These passages are transcriptions (possibly edited) of spontaneous speech, each approximately 750 words long. Examples from each of them were used to illustrate different sensory-motor meanings in Chapter 5.

The passages were classified by the two of us, working separately, into segments that we judged to correspond to sensory-motor meanings. The following categories were used (for definitions, see Chapter 5): Event (intransitive); Event$_1$ (transitive omitting the patient); Event$_2$ (transitive including the patient); Action; Location; State; Property (Entity and Person); Property (Event); and Person. When necessary, overlapping speech segments were classified in different ways. For example, *I found the telephone disconnected* is an Event$_2$; it is also an Event$_1$ (*I found*) and an Action (*the telephone disconnected*).

Under these circumstances the "maximal" reliability is approximately 90%. The greatest disagreements arise between State and Event, as would be expected from the complexity and subtlety of the definitions of these sensory-motor ideas. Such complexities can diminish agreement between experienced judges. On the other hand, it is almost always possible to reach agreement through discussion, because the application of the definitions of the sensory-motor ideas can be analyzed. With discussion, the level of agreement is about 98%, the residual corresponding, for the most part, to ambiguities.

"Minimal" reliability is obtained when naive judges are compared to experienced judges. We recruited five individuals, all social scientists who had had no prior experience at or information about classifying sensory-motor representations. They were provided with brief definitions and examples of Events (but without attempting to distinguish intransitive and transitive Events), Actions, Locations, and States. These judges classified all of the sensory-motor segments identified by Lindig and myself in the two passages mentioned above. The judges had to label segments, therefore, but not divide the text. Passages where segmentations occur on two levels (such as *I found the telephone disconnected*) were presented separately in each segmentation, and no judge was given both segmentations. Although the segments appeared on the response sheet in their original order, the instructions did not attempt to describe how this context could be taken into account in labeling segments.

The definitions given to the judges were the following:

Event = a *change* of state of any kind. For example, *the men stopped their cars,* or *the men stopped.*

State = the *initial* or *final* state in an Event. A State does *not* involve change, and it *must* be initial or final in some Event. For example, *when the cars had stopped* is the final State of the Event of the cars stopping.

Action = the *performance* due to an agent. For example, *stopped the cars* is the Action due to the men. Actions are parts of Events and are distinguished from them in the following way: Call something an Action only if just the Action alone is mentioned in the example. If the agent also is mentioned, call the example an Event. For example, *had to stop* is an action (replying to a question, "what happened?").

Location = the place at which an Event or Action occurs. For example, *the men stopped their cars at the cliff's edge.*

The percentage agreement between the labeling of the naive judges and the labeling of the experienced judges ranged from 74% to 80%. To express these reliability values more carefully, I have calculated values of Kappa (Cohen, 1960) for each judge. Kappa is a superior measure of reliability because it corrects for chance agreement. Kappa varies in theory between +1.0 and −1.0 according to the formula,

$$\kappa = \frac{P_o - P_c}{1 - P_c}$$

where P_o is the observed proportion of agreement between judges and P_c is the proportion of agreement expected by chance. P_c is calculated from the marginal frequencies of the two-fold table comparing the judgments between experienced and naive judges in each category (Event, Action, Location,

TABLE 8.2
Reliabilities of Standard Sensory-Motor Classifications

Judge	Kappa	% Agreement
1	.72	80
2	.70	78
3	.69	77
4	.68	76
5	.63	74

State). The correction is quite stringent, but it assures that the value of Kappa gives the proportion of agreement between judges that exceeds chance agreement.

Table 8.2 shows the value of Kappa and the percentage agreement between each naive judge individually and the standard of the experienced judges (in any case of disagreement over the standard, I took my own classification). The values in the table are averages, based on the two passages.

If we analyze the sources of the reliability values in Table 8.2, we can see that most of the disagreements with the standard arose over the classification of segments as either Events or States, particularly as States (see Table 8.3). The most commonplace errors were to label Events as States (43% of all errors) and States as Events (37% of all errors). This leaves only 20% of the errors in all other combinations. Given the difficulty of the definitions of Event and State and their dependence on context, this finding is hardly surprising.

The great majority of the misclassifications of Events and States falls into a small number of categories. For example, 34 of the 61 misclassifications in which Events were called States occurred because the judges took internal Events to be States—for instance, *I never questioned, I was surprised,* and so on. In these cases, the judges could not bring themselves to apply the definition of an Event (which they used elsewhere) to an internal change of state. *All* of the 52 misclassifications of States as Events were due to the judges' not noting that a segment was the initial or final condition in a change of state. For example, *if you give them coal* is the s_1 of an Event, but 80% of the judges took it to be an Event itself.

TABLE 8.3
Percentage Agreement with Standard Sensory-Motor
Labels

Labels	%
Event	74
Action	84
Location	98
State	59

TABLE 8.4
Relative Variances (× 1000) for Repeated Utterances

	Sentence 1	Sentence 2	Juncture 1	Juncture 2
Related	2.0	2.5	51.1	22.6
Not related	3.0	3.7	25.6	48.1

Assuming that naive judges could be given explicit instructions warning them against these two types of misclassifications, the percentage agreement with the standard would approach the high 80s, a level of agreement near the "maximal" level. In other words, the "maximal" skill of labeling sensory-motor segments consists almost entirely in distinguishing Events and States.

Temporal Stability

The measurement of temporal stability allows us to approach the question of whether the programming units of speech output correspond to sensory-motor or other kinds of segments. This type of experiment seems to have been invented by Kozhevnikov and Chistovich (1965). If a speaker repeatedly produces the same segment of speech, the parts that correspond to the output of a single program should be more stable temporally than the parts that correspond to different programs; the latter parts include changes of program. The duration of the programmed segments are controlled directly or indirectly, whereas the changes of program are not.

Kozhevnickov and Chistovich had subjects repeat short sentences that they anticipated would be organized as two syntagmata. The coefficients of variation (= the standard deviation of the durations of the repetitions divided by the mean) of these syntagmata were much smaller than those of the junctures between the syntagmata, suggesting that the speech output corresponding to each syntagma was programmed as a single unit.

The data in Table 8.4 are from an experiment of my own with Lindig. We followed the Kozhevnikov and Chistovich procedure as closely as possible, with the exception that we asked our subjects to produce successively two short, grammatically complete sentences. These were produced on a single breath expiration cycle (breath group), and our purpose was to ensure the presence of a semantic juncture that was independent of a breath group. Despite this change and the difference in languages, we obtained results close to those of Kozhevnikov and Chistovich. Table 8.4 gives the relative variances (= standard deviation squared, divided by the mean)[2] for pairs of sentences produced on the same expiration. Half of the sentences were semantically

---

[2]This follows the recommendation of Ohala (1970). The relative variance is independent of the size of the mean, whereas the coefficient of variation necessarily decreases as the mean increases.

related (e.g., *Lonny dropped the soup. Ted wiped it up.*) and half were semantically unrelated (e.g., *Sally read the note. Kay pulled weeds.*). Relative variances are given for both of these sentence types, for the two sentences (1, 2) that the subject produced on one expiration, for the juncture between them (Juncture 1), and for the juncture between expiration and inhalation (Juncture 2).

The lower values, by approximately a factor of 10–20, for both Sentences 1 and 2 compared to Juncture 1, correspond to the result of Kozhevnikov and Chistovich and suggest that each sentence was individually produced as a single output. Because the two sentences and Juncture 1 were part of the same breath expiration, this result cannot be attributed to any effects arising from the programming of breath groups (cf. Lieberman, 1967). The inhalation portion of the breath group (Juncture 2) also shows some evidence of programming in the case of related sentences, but not in the case of unrelated sentences. For some reason, there is no evidence in the Juncture 1 values that the related sentences were programmed together as a single output more often than the unrelated sentences; in fact, the evidence shows, if anything, the reverse. It is not known what could have caused this result.

The simple sentences used in this experiment correspond to the idea of an Event. The results accordingly suggest that this idea can be used to program speech output.

However, there is a difficulty of theoretical importance in this experiment and in the Kozhevnikov and Chistovich method in general. The difficulty is that constant repetition of the same structure can lead to semantic satiation (Lackner & Tuller, 1976). When in this state, the speaker loses the sense of the semantic and/or grammatical structure of the sentence. The sentence may no longer have a meaning for him or her, it may take on a new meaning that is often bizzare, it may appear to be segmented in a new way, and so on. When this state occurs, we can no longer predict syntagmata from the semantic organization of the utterance, as we do not know what this organization is.

To ward off semantic satiation, we have modified the Kozhevnikov and Chistovich method in the following way: The speaker never literally repeats himself. We redefine "repetition" to include repetitions under the same sensory-motor or other description, and we collect all occurrences of this description in a stretch of continuous speech as a sample of "repetitions." For example, each Event segment in a sample of continuous speech can be regarded as a repetition of the speech program based on the sensory-motor idea of an Event, and the same can be done for other sensory-motor ideas. Although these "repetitions" differ in length, words, meanings, and rhythmic pattern, they are each an instance of what could be a syntagma based on a specific sensory-motor idea. The differences between occurrences of the same sensory-motor idea will add to the temporal variability of the "repetitions," but we can assume that this additional variance is random in the sample of

TABLE 8.5
Relative Variances in Continuous Speech

	"Oscar"	(N)	"Diana"	(N)
Transitive Event$_1$	5.22	(15)	2.20	(11)
Transitive Event$_2$	2.53	(13)	1.18	(8)
Intransitive Event	1.16	(6)	3.11	(8)
State	0.68	(14)	1.21	(9)
Action	3.05	(8)	3.64	(13)
Location (spatial)	0.96	(9)	0.86	(8)
Total sensory-motor	3.65	(77)	3.00	(69)
Surface clauses	5.93	(52)	3.73	(41)

"repetitions." If we are willing to accept greater variability, it becomes possible to compare different sensory-motor segments without risk of semantic satiation effects. As can be seen by comparing Tables 8.4 and 8.5, the relative variances of the "repetitions" of sensory-motor segments in continuous speech are about 1000 times greater than those of actual complete repetitions.

Table 8.5 shows the relative variances of several "repetitions" in one individual's reading of the "Oscar" and "Diana" passages from Terkel (1970) which were discussed previously.[3]

Duration was measured from oscillographic tracings of the recorded speech, a procedure which makes possible a high degree of accuracy. Segments were normalized for syllable length by calculating the average syllable duration, and these values were used to calculate the relative variances. The shortest and longest such syllable durations were eliminated from each of these calculations, and the six longest and six shortest average syllable durations were eliminated from the two baseline calculations described in the following paragraphs.

The category of transitive Event$_1$ in Table 8.5 consists of such segments as *the farmer got,* in which a transitive verb is included but its object is excluded, and the category of transitive Event$_2$ consists of these same sentences with the object also included. These are in fact the same sentences; the object simply was not included in the duration for Event$_1$. There were no examples of true Event$_1$ segments in the two passages.

Sensory-motor segments can be compared to each other and to baseline calculations of relative variance. Two such baselines appear in Table 8.5. For one we combine the different sensory-motor samples. In this baseline, we are asking, in effect, whether it is possible to select from the total variance of the

[3]I am grateful to K. Lindig for the use of these recordings, which she made as part of her doctoral research (Lindig, 1977). The recordings were made independently and in advance of the classification of the passages into sensory-motor segments.

combined sample subsamples, corresponding to the separate sensory-motor segments, which are less variable. This would be possible, for example, if some of the subsamples differ in mean syllable duration and/or if some subsamples are less variable and others are more variable than the total sample. The other baseline is calculated from surface grammatical clauses. Only those surface clauses that coincide (as nearly as possible) with sensory-motor segments are included in this baseline calculation.

The two baselines give essentially the same results, although the evidence for sensory-motor programming is slightly stronger when compared to surface clauses than when compared to the total sample of sensory-motor segmentation. The evidence strongly supports State and Location as programming units; these yield significantly ($p < .05$) lower relative variances in comparison to both baselines, and in both passages. (The "total" sensory-motor relative variance has been calculated separately for each sensory-motor segment and excludes the particular segment.) In addition, Event$_2$ and intransitive Event both yield significantly lower relative variances in comparison to both baselines in one of the passages. There is no evidence, on the other hand, that the speaker made use of either Action or Event$_1$ as the basis of output programming.

Considering these data, therefore, we find certain evidence of speech planning at the level of several sensory-motor representations. The ideas of State, Location, transitive Event$_2$, and intransitive Event provide the bases for syntagmata. In different samples, with other speakers or altered speaking conditions, other sensory-motor ideas might also prove to be relatively more stable.

In no case is the surface grammatical clause more stable than any of these sensory-motor segmentations. There is no evidence, therefore, that such grammatical structural units correspond to psychological functional units. Surface grammatical clauses differ from sensory-motor segments in three ways that could account for their greater variability: (1) surface clauses sometimes include nonclassified segments (e.g., conjunctions) besides sensory-motor segments; (2) surface clauses do not distinguish between different types of sensory-motor segments; and (3) surface clauses may combine more than one type of sensory-motor segment. One or more of these factors may have contributed to the greater relative variance of surface clauses beyond the contribution of the separate sensory-motor segments that they contain.

When we segment speech according to the sensory-motor content, we could be sorting utterances according to the output (syllable) rate, and several of the sensory-motor segments do have different output rates. However, there is no consistent association of a given type of sensory-motor segment with a particular rate; two passages can give conflicting results (e.g., one slow, the other fast) for the same type of segment. Apparently, the speaker could vary her speech rate (and, in fact, did so) by changing the rate at which different sensory-segments were played out. But there is no evidence that a given type of sensory-motor segment has to be produced at a particular rate.

Table 8.6 gives the average syllable duration for the different sensory-motor segments. Each of these means is tested against the total sensory-motor mean with the respective subsample excluded; differences significant by t at $p < .05$ are indicated by †. This table shows a pattern similar to Table 8.5, with a few interesting exceptions. Among the similarities, transitive Event$_2$ is faster than average in "Diana," where it is also less variable; State is faster than average in "Oscar" and also less variable; Location is faster or slower than average, depending on the passage, and is less variable. However, there are two segments that are significantly less variable and are not significantly faster or slower—intransitive Event in "Oscar" and State in "Diana." These segments apparently were produced at a controlled rate that was close to the average speech rate. Furthermore, there are four segments that are not significantly less variable, but are significantly faster or slower than average. Transitive Event$_1$ in both passages was produced faster, and Action in both passages was produced slower than average. We may have weak evidence here, after all, of the speaker's use of these sensory-motor ideas, in spite of their lack of relative temporal stability. Transitive Event$_1$ and Action are faster and slower respectively in both of the passages, but other sensory-motor ideas are different in the two passages. The most dramatic of these differences is Location, which is exceptionally slow in "Oscar" and exceptionally fast in "Diana"; State shows the opposite distinction, though less sharply. These differences show that sensory-motor ideas are not necessarily associated with specific ranges of output rate, and that speakers have the option of playing out a given sensory-motor segment at either a fast, an average, or a slow rate.

Finally, it should be noted that the average syllable duration of all sensory-motor segments or surface clauses combined is approximately 190 msec, or a

TABLE 8.6
Average Syllable Duration in Continuous Speech
(msecs)

	"Oscar"	"Diana"
Transitive Event$_1$	176.9†	177.6†
Transitive Event$_2$	184.6	183.7†
Intransitive Event	193.5	200.3
State	172.3†	197.6
Action	210.3†	203.1†
Location (spatial)	212.0†	178.4†
Total sensory-motor	188.7	194.1
Surface clauses	187.3	187.8

rate of output of about 5.3 syllables a second. This value is close to the frequency of 6 Hz postulated by Lenneberg (1967) as a basic carrier frequency of the nervous system. Six events per second does approximate the syllable output rate averaged over different types of sensory-motor segment, but Table 8.6 also suggests that there is a range of nearly a full syllable of output rates (4.7 to 5.6 per second), which is correlated with different types of sensory-motor segment, and that the same type of segment may adopt different stable rates across this range. If there is a carrier frequency, therefore, it is open to modulation, and logically this must depend on the prior choice of a sensory-motor segment. This is compatible with the sensory-motor scheme being the controlling program of the syntagma.

Summary. This section has presented evidence, consisting of the temporal stability of repeated speech segments, that the sensory-motor ideas of Location, State, and Event can and do function as the basis of speech programming.

Examples of Conceptual Structure Representations

The four specimens analyzed in the present section are spontaneous utterances. Three of the specimens are from conversations in which I was a participant, although not all are from my own speech; the fourth specimen, from the speech of H.M. (Scoville & Milner, 1957), is available to me through William Marslen-Wilson.

The purpose in showing these examples is to provide demonstrations of extended analyses of the conceptual structures of naturally occurring utterances. With H.M.'s utterance, moreover, we can see the effect of a pronounced memory abnormality on the formation of conceptual structure.

It is the case, of course, that naturally occurring utterances can include aspects of structure that have not been considered in the methods of analysis discussed hitherto; some of these are important and frequent, such as complement structures and anaphoric pronominalizations. Where possible I have assumed the existence of parallels with structures already investigated and have dealt with the "new" structures as if they were analogous to other familiar structures. These assumed parallels and other tentative solutions will be pointed out as they occur.

1. *"Let's keep it over near the door*
   φ that's a dark corner."

(The φ represents a hesitation.) This specimen illustrates the importance of considering the context of utterances. The connectedness of this example is at Level 3, but this is apparent only when the context is considered; it is at Level

2 if the utterance is considered out of context. This context was a dialogue as follows:

Speaker A: where shall we put this lamp?
Speaker B: let's keep it over near the door ϕ that's a dark corner.

It is clear from the context that the second clause of Speaker B's utterance is not a relative clause. It also seems appropriate to consider this clause as the continuation of the first clause. B's utterance in the context of A's forms a logical deduction; however, the sequence of the deduction is stated backwards in the utterance, with the conclusion mentioned before one of the premises (and the other premise not mentioned at all). The steps *logically* arranged are the following:

(Premise)   1. we shall put this lamp someplace;
(Premise)   2. it will be in an existing dark corner;
(Conclusion) 3. therefore, it will be over near the door.

The first premise appears only in the context but can be assumed to be incorporated into the utterance structure. The second premise is stated in the second clause and the conclusion in the first clause.

Fig. 8.6 is the graph representation of the conceptual structure of this utterance. The initial part of the graph represents *let's keep it over near the door.* The modal verb *should* is treated as a concept in accordance with the discussion of concepts as distinguished from relations in the first section, on methods, of this chapter. The question of precisely how this concept should be related to the Action, *keep it,* has been settled on the ground that *should,* as a modulation or specification of the type of the Action, should be included within this idea. This representation may not be appropriate for all uses of the modal verb. For example, *it should be X* does include *should* as an independent component.

The pronoun *it* anaphorically refers to *this lamp* in the previous discourse. This important function is represented in Fig. 8.6 by the relation *indicates* (Entity, Entity), where the first Entity argument is part of the lexical retrieval of *it* and the second is part of the lexical retrieval of *lamp* (accomplished during B's listening to A's utterance). The anaphoric function according to this representation exists between two Entity concepts, one of which originally appeared in the previous discourse, such that the noncontextual concept indicates the contextual one. As in earlier discussions of the anaphoric function, this description is intended to apply to the conceptual structure and to parallel a pragmatic function (i.e., to remind the listener to attend to the referent of *this lamp*).

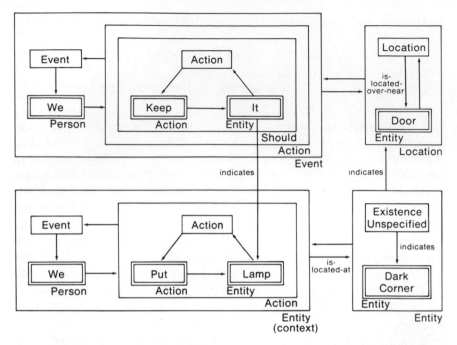

FIG. 8.6 Conceptual structure representation of *Let's keep it over near the door φ that's a dark corner.*

The second clause, *that's a dark corner,* is also connected to the first by a relation of indication. In this case, the arguments are this clause and the location phrase, *over near the door.*

The orientation of these relations causes the entire conceptual structure, including the part from the context, to be connected at Level 3. Leaving out the contextual part reduces the connectedness to Level 2. If the utterance had been produced without any prior context, if, for example, it had been the opener of a conversation, *let's keep the lamp over near the door, that's a dark corner,* the connectedness would be Level 2. Thus, the internal cohesiveness of the utterance as produced crucially depends on the anaphora of *it.* The complete utterance path leads from *let's keep it over near the door,* through the context, and to *that's a dark corner.* This is the *only* path through this Level 3 structure that does not begin or end with the context. Thus, the illogical sequence of the utterance, with the conclusion emerging before one of its premises, probably can be explained by the way in which Speaker B incorporated the prior context.

The role of anaphora in raising the connectedness of the utterance to Level 3 means that the relation *indicates* (Entity, Entity) was guaranteed by the quantum restriction to affect only the connectedness of the conceptual structure and not the focus. On the other hand, the relation *results-in* (Entity, Location) between the second premise and the conclusion and the relation *located-at* (Event, Entity) between this premise and the context, neither of which affects the connectedness, are both free to shift the focus. All of these consequences of the quantum restriction can be seen to hold in this example. Calculating the focal point of *let's keep it over near the door,* without either premise included, shows that the Action, *should keep it,* is the focus. Adding the premise, *that's a dark corner,* shifts the focus to the Event, *let's keep it.* Adding the contextual premise, *we shall put the lamp somewhere,* shifts the focus to the Location, *over near the door.* Adding the anaphoric relation to the context, *indicated* (Entity, Entity), cannot have an effect of the focus since it increases the connectedness. The focal idea of the utterance, therefore, according to the graph representation in Fig. 8.10, is *over near the door,* and this is intuitively plausible. The speaker could have started with this idea, and added anaphoric *it* without affecting the focus. The next most focal concept is the Event, *let's keep it,* and the third most is the Action component of this Event, *keep it.* The Entities *it* and *lamp* are quite low on focus, and this seems intuitively correct also. An interesting distinction exists between the idea of Location, which is focal, and the idea of an Entity, *dark corner,* which is extremely low on focus. This distinction corresponds to the logical structure. Even though *dark corner* is closely related to the idea of Location, because the speaker was attempting to make everything in the utterance relate as closely as possible to the conclusion rather than to the premise, it is distant from the rest of the utterance and hence low in focus.

Two features of this first specimen are worth re-emphasizing, because the next specimen contrasts with both of them. The first is that a representation of the context is an integral part of the internal structure of the utterance, and the second is that the role assumed in this process by the anaphoric pronoun *it* is to relate outward from the utterance to the context. In the case of the next utterance, however, prior context is absent.

2. "He has a scratch on his eye; he says."

(The ";" represents a terminal contour.) This example also involves an apparent inversion of the logical sequence (which would have been in the main-subordinate clause order: *he says something; it is that he has a scratch on his eye*), but the specimen was produced without any relevant prior context. Thus nothing can rescue it from the ignominious Level 2 of connectedness. Fig. 8.7 is the graph representation of this utterance. Part of the speaker's meaning was that the alarming statement in the subordinate clause is subject to doubt, and this is reflected in the labeling of the relation between the Events; namely, that the Event of the scratch *results* from the Event of his saying it.

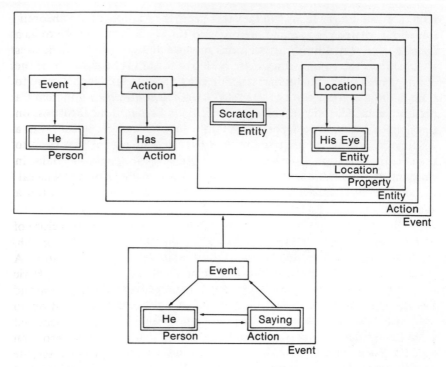

FIG. 8.7   Conceptual structure representation of *He has a scratch on his eye, he says.*

3. "You don't have to have that one because I have another one."

This example shows a number of interesting details. The dialogue in which it appeared included the following:

Speaker A: we have that table with the tape recorder on it
Speaker B: you don't have to have that one because I have another one
      (*one* referring to *table* in each occurrence)

The conceptual structure of this utterance incorporates the context of A's utterance via *another one,* a concept which receives a relation from the context; and it makes contact with the context a second time deictically with *that one,* a concept which sends a relation out to the context. In this example, unlike the first one discussed, the connectedness level does not depend on the context, because the conceptual structure is at Level 3 regardless of the context.

This conceputal structure illustrates a phenomenon mentioned theoretically in Chapter 5. The idea of an Event corresponds to the utterance as a whole, although no component of the utterance is an Event. The two clauses considered separately are based on the idea of a State. The sequence of the utterance is s_2 and s_1 in terms of the formula $s_1 T s_2$. The speaker did seem to pronounce the entire utterance as a single output (i.e., there was apparently a single phonemic clause, one terminal contour, and a single primary stress on *another*), corresponding to the idea of an Event. This achievement raises a theoretical problem, because it means that one speech program was sent to the articulatory apparatus in which the same symbol, State, was expanded in two ways. An escape from this difficulty would be to distinguish in general between initial s_1 and final s_2 State; each type of State would then constitute a distinct symbol in the speech program.

Figure 8.8 shows the graph representation of the conceptual structure of this utterance. Several assumptions were necessary in preparing this graph. The negative verb, *don't have,* is assumed to include a concept of negation. A second assumption is that the infinitive complementizer, *to* has anaphoric and deictic functions which indicate both the complementizing verb *have* and the subordinate verb phrase *have that one.* This treatment is based on an analogy with relative pronouns; i.e., *to* with respect to the complement and the complementizing verb is assumed to be analogous to a relative pronoun with respect to the relative clause and the noun phrase head. In both cases, the particle or pronoun is a kind of signpost rising out of ˙the sentence that indicates the elements that are related to each other. The complement itself is an Action, *have that one,* assumed to be contained within the idea of an Entity. The later assumption is meant to correspond to the presence of noun phrase properties of complements (Rosenbaum, 1967, preface).

The focal point of the graph in Fig. 8.8 is State$_1$, *I have another one,* a plausible description, as this presumably is the idea that the speaker would have thought of first in the context. (This context relates to State$_1$.) She added the consequent State$_2$ to form the idea of an Event. This State relates back to the context, not disrupting the Level 3 of the connectedness.

Since this structure is at Level 3, the quantum principle does not guarantee that the focus will not shift with the addition of new relations. This fact could explain the choice of the word-order sequence in which the nonfocal State$_2$ is mentioned first. If all three relations between State$_1$ and State$_2$ are reversed, corresponding to the utterance *I have another one so you don't have to have that one,* the focus becomes State$_2$. The order of clauses is the one that maintains State$_1$ as the focal point.

Representing the Utterance Path of this Example. Directed graphs cannot properly convey the dynamic changes that take place in the utterance path as it is converted into speech. It is possible to derive a different kind of

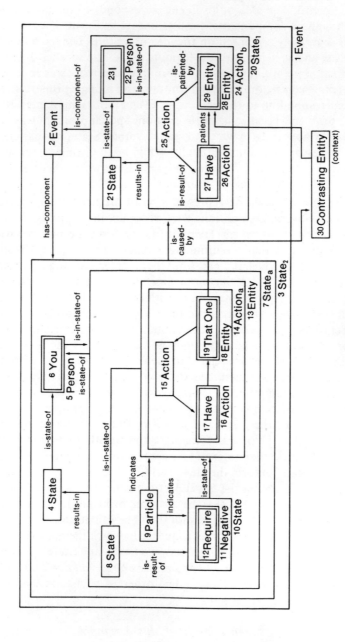

FIG. 8.8 Conceptual structure representation of *You don't have to have that one because I have another one.*

192

representation, however, based on the directed graph structure, that is better adapted to conveying these changes. This new representation contains no information not already in the directed graph structure, but it displays it in a form that corresponds to the output sequence. It also would be possible to represent the process of assembling conceptual structures, which can follow a different sequence from the output. Fig. 8.9 is an example of the type of graph that shows the output sequence. It is based on Fig. 8.8 and shows changes in the conceptual structure along the utterance path during production of *you don't have to have that one because I have another one.*

It is necessary to make certain assumptions regarding the formation of the conceptual structure in Fig. 8.8, particularly in regard to when the conceptual structure is organized and when speech comes to be produced from it. Based on comments by the speaker, we can assume in this case that the major features of the conceptual structure were assembled before *any* speech was produced. Thus, Fig. 8.9 begins (in panel a) by showing a not-yet-articulated mass corresponding to the already formed conceptual structure, which is lying to the left. This and subsequent panels correspond to the following (selected) steps in the utterance path (numbers refer to points in Figs. 8.8 and 8.9): Event (1), $State_2$ (3), *you* (6), $State_a$ (7), *don't have* (= Require) (11), $Action_a$ (13), *have* (= Possess) (16), *that one* (18), $State_1$ (19), *I* (22), $Action_b$ (23), *have* (= Possess) (26), *another one* (28). This list includes all the lexical items and the major sensory-motor ideas but leaves out 29 other transitions from the shortest complete utterance path in Fig. 8.8.

I will explain the construction of the diagrams in Fig. 8.9 later, but first I should suggest how they can be viewed. There are two main possibilities. In one, the sequence of panels a through m corresponds to a series of elevation views of an epigenetic landscape through which the utterance path moves in a valley. This valley commences in the upper right corner of the epigenetic landscape and cuts through it to the lower left. A ball representing the output of the speech apparatus would roll along the valley and through the conceptual structure.

The second way of viewing Fig. 8.9, which I prefer, is that the succession of panels shows the effects of unfolding the utterance by pulling the mass displayed in panel a through a small aperture (the equivalent of the articulator). As this mass is pulled through the articulator, it unfolds, and the contents (a concept or word) are exposed. As the conceptual structure unfolds in this way more and more of the utterance path is revealed, and the unfolding conceptual structure itself takes on a particular shape that changes through degrees from panel to panel. At first it fans out, as the mass on the left is pulled through the aperture, and then begins to curl over. The last panel (n) shows the conceptual structure refolded, seen from the perspective of the last step in the utterance path (with the mass now to the right). Inasmuch as these panels are based entirely on the information contained in the graph structure, we can

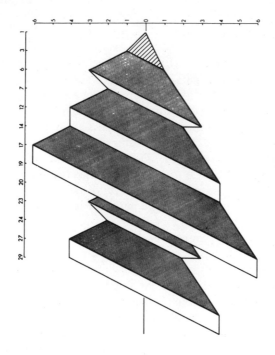

FIG. 8.9a *You dont have to have that one because I have another one before any speech is* produced. Subsequent panels (b–m) show the stages of producing this utterance.

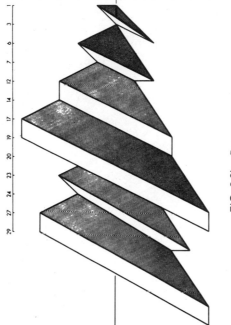

FIG. 8.9b State₂.

195

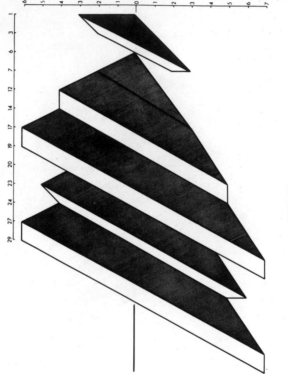

FIG. 8.9c *You.*

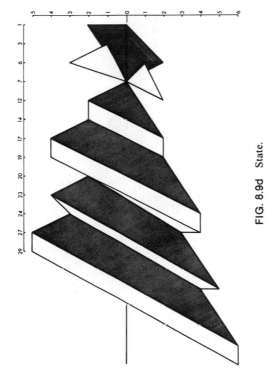

FIG. 8.9d State.

197

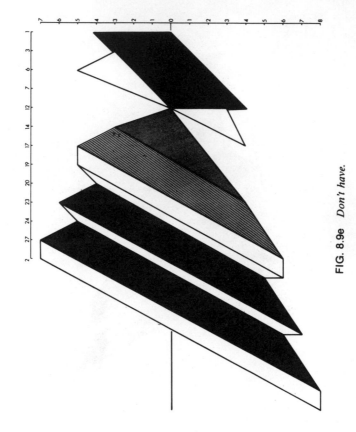

FIG. 8.9e *Don't have.*

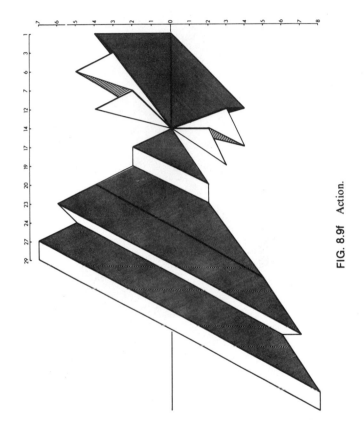

FIG. 8.9f   Action.

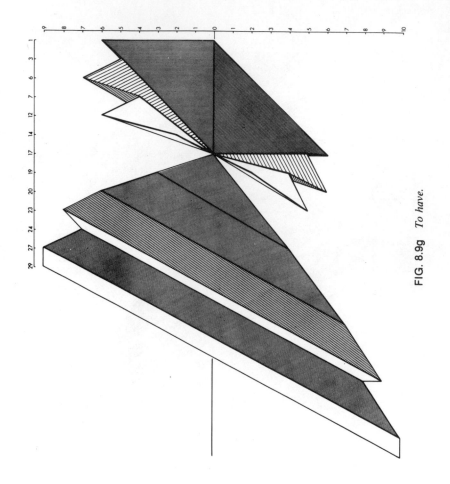

FIG. 8.9g *To have.*

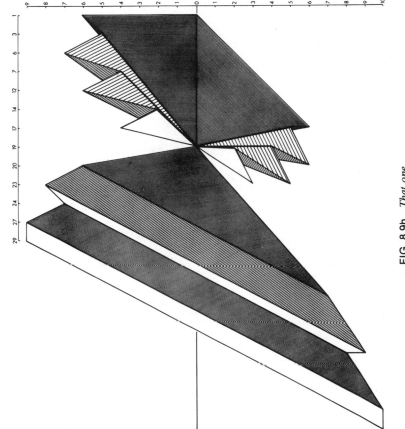

FIG. 8.9h *That one.*

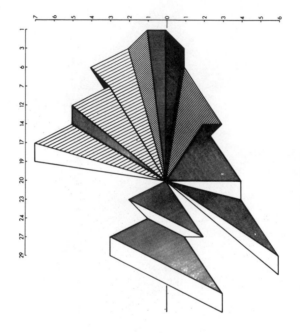

FIG. 8.9i State₁.

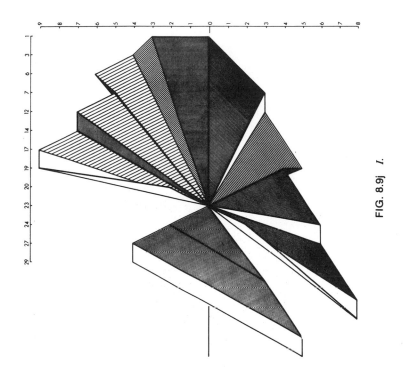

FIG. 8.9j *I.*

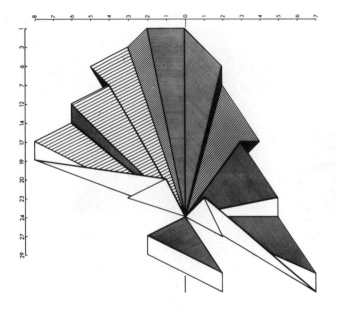

FIG. 8.9k Action.

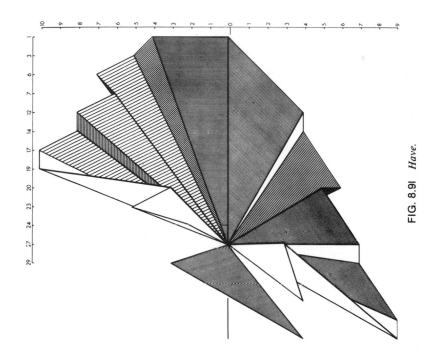

FIG. 8.9I *Have.*

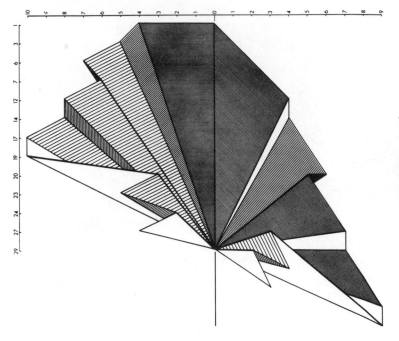

FIG. 8.9m *Another one.*

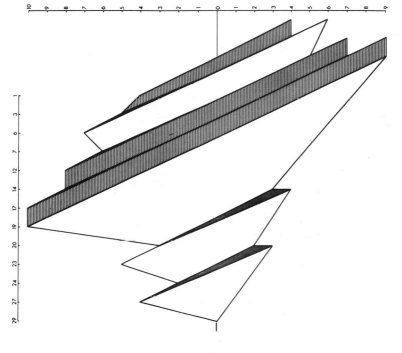

FIG. 8.9n *You don't have to have that one because I have another one* completed.

see that this structure must contain within it the notion of completion of the utterance (producing the curl-over). The example in Fig. 8.9 is exceptionally symmetrical. Other utterances may run down relatively early, and others relatively late. These dynamic characteristics are easily seen in diagrams of the type shown in Fig. 8.9.

The diagrams in Fig. 8.9 are based on the distance matrix of the directed graph structure. For each point in the utterance path there is a separate diagram. In every diagram all the points on this path are arranged in order along the horizontal x-axis (alternatively, they could be analyzed in order of assembly). One finds the distance *to* each of the 13 points from the point in question (corresponding to the entries in its row of the distance matrix) and plots these distances on the vertical y-axis of the diagram. These points are connected to one another. One also finds the distance *from* each of the 13 points to the given point (corresponding to the entries in its column of the distance matrix) and plots these distance on the depth z-axis of the diagram. These points are also connected to one another. In this way, each diagram includes all the distance information regarding its particular point. The particular point itself appears at zero y and z distance. On the still folded (left) side of the aperature, the outer surface of the conceptual structure is visible. This is shown by connecting corresponding points in the y and z fields: point 1 with point 1, 2 with 2, and so on. On the unfolded (right) side of the aperture (except for panel n), the interior of the conceptual structure is visible looking into the aperture. This is shown by connecting every point in both the y and z fields to the zero point, the aperture.

By noting whether surfaces are inside or outside the open space of the unfolded part of the diagram, we can diagram the unfolding and refolding of the conceptual structure. The source of this effect is easily understood. As the utterance path proceeds, the distances to or from the different points may increase, remain the same, or decrease, compared to earlier distances. If these distances increase, the diagram unfolds, and if they remain the same or decrease, the diagram refolds. The distances increase as long as the utterance path is reaching more and more embedded concepts, and they decrease as it leaves these concepts and reapproaches the outer boundary of the utterance— hence the initial fanning followed by curling. Utterance paths that quickly enter the most deeply embedded concepts will form diagrams that just as quickly start to curl over, and those that quickly leave the most deeply embedded concepts after slowly entering them will curl only at the end. (*He has a scratch on his eye* is of this latter type.)

Panel n of Fig. 8.9 is constructed with the depth z-axis viewed from the opposite perspective and is a plot of the same distances as in panel m. The only difference is that the exterior surface is shown (lying to the right), rather than the interior (lying to the left), and it is formed by re-sealing the figure in panel m.

The horizontal y-axis of Fig. 8.9 has equal spaces. This is arbitrary. If distances were shown between these points instead, however, the spacing of points along this axis would be nearly the same as shown except at one point. It did not seem necessary to represent this small variation from equal spacing.

4. *"You run through it and you find out what's good but you go through them all again and that because you know which one is good φ but you go through them all to get the bad ones too φ instead of get the good ones right off."*

(The φs mark hesitations.) This utterance appeared in a conversation which William Marslen-Wilson had with the amnesic patient known as H.M. (Scoville & Milner, 1957), and it is H.M.'s description of the experiences he has when attempting to recall information from memory.

H.M. was subjected to bilateral removal of the amygdala, large parts of the hippocampus, and the hippocampal gyrus. This operation was performed in 1953 in an attempt to treat a severe lifelong epilepsy. The result for his memory function was extreme and dramatic. It has been shown that his usable memories for preoperative events are reasonably accurate given their age, but those for postoperative events are practically nonexistent. He is characterized by an extreme forgetfulness in his daily affairs. However, he responds to prompts and can recognize political and entertainment figures who would not have been known until after 1953 (Marslen-Wilson & Teuber, 1975). Thus, he retains a capacity to form memory traces in some form.

The utterance above is remarkable and unlike any others I have analysed in respect to its extreme repetitiveness. In the speech of normal persons, several related ideas may occur at different places but never the same ideas several times. It is possible that this repetitiveness is a consequence of H.M.'s amnesia. There seem to be problems for H. M., in addition to those involving sheer storage and retrieval, in organizing the information retrieved so that it will correspond with the organization of the conceptual structure of his utterance. He uses the same conceptual structure schemata repeatedly although the specific content of the information that he is trying to convey changes. One can speculate that this repetitiveness arises from H.M.'s attempt to find a match acceptable to him between this retrieved information and conceptual structure, a search he carries out by changing the information as well as the conceptual structure in an uncoordinated fashion. The effects of this groping can be seen in Fig. 8.10.

Several assumptions had to be made in preparing the graph in Fig. 8.10, in particular about the effect of adverbs. These words function as concepts in the graph structure, as can be shown with *again,* which is made into a weakening point in the following:

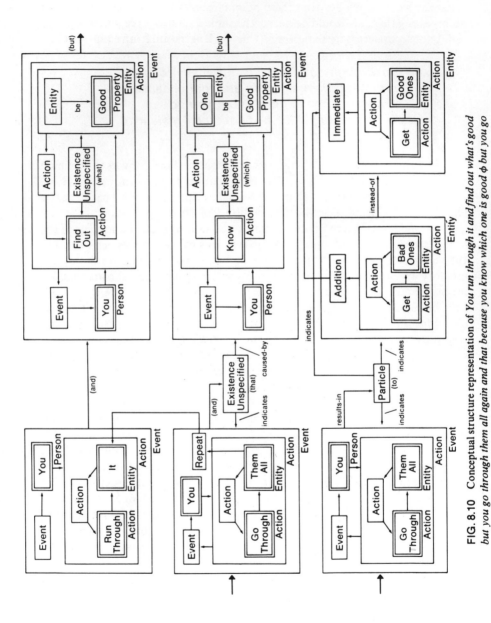

FIG. 8.10 Conceptual structure representation of *You run through it and find out what's good but you go through them all again and that because you know which one is good φ but you go through them all to get the bad ones too φ instead of get the good ones right off.*

210

Level 2: go through them all again
Level 0: go through them all again in addition
Level 2: go through them all in addition

The following adverbs were used by H.M. and are assumed to have the indicated meanings and functions:

again = (Repeat), which relates two ideas of Action
too = (Addition), which relates two ideas of Action
right off = (Immediate), which relates to one idea of Action

Other assumptions in constructing the graph are that *to, which, what,* and *that* all serve an indicating function (as well as other functions) and appear with the relation *indicates* (Particle, Concept). Also, *instead of* is assumed to correspond to another relation, *instead-of* (X, Y).

In the graph structure are two types of Event and one type of Action (converted to Entity as part of the complement), all of which are repeated. One type of Event occurs three times:

you run through it
you go through them all again
you go through them all

The other type of Event has an internal indicating term and occurs twice:

you find out what's good
you know which one is good

The Action also occurs twice:

get the bad ones too
get the good one right off

Moreover, the sequence of these types is always the same. The first type of Event precedes the second and also precedes the Actions. Also, as will be shown, the same idea is the focal point in two of the three strong components of the graph structure.

The connectedness of the entire graph is at Level 2. However, it divides into three strong components, each of which, except for the last, is formed via the effects of one or another of the adverbs mentioned above. H. M. inserts the adverbs to create strong components, a procedure that avoids the necessity of reorganizing the conceptual structure. This method should be viewed in the light of the repetitiveness mentioned previously. The resulting strong components and their focal concepts are the following:

First: *you run through it and you find out what's good but you go through them all again and that,* with the focal concept being the last Event, *you go through them all again*—an intuitively correct designation.

Second: *you know which one is good φ but you go through them all to get the bad ones too,* with the focal concepts being the same last Event, *you go through them all,* again intuitively correct.

Third: *get the good ones right off,* with the focal point being the Action, *get the good ones,* rather than *right off.* In this case, the intuitively correct choice would seem to have been *right off.* Since this concept, however, was only fourth in terms of focus, a fairly radical reconstruction of the conceptual structure would have been needed to bring it into the focal position, and apparently it was not possible for H.M. to manage that degree of flexibility without losing the representation of meaning.

The two hesitations in the utterance occurred between major sensory-motor segments, as one would expect, and the second of them occurred between strong components.

It should be noted that apart from the presumed effect of H.M.'s memory defect, there is no evidence of any speech or intellectual abnormality. This is consistent with the impression of primary observers of H.M., that he is intact in all respects except memory function (Marslen-Wilson & Teuber, 1975).

Primary Focus Sets

The primary focus set consists of one or more points that are, or have the potential to become, the primary focal point. According to the quantum restriction (Chapter 6), an added line in a graph can increase the connectedness of the graph or can shift the focal point outside of the primary focus set, but it cannot do both of these things at the same time. One interpretation of the quantum restriction is that the primary focal set contains all the concepts that the speaker has in mind as possible focal points from the beginning of the utterance, and that the conceptual structure is constructed by adding relations that increase the connectedness of the structure. None of these relations can shift the focus outside of the primary focus set.

In the first example I discussed, *let's keep it over near the door φ that's a dark corner,* the level of connectedness is Level 2 before the context is taken into account. Only concepts with infinite incoming distances in this Level 2 structure (i.e., *that's a dark corner*) could possibly be hidden members of the potential focus set, but none of these concepts can be made into the focal point no matter what line is added to increase the connectedness. Thus *that's a dark corner* is not in the primary focus set. Therefore, the speaker apparently had the idea of Location in mind as the focal point from the first, and the quantum restriction assured him that the addition of a relation leading to the context that increased the connectedness would not cause the focus to shift from this concept.

In the second example, *he has a scratch on his eye; he says,* the connectedness is at Level 2 and the focal point is the Action *has a scratch on his eye.* This point is the only member of the primary focal set. There is no way in which the focal point could shift away from this Action even if the connectedness were at Level 3. Therefore, the speaker apparently had this concept in mind from the start (a plausible circumstance given this utterance).

In the third example, *you don't have to have that one because I have another one,* there is no point on the utterance path at which the connectedness is not at Level 3. This is because the overall structure of the Event, consisting of two States, dominates every point. In this situation, no point has infinite incoming distances. The focal point was thus known from the start, a fact confirmed by the speaker's subsequent report.

In the three examples from nonpathological speakers, the primary focal set contained only one member, even when the level of connectedness was less than Level 3. Apparently these speakers were able to select a focal point and construct a conceptual structure around it. In contrast, the H.M. example seems to show a failure to mesh the conceptual structure with the choice of focal point.

The H.M. utterance consists of three strong components. The second of these, *you know which one is good φ but you go through them all to get the bad ones too,* owes its Level 3 connectedness to the adverb *too.* This word accompanies the relation that links *bad ones* to *one is good.* This strong component has the Entity *one is good* as its focal point, as noted before. The focal point in this strong component is one of *five* points in the primary focal set within the structure that exist before the adverb is involved. The other points are the Event *you go through them all;* the idea of an Event within this Event that is necessary for representing the semiotic extension; the idea of a Person *you;* and the Action *go through them all.* By selecting *too* as the adverb, H.M. made *one is good* into the focal concept. If H.M. had not chosen this adverb, if he had said *but you go through them all to get the bad ones,* there would have been no line in the graph from *bad ones* to *one is good,* and the five points mentioned would have remained members of the same primary focal set. Four members of this set are from the same sensory-motor idea of an Event, but the fifth member (eventually the focal point) is not from this same idea of an Event. Thus H.M. had a semantically ambiguous primary focus set until he reached the adverb *too.* The heterogeneity of this set seems to be another effect of H.M.'s inability to vary the sensory-motor representation of the segments of his utterances. This heterogeneous set can be placed together with the misplaced focus of the final strong component, mentioned previously, as an example of the uncoordinated use of sensory-motor schemata. This lack of coordination is possibly due to H.M.'s memory disorder and is perhaps a cause of the extraordinary repetitiveness of his speech.

SUMMARY

This chapter discusses methods used for analyzing conceptual structures and miscellaneous findings regarding these structures. Among the methods are the following:

1. A formal distinction between concepts and relations, which leads to a test of whether a given element of meaning should be represented as a point or line in a graph representation.
2. The pseudocleft construction, which permits probing the sensory-motor content of conceptual structures.
3. A hierarchical clustering method, in which constituents are directly related to each other, and which permits reconstructing some of the effects of syntactic devices.
4. Various rules of thumb for labeling concepts and relations.

Among these the findings are these:

1. Reliability of sensory-motor classifications of speech segments.
2. The temporal stability of the different sensory-motor segments in speech output, which provides evidence of speech programs based on sensory-motor representations.
3. Examples of conceptual structure analyses of spontaneous utterances.

9 Spontaneous Speech

Various traces appear in speech showing that speech output tends to be segmented into units that correspond to content. This chapter surveys certain of these traces of content in speech output, including phonemic clauses, hesitations, and dysfluencies of various kinds.

Much of the data I report are based on a two-person conversation recorded and transcribed by S. Duncan, Jr. (Duncan & Fiske, 1977). I am grateful to Duncan and Fiske for providing me with this transcript to study. The conversation took place between two well-acquainted men, both psychotherapists, who were discussing a patient, and it lasted about 18 minutes. The method of transcription employed the conventions of Trager and Smith (1951) and included segmental phonemes, primary stresses and terminal contours.

A phonemic clause is defined by Trager and Smith as a sequence of segmental phonemes bounded by silence and/or a terminal contour. It contains one and only one primary stress. In addition, a phonemic clause has one of a restricted set of intonation patterns. Each combination of these features (a particular tune and stress assignment and the choice of a terminal contour) can be proposed to be the output of a single speech program. Not all instances of phonemic clauses can be regarded in this way, but nonetheless we can raise the question of what fraction of the phonemic clause segmentation of a speech corpus appears to be the output of syntagmata. Do phonemic clauses tend to coincide with independently determined semantic segments, the ideas of Event, Location, and others? (A phonemic clause, of course, should not be confused with a grammatical clause; the definitions of the two are entirely independent.)

A second approach to locating natural processing units of speech is to make use of the dysfluencies which appear in a speaker's output. For example, when the structure of the utterance breaks down and some new structure replaces it, what elements are retained and what new ones added? If there are hesitations, can they be interpreted as occurring at points where the speaker shifts speech programs?

Altogether the two speakers in the Duncan corpus produced 1,438 phonemic clauses, 561 from speaker L (lower on Duncan's transcript) and 877 from speaker U (upper). This mass of information will be approached in a variety of ways.

First, as suggested above, I will analyze the entire conversation in terms of the types of dysfluencies that occur. A classification of these is described in the following paragraphs and consists of the following types: hesitations, breakdowns, buildups, anticipations, and errors of articulation. Second, I will analyze the distribution of phonemic clauses in relation to a sensory-motor segmentation of the corpus. Third, I will examine all examples of the three syntactic devices analyzed in Chapter 7—the passive, the relative clause (restrictive), and the pseudocleft.

TYPES OF
SPEECH DYSFLUENCIES

In the examples that follow, a vertical line marks the end of a phonemic clause; ϕ indicates an unfilled hesitation (i.e., no vocalization); *eh* or *uh* shows a filled hesitation; (inhale) shows an audible inhalation; and (click) indicates an audible glottal click.

A catalogue of the speech dysfluencies in the Duncan corpus shows the following:

1. *Hesitations.* These are any interruptions in the flow of the speech output, specifically unfilled pauses, filled pauses, glottal clicks, and audible inhalations. Unfilled pauses have been detected subjectively, by Duncan, and probably tend to be longer than those found by automatic methods (e.g., Jaffe & Feldstein, 1970). Hesitations are the most common type of dysfluency, appearing in 19% of all phonemic clauses in the speech of L and in 14% of all phonemic clauses in the speech of U.

2. *Breakdowns.* These are collapses of structure followed by new structures. A change of direction is the distinguishing feature of the breakdown. These dysfluencies are often called "false starts," but this term misleadingly implies that they occur only at the beginning of utterances, whereas they may actually occur in a variety of positions. Often breakdowns are accompanied by hesitations, but these are not part of the definition of this dysfluency. Interruptions of a speaker's turn, even though they may produce a

collapse of structure, are not counted as breakdowns. Breakdowns are the second or third most common type of dysfluency, although they lag far behind hesitations, appearing in 4% of all phonemic clauses in the speech of both L and U.

3. *Buildups.* Like a breakdown a buildup involves a structural collapse. However, there is no change of direction. The speaker repeatedly encodes the same structure, each time including a different part of it. Some buildups are quite extended but are still counted as a single dysfluencey. Buildups are about as frequent as breakdowns, appearing in 5% of the phonemic clauses of L and in 2% of the phonemic clauses of U.

4. *Anticipations.* The speaker encodes a portion of an utterance prematurely. The essential characteristic of an anticiaption is that subsequently an appropriate element of structure should appear in speech that incorporates the anticipated element, but the element is out of place the first time it appears. Anticipations occur in less than 1% of the phonemic clauses of each speaker.

5. *Errors of articulation.* These are articulatory errors not accompanied by any other form of speech dysfluencey. Such errors mainly degrade intelligibility; they occur in less than 1% of the phonemic clauses. Errors of articulation that accompany other kinds of dysfluency are slightly more frequent and are described later.

The above mentioned categories are proposed merely for convenience of exposition. Individual occurrences of dysfluency often have characteristics that place them into more than one category. In particular, breakdowns, buildups, and anticipations are difficult to distinguish. No suggestion is made that different mechanisms are involved in these varieties of dysfluency.

Not every disturbance of speech is included in this classification. In particular, two categories are left out. Sociocentric expressions, *but (uh), you know, well,* and others, although frequent, have been excluded. Some of these can plausibly be regarded as part of a disturbance of speech programming (and are thus a kind of hesitation), but not all can be; distinguishing those that reveal a disturbance of programming from those that are truly sociocentric is often arbitrary, and the whole set has been excluded.

Also excluded are 11 utterances at the ends of turns that were not completed. It is impossible to tell whether the breakdown was the result of the other speaker interrupting or had some other cause.

Finally, omissions of required words that were not also accompanied by dysfluencies are excluded. Although the structure was interfered with, speech output was not. Some of these errors occur in the context of the syntactic devices I will discuss.

Apart from these exceptions, the aforementioned categories encompass virtually every disturbance in the corpus, and hence nearly all the disturbances that occurred in the process of integrating speech.

No examples of metatheses of the kind described by Fromkin (1971) or Garrett (1976) occur in the 18 minutes of the discourse.

The following sections provide examples of these different categories of dysfluency:

Articulatory Errors

An example from L is the following:

AR1   with her | bəbɨrn that |

Articulation errors (as defined) are so rare because any faltering of articulation is usually accompanied by some other failure of speech output. Articulatory errors that accompany other types of dysfluency are four times as frequent as ones that occur alone.

Breakdowns

These dysfluencies create a vivid impression of the dynamic course of speech production. The speaker seems to pursue a zigzag course. He or she begins on a certain tack, then encounters some difficulty. The speaker may commence a rapid alternation of different structures, trying one after another. These variants appear to be on almost instantaneous call. Finally one is found that succeeds in carrying speech onward a little further. Often the new structure has a conceptual direction if its own, however, and the line of speech takes a slight turn. After a while there is another substitution, new structures, a new tack, and so on; the process continues this way, much as if the speaker were beating a path upwind.

Although the choice of structures at each point is clearly far from random, it is also the case that there is not always an instantaneous meshing of the production apparatus and the meaning that the speaker tries to communicate. The intended meaning points in the general direction, and the problem then is to find a version of this idea that can be uttered.

The following are some examples of breakdowns (italics marking the portion of the utterance considered to be directly involved in the dysfluency):

B1   she was so *reluctant* | *tow* | *to* uh φ well | *the* | *m* | *the* | *the thing* | *I reacted to* | was when | I asked her |

B2   personal | situations | where | (inhales) *where* | *with a* | *I think* | *what she said* | was that with a person |

B3   *that's* uh | *asking* | all these questions | is too much

These demonstrate the substitution of concepts in breakdowns. It is not always the case that the first concept is completely encoded. Rather, there is an indication that this construction is launched expressing a certain idea but then is stopped and replaced (sometimes after a confused stretch) by another construction and a different idea (hence the term "false start"). The motivation in some breakdowns could be that initially the speaker fails to preserve a focal point selected in advance, and this leads him to abandon the structure. In B1, for example, the speaker started a complement, then shifted to a pseudocleft and to the structure (Unspecified (Event)). The focal point of this pseudocleft is the phrase, *I reacted,* but this would not have been the focal point in any plausible continuation of the utterance before the breakdown (for example, *she was so reluctant to* (Action) *and I reacted to this* has as its focal point *she was so reluctant* not *I reacted*). In B2 there is a shift from (Unspecified (Location)) to (Unspecified (Action)), possibly to avoid focusing on the idea of Location. B3 started with (Unspecified) and shifted to (Entity (Action)), possibly to focus on this Entity.

Such examples can be viewed as an alternation of speech programs. The interval after the breakdown shows a single integrated output of speech (unless this too ends in a dysfluency) that extends to at least to the next terminal contour. By examining phonemic clauses preceded by breakdowns, therefore, we can investigate what plausibly are the outputs of single utterance programs.

This first phonemic clause usually corresponds to a single strong component in the conceptual structure. In B1, for example, | *the thing* | is (Unspecified (Entity)). In B2, the first phonemic clause, | *I think* |, is (Event), and in B3, the first phonemic clause, | *asking* |, is (Entity (Action)), introduced by a nominalization.   We do not observe such outputs as | *the thing I* | , | *with a I* |, or | *asking all* |.

The process of shifting speech programs can proceed through a rich variety of combinations, different elements of which are kept in the ultimate structure. This is shown in example B4 (which also includes aspects of a buildup, as discussed later).

B4   yeah | (inhales) *how 'bout* | *the* | ϕ *the* | ϕ *does that* | *how much do* | *how has* | that affected you |

The speaker seems to have had (Unspecified) and a question in mind from the start, as shown in the word *how* and the construction *how 'bout,* but could not find a way to use this concept is a form that did not contain extraneous ideas, or that did not lose an essential idea. The ultimate conceptual structure that emerges from the breakdown is (Event (State (Q Unspecified)) (State$_2$)) (State$_1$)) underlying *how has that affected you?* The focal point of this structure is (State (Q (Unspecified)) (State₂)), *how has,* and the secondary focal point is (Q (Unspecified)), *how.* The breakdown appears to have been motivated by the speaker's inability to integrate the complete focal point into the speech program from the start. The first candidate structure leading into the breakdown, (inhale) *how 'bout* |, contains (Q (Unspecified)) but lacks (State₂). In fact, this is the secondary focal point. The second candidate, *the*| *ϕ the*|, is so fragmentary as to be almost mysterious, but it seems to have been (Entity) or (Event), which is not inconsistent with another go at (Unspecified). The third candidate, *ϕ does that* |, is a question but lacks other relevant conceptual content (the *that* appears to be an anticipation of the demonstrative pronoun). The fourth candidate, *how much do*|, contains (Q (Unspecified (Process₂)) but lacks (State₂) and includes an idea of quantity that is rejected. (*How much do* introduces Process₂ assuming that the verb yet to come was *affected.*) This fourth candidate, nonetheless, is very close to the next structure, the successful one, in that Process₂ is related to State₂ and the utterance at this point includes both Q and Unspecified.

There is a kind of progression through the breakdown as the speaker attempts to build up a conceptual structure. Each candidate retains elements from previous structures and contributes something to following structures. This progression is shown in Fig. 9.1 by the arrows that trace the retained elements. Accumulation can be seen in the irregularly increasing number of elements that anticipate the ultimate version, namely, two in the first candidate, one each in the second and third candidates, each one different, and three in the fourth candidate. (The second candidate is taken in its most relevant interpretation.)

Buildups

The evolution already apparent in B3 becomes the dominant feature of buildups. The same conceptual structure of the utterance is organized more than once in repeated attempts. The unique aspect of the buildup is the

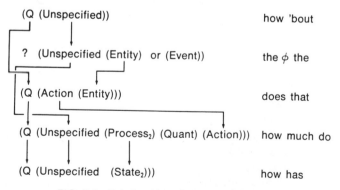

FIG. 9.1   Relationships within a breakdown.

conceptual structure that is held constant. There is not a shifting of complete utterance programs during this type of dysfluency, but a process more like an internal adjustment of the same program that is repeatedly activated.

In BU1 the maintained concept is (Entity) with an adjustment or expansion that is rejected, presumably the word *main*:

BU1   well| *the* | *m* | *the* | *the thing* | I reacted to

In Bu2 the maintained concept is (State₂), which starts to be encoded first without a form of *be:*

BU2 | *I* | yeah *I'm* | *surpri* | (inhale)

In BU3 the maintained concept is (Event):

BU3   *I* | *I felt that* | *I felt that* | *about her* | very much |

Buildups thus show persisting control by single sensory-motor ideas—Entity, State, and Event in these examples.

Anticipations

Anticipations consist of something that appears initially in the wrong place and subsequently is integrated into the utterance. It is apparent that the initial fragment, whatever it is, is capable of being activated independently of *both* the context in which it first appeared *and* the context into which it is later integrated, and thus reflects a possible speech program.

In A1 the concept of (State₂) behaves as such an independent element:

A1 | I think| she said| that *she had felt* | (inhale) she feels bad| now| and| *it was that way* | *she felt* | when she was last | in school |

In A2 (Unspecified) behaves as an independent element:

A2   *what* is| *what* are| d| when you said| at the beginning| about the| (inhale) good prognosis| *I wonder what* | you | meant by that |

In A3 there is a double anticipation:

A3 | rather than| saying like| well wait| *cou'*| *mab'*| *my*| *maybe*| i| *you could give me* | a little better |

Two aspects of conceptual structure are simultaneously worked out on semi-independent tracks and eventually integrated. One of these includes the idea of potentiality, which is manifested in the auxiliary *cou'*, the adverbials *mab'* and *maybe*, and possibly a conjunction, *i (if)*. The other anticipation involves the idea of self-reference manifested in the pronouns *my/me*.

cou' → mayb' → maybe → i → could (potential)
my → me (self-reference)

There may have been phonetic influence between these tracks at the point where the speaker said *my*. Considering the appearance of stereo programming in this example, the ideas of potentiality and self-reference were simultaneously active, though not yet combined. Of course, the absence of such a combination may have been the cause of the error in the first place.

Hesitations

Hesitations of various kinds are by far the most common form of dysfluency in Duncan's corpus, and several types occur: filled pauses consisting of unarticulated vocalizations; unfilled pauses consisting of intervals of no vocalization; and audible inhalations and glottal clicks, which are classified with the unfilled pauses.

A problem with hesitation data is that sometimes the hesitation may be part of the programmed speech output, whereas our interest focuses on unprogrammed hesitations. These could show when speech programs are changed, but programmed hesitations must occur within a speech program. We should therefore try to identify and remove the programmed hesitations from the sample.

Inhalations, it seems, are programmed. There is evidence of the smooth control of the breathing process during speech, and this is different from normal breathing (Lieberman, 1967). Thus, if we remove all audible inhalations from the sample of hesitations, the remainder should be more nearly a collection of hesitations that occur as speech programs change.

In a further attempt to purify the sample, we can apply the distinction drawn by Goldman-Eisler (1968) between "grammatical" and "nongrammatical" hesitations. Presumably a speaker's ability to program hesitations would be greater when they occur at grammatically definite points. Therefore, if we remove all the "grammatical" hesitations, what remains should come still closer to the desired sample of hesitations that occur at the point of changing programs.

Each hesitation in Duncan's corpus has been classified into one of 11 categories. Nine of these correspond to the definitions given in Goldman-Eisler (1968) for "grammatical" hesitations (her six categories plus the three in italics): sentence ϕ; ϕ conjunction; *conjunction*; ϕ; ϕ wh-term; *wh-term ϕ*; ϕ quotation; *quotation* ϕ (quotes may be direct or indirect); ϕ adverbial of manner, time, or place; ϕ parenthetical clause (or phrase) ϕ (i.e., at either end).[1]

This process of elimination leaves the two following categories as the most likely to contain unprogrammed hesitations:

1. *Concept ϕ Concept.* The hesitation occurs at a nongrammatical point between two sensory-motor ideas. For example,

I just want to ϕ talk with somebody

The first segment corresponds to (State$_1$) plus the complementizer, which functions as a relation and is assumed to perform a deictic function. The second segment is an (Action). This example suggests that the speaker shifted speech programs at the onset of the idea of an Action.

2. *Con ϕ cept.* The hesitation occurs in the middle of a sensory-motor idea. For example,

a very real ϕ thing she was doing

Here a hesitation occurs in the midst of the idea of an Entity, and it seems that this idea should have been programmed as a single output. The hesitation therefore interrupts a presumed programming unit.

There are necessarily more places where hesitations could occur within concepts (2) than there are between concepts (1). This is simply because each between-concept position requires two concepts, each of which is a potential within-concept position. In spite of this greater opportunity, however, there are far fewer within-concept hesitations than between-concept hesitations.

Table 9.1 shows the result of classifying the four types of hesitation mentioned above into the different varieties of "grammatical" and "non-grammatical" category. Speakers L and U have been combined in this table. To evaluate Table 9.1, we eliminate all the hesitations that consist of audible inhalations and all the hesitations deemed to be grammatical. The remaining 118 hesitations consist of filled pauses, unfilled pauses, and glottal clicks, which are classified as either "concept ϕ concept" or as "con ϕ cept." Of these hesitations 87% are in the category of "concept ϕ concept." Thus, we can conclude that hesitations that are likely to be unprogrammed occur at points where, on theoretical grounds, we expect one syntagma to be available to take over from another.

---

[1]The symbol ϕ in this section stands for any kind of hesitation.

TABLE 9.1
Number of Hesitations in the Speech of Two Speakers

Environment	Type of Hesitation				
	Filled Pause	Unfilled Pause	Glottal Click	Inha-lation	Total
concept φ concept	40	61	2	48	151
con φ cept	6	9		4	19
sentence φ	4	24	2	41	71
φ conjunction	1			7	8
conjunction φ	8	3	3	4	18
φ wh-term					
wh-term φ	3	3		2	8
φ quote	4	3		4	11
quote φ	2	1		1	4
φ adverb				1	1
φ parenthetical φ		2			2
Not classified	2	2		5	9
Total	70	108	7	118	303

The 67 "grammatical" hesitations in Table 9.1 also can be described in terms of syntagmata, and including them in the "concept φ concept" category increases the percentage to 91%.

THE EFFECTS OF COMPLEXITY

When a speaker is trying, under the pressure of time, to organize the plan of an utterance, the complexity of this plan could affect concurrent speech output. This should be particularly true if the speech arises while the plan is being organized. More complex plans, if they are harder to organize, should be more often accompanied by dysfluencies. Among the different types of dysfluency, the one that should most directly reflect failures of planning is the breakdown. The speaker, in these cases, is not able to carry out or does not completely formulate a plan, as evidenced by the utterance structure collapsing and being replaced by another structure.

To test this hypothesis we can compare the number of sensory-motor concepts that were expressed immediately before and immediately after breakdowns, for both L and U. The number of concepts after the breakdown is a measure of the complexity of the conceptual structure that the speaker was trying to organize. For example, *she told me about the trip* includes five sensory-motor ideas as follows: Person, *she;* Person, *me;* Action, *told;* Action, *told [about] her trip;* and Entity, *her trip* (the *about* arises from a relation). In contrast, *she was depressed* contains two sensory-motor ideas:

Person, *she,* and Property, *depressed.* This method of counting takes into account the number of sensory-motor concepts but not their arrangement. To achieve comparability with the count described in the next paragraph, only breakdowns that occurred between complete, intact Events were included.

Compared to breakdowns, unfilled pauses can arise from encoding obstacles not involving construction, in particular delays in the lexicalization of words. I have counted the number of sensory-motor ideas immediately before and immediately after each unfilled pause in the speech of L and U. Only unfilled pauses that appear in the middle of an otherwise intact Event were included in this count. This was to insure that no breakdowns of utterance structure also occurred.

The average numbers of sensory-motor ideas in the positions before and after both breakdowns and unfilled pauses are given for L and U combined in Table 9.2. There is no evidence of greater complexity in terms of the number of sensory-motor ideas before or after unfilled pauses ($t < 1$). This contrasts with the greater complexity of utterances in such terms after breakdowns ($t > 5$, $p < .00001$). Since only intact Events have been considered at these two positions, this result cannot be explained as reflecting merely the incompleteness of the first Event.

It is the case that the speaker did not produce, in the initial Event, the number of sensory-motor ideas contained in the final Event. This could occur if breakdowns tend to take palce when the speaker is momentarily unable to build up the degree of complexity needed and reached after the breakdown.

Dysfluencies in Various Contexts

A possible output segmentation of an utterance that includes a transitive verb is one that places the subject and verb into one segment and the rest of the verb phrase into another. Although this arrangement disrupts the grammatical constituent structure, it preserves a sensory-motor combination, namely, Event + Entity. The Event would consist, for example, of Person + Action. In the Duncan corpus, L's and U's dysfluencies produce this kind of segmentation ten times more frequently than a segmentation into the

TABLE 9.2
Number of Sensory-Motor Ideas Before and After
Two Types of Dysfluency

Type of Dysfluency	Relation of Content to Dysfluency	
	Before	*After*
Breakdown (N = 31)	3.10	6.32
Unfilled Pause (N = 38)	2.43	2.53

grammatical constituents of NP and VP. Table 9.3 shows the distribution of all the dysfluencies (all types combined) that occurred before or after transitive verbs. The distribution of dysfluencies is shown also for complementizers (*that* and *to*), prepositions, articles, and auxiliary verbs.

Table 9.3 suggests that speakers L and U *as a rule* break up grammatical constituent structure in their speech output. For example, besides transitive verbs, they tend to produce prepositions with antecedents rather than with the NPs of the same prepositional phrases. Similarly, they tend to produce articles with antecedents rather than with the Ns of the same NPs. In both of these cases, conceptually, the speakers are encoding relations with their antecedent concepts (see Chapter 8). An on-line uncertainty in lexicalization would bias the speech output in this direction.

The complementizing words *that* and *to* also tend to be produced with their antecedents (although the number of examples is small). Complementizers are thought to belong with the sentence underlying the complement. In their function as anaphoric or deictic particles, these complementizing words could equally be programmed with the antecedent concept, and again any uncertainties in on-line programming would create a bias in this direction.

The only exception in Table 9.3 to the tendency for dysfluencies to disrupt grammatical constituent structure is that auxiliary verbs tend to be produced with their main verbs. This tendency is not particularly strong, however. In this case, the pairing of each auxiliary with the corresponding inflection (*be-*

TABLE 9.3
Dysfluencies in Various Contexts[a]

	Speaker L	Speaker U	Total
Prepositional Phrase			
X ϕ Prep NP	1	2	3
X Prep ϕ NP	3	8	11
Noun Phrase			
X ϕ Art N	0	1	1
X Art ϕ N	14	8	22
Trans. Verb Phrase			
X ϕ V NP	1	2	3
X V ϕ NP	15	19	34
That Complement			
X ϕ that C	1	0	1
X that ϕ C	8	2	10
To Complement			
X ϕ to C	1	0	1
X to ϕ C	3	0	3
Auxiliary Verb			
X ϕ Aux V	13	6	19
X Aux ϕ V	6	7	13

[a]The symbol ϕ signifies any type of dysfluency.

ing, hav-en) would have worked against any biases that might be established by on-line programming uncertainties.

Examples of each of the types of the nongrammatical segmentations in Table 9.3 are as follows:

Preposition ϕ NP
I mean she sort of spiral into...(it)

Article ϕ N
but just memory of the my interview with her

V ϕ NP
she said uh something like

that ϕ Complement
and like there she's really frightened that did this mood mechanism

to ϕ Complement
I just want to uh...talk with somebody

PHONEMIC CLAUSES

Phonemic clauses appear to be based on a single organized phonological effort by speakers. They accordingly offer themselves as plausible candidates for the output of single speech programs.

Distribution of Phonemic Clauses

Table 9.4 gives tabulation of the phonemic clauses in the Duncan corpus classified according to the correspondence with a sensory-motor segmentation of the same utterances. (No dysfluencies included.)

Four cases appear in this Table as follows:

1. In this case, the phonemic clause coincides exactly with some sensory-motor idea, for example,

I wonder what | you | meant by that |

The first segment corresponds to an Event, *I wonder (something)*, the second to a Person, *you*, and the third to an Action, *meant by that*.

In Case 1, the evidence is that the articulation program that produces the phonemic clause corresponds to a single sensory-motor meaning. This evidence is lacking in the other cases.

2. In this case, a sensory-motor idea corresponds to more than one phonemic clause. The ideas that span more than one phonemic clause show a real connection, and at least one of them would not be expected to be

TABLE 9.4
Phonemic Clauses Compared to Sensory-Motor Segments

			Speaker L		Speaker U		Total	
			Freq.	%	Freq.	%	Freq.	%
Case 1								
PC	⊢——⊣							
SM	⊢——⊣		249	84.7	500	84.0	749	84.3
Case 2								
PC	⊢—+—⊣	2 PC	34	11.6	76	12.8	110	12.5
SM	⊢——⊣	2 PC	3	1.0	8	1.3	11	1.2
		4 PC			1	0.2	1	0.1
Case 3								
PC	⊢——⊣	2 SM	5	1.7	6	1.0	11	1.2
SM	⊢——⊣	3 SM	1	0.3			1	0.1
Case 4								
PC	⊢+—+⊣		1	0.3			1	0.1
SM	⊢—+—⊣							
	Unclassified		1	0.3	4	0.7	5	0.6
	Total		294	100.0	595	100.0	889	100.0

produced by itself. Table 9.4 distinguishes among the number of phonemic clauses over which the single sensory-motor idea is spread (2 PC, etc.). An example of Case 2 is this:

that was a | beautiful | thing she did |

These form a single idea of an Entity, *a beautiful thing she did. Beautiful* should not stand alone from the Entity it modifies, yet is appears in a separate phonemic clause.

3. In this case, the phonemic clause contains more than one sensory-motor idea, one of which one would expect to have been produced separately. Most of these examples involve adverbials that can optionally appear in alternate sentence positions. The adverbial would seem to require separate programming, and such adverbials in the Duncan corpus generally do, in fact, occupy their own private phonemic clauses, but in Case 3 they jointly appear with other sensory-motor ideas. An example is the following:

however it was | she went to school previously |

The offending adverbial is *previously,* which could have occurred after the *was* with a difference in meaning. That it occurred at the end of the sentence should therefore have called for separate programming.

4. In this case, there is no correspondence whatsoever. The only example is:

then on | that there | was a good year |
          Location Existence Entity

Degree of Correspondence

The degree of correspondence between the phonemic clause segmentation of the speech of L and U and the sensory-motor content can be estimated in two ways. First, we have the percentage of sensory-motor ideas that appear in one phonemic clause; this is the fraction (Case 1 / Case 1 + Case 2). Next, we find the percentage of phonemic clauses that contain just one sensory-motor idea (which might be complex); this is the fraction (Case 1 / Case 1 + Case 3). These fractions are similar for L and U, as shown in Table 9.5.

From these results we can conclude that nearly all of the phonemic clauses in the Duncan corpus are segregated into their own sensory-motor segments, and more than 85% of the sensory-motor ideas coincide with single phonemic clauses. Although the phonemic clause boundaries, which represent an independent phonological segmentation by Duncan, could have occurred in a variety of positions, they are in fact highly constrained by the speaker's meaning, and this aspect of the phonological output accurately reflects the underlying sensory-motor content.

TABLE 9.5
Correspondence Between Phonemic Clauses and
Sensory-Motor Ideas

	% SM Ideas in One PC	% PC in One SM Idea
Speaker U	85.5	98.8
Speaker L	87.1	97.6

Second Study of Phonemic Clauses

Although the classification of L's and U's speech into phonemic clauses was performed by Duncan and is independent of my description of the sensory-motor content of their speech (having been done first), it is possible that I may have been influenced by Duncan's phonemic clause segmentation. I have carried out a second study of the correspondence between the phonemic clause and sensory-motor descriptions, where neither type of description was performed with the knowledge of the other.

TABLE 9.6
Correspondence Between Phonemic Clauses and
Sensory-Motor Ideas (Blind Ratings)

	% SM Ideas in One PC	% PC in One SM Idea
Event$_1$ or $_2$	94	100
Event$_1$	83	45
Event$_2$	50	100
Event$_{intrans.}$	89	100
State	75	100
Location	100	90
Action	100	86

The speech I used is the "Diana" passage read by K. Lindig (see Chapter 8). A tape recording of this reading was divided into phonemic clauses by a third colleague who was not shown the sensory-motor classification. Table 9.6 shows the correspondence between sensory-motor segments and phonemic clauses. The level of agreement is in fact superior to that with the Duncan corpus, with the exception of Event$_1$ and Event$_2$. In the case of Event$_1$ (subject and transitive verb with the object excluded), the percentage of phonemic clauses that are contained in this one sensory-motor idea is exceptionally low. In the case of Event$_2$ (subject and transitive verb with object included), the percentage of these sensory-motor ideas that are contained in one phonemic clause is exceptionally low. These discrepancies might mean that the speaker was matching, on different occasions, both Event$_1$ and Event$_2$ to phonemic clauses in different utterances. When we look at the correspondence of phonemic clauses with Event$_1$ *or* Event$_2$, indeed, the level of agreement becomes very high. Thus, there is evidence of a correspondence between the idea of an Event and the phonemic clause segmentation.

It is important to note, in Table 9.6, that the idea of Action agrees very well with the phonemic clause segmentation, supporting this sensory-motor idea as a basis for speech programming, although the evidence for it in this function in Chapter 8 was equivocal.

Length of Syntagmata

Syntagmata appear to be quite short, to judge from the length of the phonemic clauses in L's and U's speech. Table 9.7 gives the distribution of the number of syllables in the first 102 phonemic clauses produced by each of the speakers L and U (excluding phonemic clauses preceding dysfluencies and sociocentric phonemic clauses). The average length is 3.02 *syllables* for L and 3.08 *syllables* for U. In L's speech, the modal length is only two *syllables*. At such extremely short lengths, the typical programming segment must be a

TABLE 9.7
Length of Phonemic Clauses

	Number of Syllables								
	1	2	3	4	5	6	7	8	9
Speaker U	9	28	34	15	13	1	1	—	1
Speaker L	13	30	24	20	9	5	—	1	—

simple (i.e., most subordinate) sensory-motor idea, often corresponding to a single lexical item. Programming at such a low level suggests that these speakers were rarely planning far ahead but were able to produce speech output nearly at the same time as they planned it. (This does not affect the connectedness level of their speech.)

SYNTACTIC DEVICES

The number of passive, restrictive relative clause, and pseudocleft constructions is small in the Duncan corpus. Only six passive (not including predicate adjectives), 14 relative clause, and six pseudocleft examples appear. Six additional transcribed conversations supplied by Duncan contain a few more examples, and I have added them to the sample.

The Passive

In all, nine examples of the passive (excluding predicate adjectves) occur in the combined conversations. These nine contain seven errors or dysfluencies, a level of difficulty that should be judged against the generally high levels of dysfluency in the corpus. Four of the disturbances (= 70%) involve the concept of Property—either it fails to be marked by the past participle or the verb converted into a Property by the passive does not appear at all. The other three errors involve modal verbs in two cases, and the *be* passivizer in the other.

P1   I was most| uncomfortable| with her| and most| acutely| aware| (inhales) of it being on| uh| *being videotape*|

P2   *I was*| *a little uncomfortable*| by what I thought|

P3   and I immediately like| feel like| *I'm being deceived*| or maybe that's not| really true|

P4   she's afraid| *she's being deceived*| by those feelings| φ th' in fact| school| isn't really bad|

P5   she wouldn't | say | anything | because she was afraid | *she would be found* | φ to be | stupid |

P6   *I get* | you know | I'm tired |

P7   you know *you kinda get draw away*

P8   *that ha'* | φ *had been manipulated*

P9   we were told that *we be* | (inhale) *probably be* | asked | to leave | *the country* | by | the Koreans |

The past participle inflection is missing from P1 and P7, the verb converted to Property is missing from P6 and possibly from P2, the modal verb is disrupted in P8 and P9, and the *be* passivizer is missing from the first attempt in P8. Three passives not accompanied by errors or hesitations are P3, P4, and P5.

According to the passive PATN, the past participle inflection and the concept of Property, where most of these errors occur, are generated in the first time segment but are not actualized as speech until the second time segment. Property is one of two concepts so delayed in the PATN, the other being Person or Entity. The relation *be-X* also is generated in the first time segment, but aspect is not determined until the second time segment. There is one error of not producing the *be* passivizer and two errors of omitting modal verbs (which depend on replacing the *be-X* relation). A common feature of all the passive errors or hesitations, therefore, is that the speech segments involved depend on information that must survive an increment in the T-count. It is also the case that these PATN steps are relatively complicated, in the sense of involving complex conditions, and this complexity would add to their vulnerability.

Thus, a valid hypothesis concerning the speech production mechanism may be that whenever information is moved through time there is an increased possibility of error. Depending on the organization of the syntactic device, errors may appear in different places. The following section shows that this principle holds in another context.

The Restrictive Relative Clause

In 14 restrictive relative clauses from the principal Duncan corpus and 26 from the supplementary conversations, 24 errors and hesitations occur. There are approximately equal numbers of right-branching and center-embedded relative clauses. Center-embedded relative clauses have comparatively more disturbances that occur both before the head noun is uttered and at the conclusion of the relative clause, and right-branching relative clauses have comparatively more disturbances that occur immediately after the relative

TABLE 9.8
Dysfluencies and Errors in Relative Clauses

	ϕ N rel pro	N ϕ rel pro	rel pro ϕ R	rel pro R ϕ R	rel pro R ϕ
Right-branching	0	3	3	4	1
Center-embedded	4	3	0	3	3

pronoun has been uttered. This distribution of dysfluencies is shown in Table 9.8 (the symbol ϕ representing all types of disturbances and R the relative clause).

According to the relative clause PATN, in right-branching structures, Event$_R$ is retrieved in the second time segment after Event$_M$ has been encoded. The relative pronoun and head noun themselves are reached from Event$_M$; therefore errors immediately after the relative pronoun correspond to the beginning of the second time segment and the retrieval of Event$_R$.

In a center-embedded structure, Event$_M$ is retrieved in the second time segment, which occurs after the relative clause has been encoded. This corresponds to errors in the rel pro R ϕ category above. The peak of center-embedded errors before the head noun (ϕ N rel pro) corresponds to the point in the PATN where Event$_M$ is stored, which depends on the prior intersection of the two Events at the concept underlying the head noun. The right-branching storage of Event$_R$, on the other hand, is accomplished before this concept is encoded and hence could not disturb it.

The distinctive patterns of dysfluencies in right-branching and center-embedded relative clauses, therefore, correspond to the specific PATN steps of these constructions in which information is moved sequentially in time. Two dysfluency sites occur in the second time segment when Event$_R$ or Event$_M$ is retrieved, and a third site occurs in the first segment when Event$_M$ is stored. It is the case that these operations of the PATN manipulate highly complex concepts, in fact entire Events, a factor that would also create greater vulnerability to disruption.

As for the two remaining sites of errors and dysfluencies, the position between the head noun and the relative pronoun attracts errors in both the versions of the relative clause device. This position corresponds to a step (Step 6c) that involves storage of Concept 1. This idea must be moved forward in time regardless of the type of relative clause, and dysfluencies could (and do) occur here with either type. The site of the dysfluency within the relative clause itself (R ϕ R), however, is not predicted by either version of the PATN. Examples of the four predicted types of dysfluency are the following (CE means center-embedded, RB right-branching):

φ N rel pro
CE1   there was *φ um a young man who* I'd never seen in there

N φ rel pro
RB2   that'd be the place maybe to look for *a teaset φ that* I could use as demitasse cups

CE3   with *a person (inhale) that* she wasn't interested in or didn't care particularly about she wouldn't say anything

rel pro φ R
RB4   the one *that φ took* and then the one

rel pro R φ
CE5   those who stayed shifted *uh by the end (inhale) they uh* [interrupted]

The Pseudocleft

Nine examples of the pseudocleft occur in the Duncan corpus as supplemented from the additional conversations, but only two contain errors or dysfluencies. Both of these take place after the pseudocleft *be*, that is, in the second time segment.

PC1   what she'll do *is φ withdraw*
PC2   what for me that means is that she seemed to *(inhale) φ uh* [structure collapses]

The most we can say of the pseudocleft is that it does not contradict the hypothesis that the speech mechanism is particularly vulnerable when information is moved through time.

SUMMARY

Spontaneous speech output reveals the underlying conceptual structure of utterances in the form of various traces. The traces considered include four kinds of hesitation (unfilled pauses, filled pauses, audible inhalations, and audible clicks), three kinds of structural error (breakdowns, buildups, and anticipations of structure), and the distribution of phonemic clauses. The places where hesitations and the boundaries between phonemic clauses occur are taken to show potential points where speech programs change, and these are almost always where one sensory-motor–based syntagma is available to take over from another. Breakdowns, buildups, and anticipations show that the speaker manipulates, on line, speech segments that can be seen to be based on sensory-motor ideas, even when this sensory-motor structure is changing. Some of the errors, breakdowns in particular, reveal the dynamic alteration of conceptual structure. Errors that speakers make when using syntactic devices (passive, relative clause, and pseudocleft) occur at points in the speech output where, according to the PATN models in Chapter 7 for these devices, information is placed into or taken out of memory stores.

10 Ontogenesis

Considerations of ontogenesis have played an important part in evolving the arguments of this book and they have supplied several of the key concepts, among them the ideas of sensory-motor representation, signs, and semiotic extension. This chapter examines the data of children's language from the point of view of these concepts. In part, my purpose is to gather evidence in support of the analysis of conceptual structures in terms of syntagmata and semiotic extension and to do this by showing that the various theoretically proposed ingredients of the speech system can be seen emerging in language ontogenesis. In part, also, my purpose is to shed further light on the concept of semiotic extension itself, by taking the unique perspective of language ontogenesis. The topics to be considered are the following:

1. Semiotic extension can be demonstrated at the same time the child begins to form multiword utterances.
2. The child discovers the orientation of its language at an early point.
3. The age of acquisition of syntactic devices depends among other things on the type of semiotic extension that the devices make possible.

Before discussing these topics, it may be well to remind the reader of the main points that have been raised about ontogenesis; most of my discussion of these points is found in Chapter 4.

It was proposed to look upon the ontogenesis of syntagmata in terms of an AB model. According to this model, the child comes to fuse two separate action control hierarchies, making possible a new type of action, organized speech output (both single-word and multiword). The A hierarchy originally controls nonspeech action. It gradually becomes organized during the first two years into representational sensory-motor schemata. The A hierarchy contributes these sensory-motor schemata in its fusion with B. The B hierarchy is the control process for articulation. The fusion of B under the schemata of A eventually forms syntagmata, sequences of articulatory action that are organized by sensory-motor representations. This process goes on from 8 or 9 months of age, perhaps earlier, and reaches its climax at the conclusion of the sensory-motor period of cognitive development. The most important change, according to this theory, is the interiorization of sensory-motor representations.

We can look upon this development in terms of sign relationships. The interiorization of sensory-motor representations makes possible indexical signs which could not have existed without the interiorization. In these indexical signs, the sign vehicle is the activation of a speech program, AB, and the object is the sensory-motor idea, the A part of this program. The emergence of these indexical signs is noticeable during the single-word period of development in the increasing semantic value that children's speech appears to adults to have. Whereas previously speech was part of the child's overt action, it eventually comes to denote the child's internal mental (sensory-motor) representations.

Once interiorized to a sufficient degree, a sensory-motor scheme is able to enter into relationships with other kinds of signs. Semiotic extension is defined as the extension of syntagmata to content that is represented at higher conceptual levels. In this semiotic extension, the sensory-motor idea (the object of an indexical sign) is simultaneously regarded as the sign vehicle of an iconic or symbolic sign. In this way, the three types of sign interlock, and speakers can find syntagmata that relate to non–sensory-motor meanings.

Multiword utterances, according to this view, can arise when semiotic extension becomes possible. (Multiword speech that does not involve semiotic extension may also occur, as described in the first section below). More exactly, when the process of interiorization that makes semiotic extension possible is sufficiently complete, the child then can construct iconic and symbolic sign vehicles that include sensory-motor ideas, and this leads to the programming of speech output with more than one word. The words in these multiword utterances will be semantically interrelated in terms of sensory-motor representations.

With this review in mind, we can now consider our major topics.

SEMIOTIC EXTENSION

It is difficult to tell whether a child is capable of semiotic extension when utterances are limited to single-word outputs. Most unambiguous diagnostics of the process in English assume multiple-word outputs. Semiotic extension should be quite marginal when sensory-motor representations are not differentiated from overt action performances (Chapter 4), but it is possible for a speaker who has made this differentiation to use single word speech-programs as the sign vehicles of iconic or symbolic signs. The diagnostics of semiotic extension include (for English speech) preferences for VO sequences; for entity–location sequences for nonmoveable entities (*nose face*); and for possessor–possessed sequences for inalienable possessions (*John ear*). Each of these reveals the use of word order as a sign of an operative orientation, and the word order cannot be explained as having been modeled by the direction of performing actions.

We should consider the contrasting nondiagnostic cases of alienable possession, location of moveable entities, and SV sequences. These are not unambiguous indicants of semiotic extension. This is because the sensory-motor representation of these meanings could include information about temporal sequences of movements, and these movement sequences could model word-order sequences. This could be the case because the interiorized action scheme, A, is indexically related to the speech sequence, B. For example, the sensory-motor representation of the location of a moveable entity includes information about movements of fetching or depositing. The sensory-motor representation of this type of location, therefore, could include a model of an utterance sequence in which the location word appears after the entity word (for depositing) or before it (for fetching). Such an utterance sequence would have the sensory-motor representation as the object of an indexical sign. Such a sequence would therefore not unambiguously involve semiotic extension.

Menn (1973) has described several examples of very early child utterances in which the word-order sequence corresponds to the direction of a movement. In one example, a movement was actually incorporated:

Cracker—(finger into mouth)—bye-bye

That is, "cracker into the mouth and gone." In another example, the child mimed throwing a bit of food and said:

Throw duck eat

That is "Throw the bit of food to the duck for it to eat." As Menn points out, the existence of such accompanying movements is evidence that the child had a mental (i.e., a sensory-motor) representation of the sequence of states in the events he was describing, and to which the sequence of the utterance corresponded. Such word-order sequences, however, might not involve semiotic extension.

Now consider the diagnostic situation in which the entity is not moveable. The sensory-motor representation of this type of location cannot include fetching or depositing. It might include pointing, but pointing is not ordered with respect to the entity in any unique action sequence corresponding to the meaning of location. For example, one can say "nose" and point or point and say "nose," and both could have the same location meaning. The sensory-motor representation of the location of a nonmoveable entity does not provide a model of word order. Hence if there is a word-order preference we should be able to infer a semiotic extension of this sensory-motor representation. (For more discussion of these signs, see Chapter 3.) The same kind of analysis can be made of inalienable possession, because an inalienable possession cannot be moved from its possessor. If there is a word-order preference involving either inalienable possession or nonmoveable location, therefore, we should be able to infer semiotic extension.

An argument to the same effect can also be made with respect to the idea of a transitive action, although here the reasoning is different. The patient of a transitive action is not a patient until the action is performed on it. And a transitive action does not exist if there is no patient on which it is performed. There is no inherent order between the action and the patient, therefore, and either OV or VO is an option for the idea of a transitive action. Thus if a preference for one of these orders appears, we can infer semiotic extension. Subject–verb sequences, on the other hand, can arise indexically from the model of the child him- or herself taking the role of the actor (the dominant choice in early utterances). The decision to act can be identified with him- or herself—the idea of a Person—and this decision does necessarily precede the action. Thus a preference for subject–verb sequences is ambiguous as a diagnostic of semiotic extension.

Since OV, location of nonmoveable entities, and inalienable possession are diagnostics which depend on word-order sequences, they are useless with single-word speech. Also diagnostic of semiotic extension would be the occurrence of morphemes that are introduced by syntactic devices. Some morphological changes can occur on single words if the speaker is able to use the device producing them, but by themselves they do not lead the child to program multiword utterances. However, nearly all such devices (for English speech) have specialized meanings that are so late in ontogenesis, that they are of no use for detecting the earliest forms of semiotic extension. The progressive -ing used on main verbs (without the auxiliary verb) may be the output of a syntactic device, however, and this form does occur quite early.

Among the diagnostics for English of semiotic extension in early children's speech, therefore, are the following:

preferential VO sequences
preferential possessor–possessed sequences (inalienable)
preferential entity–location sequences (nonmoving)
use of present progressive (-ing)

Other kinds of sequences that occur in early children's speech, such as SV, possessor–possessed with alienable objects, and moveable entity–locations, are not unambiguous indicants of semiotic extension.

If one examines children's earliest multiword utterances, one or another— and very often several—of these diagnostics of semiotic extension is always involved. Progressive inflections that could reflect semiotic extension might occur before the onset of multiword speech, but the evidence is unclear on the point. (Slobin, in a lecture at The University of Chicago, revealed that Turkish children sometimes use inflections during the single-word period.) In Bloom's (1973) longitudinal study of her daughter Allison, the progressive -*ing* did make a limited appearance one or two months before there was conclusive evidence of multiword speech. Perhaps a syntactic device, and thus semiotic extension, preceded her multiword speech. However, the progressive occurred with just three different verbs and was not always used appropriately, whereas there were nine different verbs and the usage was invariably appropriate later when speech was multiword. The progressive -*ing* and multiword speech apparently emerged in Allison's development at the same time.

The preferential occurrence of VO sequences can be inferred from Bloom's (1973) Appendix, where are reproduced 107 pages of transcripts (including contextual notes) covering the emergence of Allison's multiword speech. At 22 months, the age at which Bloom regards multiword speech to be unquestionably present, I counted 27 tokens of VO sequences (not including three that are somewhat dubious) and no occurrences of OV. These VO sequences correspond to the sensory-motor idea of an Action and represent performances due to some performer who is not mentioned. (There also are 10 occurrences of Event where the performer is mentioned.) Examples are: *eat cookie; get Mommy cookie; open can; spill it; pour Mommy juice,* etc. VO was clearly favored by Allison at 22 months. Before 22 months, in contrast, I can find no definite examples of either VO or OV sequences. It is remotely possible that *coat on* at 20 months and 3 weeks, which Allison said as she put a coat on the chair, is an example of OV. *Mike on,* referring to the microphone in the same session, may also have been OV. These two utterances are the only examples of word sequences before 22 months that could have been based on the sensory-motor idea of an Action. This evidence, therefore, suggests that semiotic extension of the idea of Action to iconic VO sequences with an operative orientation coincides with the first occurrence of multiword speech.

It is instructive to compare Allison to a Japanese child (a girl whom I have called Izanami) at the same mean length of utterance (1.75 morphemes). (Bloom either does not say, or I have not found it if she does say, whether she calculated mean length of utterance in words or morphemes; I calculated it in morphemes for Izanami.) Izanami's level of performance is similar to Allison's, but Izanami's preference is for OV sequences. There are 26 tokens of OV and one of VO. Some examples are: *kore misete yo* (lit. this show = *show (me) this*); *kimono kite* (lit. kimono wears = *wears a kimono*); *hikōki shite yo* (lit. airplane make = *make an airplane*). The one VO sequence was *chuki kore* (= *suki kore,* lit. like this).

Nothing could present the problem that I will consider in the section of this chapter dealing with orientation more clearly than the comparison of these girls. At the beginning of their development of multiword utterances, they strongly prefer opposite word-order sequences for the same idea of Action. They have discovered some property of their respective languages that sets them going in different directions.

The second diagnostic of semiotic extension—inalienable possessor-possessed sequences, such as *Patsy hair*—has the disadvantage of being an uncommon semantic type in the speech of young children (Brown, 1973). In the data reported by Bloom, Lightbown, and Hood (1975), alienable possessor–possessed sequences such as *mine clay* are many times more frequent.

These authors continue Bloom's commendable practice of publishing abundant examples, but I am able to find only three instances of inalienable possession in their Appendix of more than 1000 utterances. Each of these is in the possessor–possessed order, which can be explained on the basis of the operative orientation of the possession relation, *possesses* (A, B). However, with so few examples it is impossible to conclude that a "consistent preference" has been demonstrated. The examples occur in the speech of three different children, and each appears at a relatively advanced level (mean length of utterance of 2.4 or more). This suggests that inalienable possession does not play a role in the first multiword utterances.

Alienable possession is far more frequent but is ambiguous as a diagnostic of semiotic extension. The alienable possessor–possessed order might or might not correspond to an oriented iconic sign. There are more than 100 alienable possession utterances in Bloom et al.'s Appendix, some occurring at mean lengths of utterance of 2.0 or less, and all except six are in the possessor–possessed order. For example, *my pen; my paper; step my Kathryn book;* etc. Possibly some of these 100 utterances are iconic sequences, although we cannot identify which ones. In these cases, assuming they exist, the possession relation could be said to be part of the semiotic extension that coincides with the occurrence of multiword speech. The possessed–possessor sequences involve deixis, as in, for example, *that Patsy* (pointing to paper). In these utterances, the speech order again corresponds to the direction of an action (indicating the referent before speaking), so it may be correct to classify the utterance as indexical and based on an action scheme, but it is not the same action as underlies the sensory-motor representation of possession.

Izanami's speech contains very few utterances of any kind with a possessive meaning. There are only five examples in the sample, and all are in the possessor–possessed order, which is the order of Japanese speech. Of these five, three refer to inalienable possessions. Thus, by chance, Izanami produced the same number of unambiguous semiotic extensions as the children in the Bloom et al. sample.

The genitive suffix (English) and genitive postposition (Japanese) are both generally lacking at this stage of development. The children in Bloom et al.'s sample included possessive pronouns in their speech, but this can not be taken to signify semiotic extension of the sensory-motor representation. This type of pronoun could be controlled directly by the sensory-motor representation (one of the lexical commands inserted by the program).

All in all, then, the evidence of semiotic extension occurring with the earliest possession utterances is not as strong as with the earliest action utterances. This weakness has to do with the low frequency of possession utterances. Such as it is, nonetheless, the evidence is consistent with the proposal that the earliest utterances involving possession include semiotic extension of this idea.

The third diagnostic of early semiotic extension—entity–location sequences with nonmoveable entities—shows itself in the large sample provided by Bloom et al. Of 217 utterances recorded with location meanings, 13 do not involve movement of the entity. And of these, 11 are in the entity–location order. Such location utterances could arise from *located-at* (A, B) in the operative orientation. Examples are: *red dragon in book; bees in there* (picture of a beehive); *pin in it* (spindle of tape recorder); etc. Since the entities located (red dragon, bees, pin) are not moveable in these cases, a sensory-motor representation of location based on the actions of fetching or depositing would not produce a consistent word-order preference. From the observed word-order preference, therefore, we can infer semiotic extension in which the sensory-motor representation serves as the sign vehicle.

Nonmoveable entity–location utterances occur at mean lengths of utterance of 1.69 and above in the Bloom et al. samples. Thus they coincide with the emergence of multiword speech. (Allison's speech at 22 months, when the mean length of utterance was also about 1.7, contains no examples where the entity was nonmoveable.)

When we consider Izanami's speech, we discover an interesting example of the situation that should be preliminary to semiotic extension. There are only two location utterances with nonmoveable entities, one in each word order. However, with moveable entities, the child shows the word-order preferences that would be predicted from the action scheme of depositing objects in locations. These utterances appear to be indexical signs with sensory-motor representations as the objects. This word order appears even though in the Japanese of her mother both entity–location and location–entity sequences are acceptable and occur. If there is any bias in her mother's speech it is in the direction of location–entity. But Izanami consistently uses entity–location. Some examples are (location term underscored): *Obachan Kyūshū* (lit.

Grandmother Kyūshū); *Mama kōki itterasshai* (lit. Mommy (air) plane goodbye); and *bata wa koko tsukete* (lit. butter–topic postposition–here (I) spread). Thus Izanami may be making use of a model based on the action of moving to locations or moving and depositing entities (both of which have their locations at the end), and she produces word sequences based on this model. This would be an indexical sign that does not involve semiotic extension.

This indexical sign, however, would be preliminary to semiotic extension if the child can turn the indexical object into an iconic sign vehicle. The same sensory-motor scheme would be involved and regarded in two ways. For example, the expression *butter here* indexes the scheme for depositing the butter on the toast; the next step would be to regard this same scheme in turn as resembling, in its arrangement of parts, the logical structure corresponding to the action, *located-at* (A, B). Thus, utterances like *butter here*, where the sensory-motor scheme is the object, can be a step toward semiotic extension of the same sensory-motor scheme when it is regarded as the sign vehicle. The same transitions should exist in the ontogenesis of other children.

Reviewing the evidence of the four diagnostics of semiotic extension, it appears that in some form semiotic extension is present from the earliest occurrences of multiword speech. Since this co-occurrence was predicted by the theory developed in Chapter 4, the evidence supports this theory. By far the strongest evidence of semiotic extension is the direction of verb–object pairings, which is opposite in Japanese and English from the beginning stages. This difference can be deduced from the definition of iconic signs in such operative and receptive languages.

The diagnostic of inalienable possession is handicapped by a paucity of relevant observations. The diagnostic of nonmoveable location is somewhat more frequent and shows a preference for entity–location sequences among English-speaking children. To this may be added the evidence of the *-ing* suffix in English, which appears as soon as there is multiword speech, if not sooner. All of these diagnostics point to the conclusion that some forms of semiotic extension can be demonstrated as soon as a child begins to form multiple-word utterances.

Slobin (1978) has provided new information regarding the remarkable linguistic performances of young Turkish-speaking children. Turkish children show a quite ferocious precocity in the use of what seem to be (from Slobin's description) devices for achieving symbolic semiotic extensions. Turkish has a highly regular and transparent system of inflectional morphology. When the subjects and objects of sentences are morphologically marked for nominative and accusative case, Turkish children are able to comprehend correctly all six permutations of S, V, and O. This performance is established by 2 years. Serbo-Croatian children, in contrast, are much slower in working out the morphology of their less transparent language. This difference between the languages is presumably due to the greater clarity of the Turkish morphological system plus the almost exclusive use, in Turkish, of word-order contrasts to signal pragmatic (rather than semantic) meanings. Both of these characteristics could make the symbolic morphological aspects of Turkish highly salient to children, as Slobin points out.

Turkish therefore seems to prove that a type of semiotic extension that is achieved symbolically can occur at the same time as the emergence of multiword speech. The Turkish evidence joins that of English and Japanese, given above, where the earliest semiotic extensions were iconic.

Slobin, in the same paper, argues quite mistakenly that the example of Turkish acquisition provides evidence contrary to any form of indexical relationship of speech and sensory-motor meaning. Slobin's argument is flawed, because it overlooks the implications of semiotic extension. Slobin thinks that every word-order sequence must be traceable to the inherent direction of some action or other. To test the idea that sensory-motor action schemata can provide direct models for programming speech output, however, it is necessary to find examples where semiotic extension could not have been involved. Because of the very precocity of semiotic extension mentioned previously, Turkish is a poor choice of a language for testing this idea, but nonetheless there are some relevant observations. One of Slobin's experiments had the Turkish children try to understand and carry out instructions conveyed with all three permutations of *uninflected* N, N, and V sequences. Among the consistent responses, most (13) involved NNV, a smaller number (7) involved NVN, and the smallest number involved VNN. That is, 20 of 24 cases involved V in other than initial position. Slobin also collected imitations of the same unmarked sequences. NNV was never reordered in imitation; NVN was sometimes reordered to NNV; and VNN was most often reordered, usually to NNV. These reorderings, moreover, were most characteristic of the younger children.

Similar observations are made with Serbo-Croatian speaking children. Unmarked NN sequences that are grammatical in this language are interpreted so that the first N is the performer of actions.

Turkish-speaking and Serbo-Croatian-speaking children's own speech production (where the correct morphological inflections appear in the case of Turkish) similarly shows a strong preponderance of sequences in which the performer is in initial position. This occurred in 63% of the Turkish sentences (compared to 20% in final position), and in 82% of the Serbo-Croatian sentences (compared to 4% in final position).

Slobin's rejection of the idea of indexical word sequences is not supported by his own data. It is only by forgetting about the consequences of semiotic extension that Slobin believes that he has evidence against the existence of indexical word sequences.[1]

ORIENTATION OF LANGUAGE

Certain characteristics of children's early multiword speech suggest that they are able to discover at an early point the orientation of their language as a whole. Across a range of constructions, English-speaking children, for example, are generally operative and rarely if ever receptive, whereas Japanese children are generally receptive and rarely if ever operative.[2]

The preference for VO sequences by English-speaking children and for OV by Japanese-speaking children was shown in the preceding section. The VO sequence is operative and the OV one is receptive, as can be seen from the logical formula, *patients* (V, O). This word-order preference is noticeable as soon as there is any evidence of multiword speech (Bloom, 1973) and could be explained by a general tendency to regard language as operative in the case of English and as receptive in the case of Japanese. (From the child's point of view, of course, the language has neither orientation; he or she simply behaves in a way that presents certain uniformities, and we, the observers, note the uniformities and the contrasts between languages.)

In a completely different domain, the child's use of prepositions (English) or postpositions (Japanese) shows a consistent operative or receptive orientation, and this also appears at an early point in development. As described in Chapter 8, prepositions and postpositions can be regarded as particles that mark basic logical relations. From the same basic logical relation, the particle will appear as a preposition in a language that is oriented operatively, and as a postposition in a language that is oriented receptively. For example, with a locative relation, *located-on* (Entity, Surface), the operative expression *entity on surface* leads to a preposition, and the receptive *surface ni entity* to a postposition. (*Ni* is one of the locative particles

---

[1]Another of Slobin's arguments is that languages that have an inflectional morphology and employ word orders that depart from "intrinsic" word orders should be harder to learn. Turkish is such a language. Yet Turkish is easy to learn as regards word order and inflectional morphology. Therefore the idea of an "intrinsic" word order loses credibility. Slobin appears to assume that an iconic method of semiotic extension (involving word order) should be easier to learn than a symbolic method (involving inflectional morphology or other devices). All the evidence suggests, however, that children can use both forms of semiotic extension at the same time they start to produce multiword utterances.

[2]In Turkish, on the other hand, where iconic factors apparently play a smaller role, the salience of the overall orientation is probably less.

in Japanese.) Japanese also makes use of the operative form with the same postposition, *entity surface ni*; the postposition depends on the basic logical form, in other words, and follows the same principle when the word order changes to an operative orientation.

Table 10.1 gives all 12 instances of prepositions in Allison's speech as recorded in the Appendix of Bloom (1973)—this is the entire sample. Of these 12, 10 are operatively oriented and two (*out truck, out school truck*) are indeterminate as prepositions or postpositions but may have functioned as verbs. To explain the orientation of these examples, consider the utterance *diaper out,* in which the preposition is final. The logical formula corresponding to this meaning is approximately *located-out-of* (Diaper, Bag), and the utterance itself therefore consists of the referent of the relation and a particle marking the relation in an operative orientation. A parallel analysis can be made of *in bag,* with initial preposition, in which the logical formula is approximately *located-in* (X, Bag). The utterance includes the relatum, and again the orientation is operative.

The two renegade examples, *out truck* and *out school truck,* are indeterminate rather than counterexamples because *out* does not function either as a preposition or postposition. (To be a postposition, the utterance would have to have been *location out.*) In the context, which involves Allison's simultaneously pushing a toy vehicle, it is possible that *out* functioned as a verb, in which case the utterance is in the VO direction and operative.

Table 10.2 gives all occurrences of postpositions in Izanami's speech when her mean length of utterance was 1.75 morphemes. The receptive orientation of 52 of these 55 tokens can be demonstrated with *papa ga ii* (papa (I) want; i.e., *it's papa I want*) as an example. The logical formula corresponding to this utterance would be *patients* (Want, Papa), and the utterance therefore begins

TABLE 10.1
Prepositions in Allison's Speech (based on Bloom, 1973)

Age	Orientation	Example	Context
20–3	O	coat on/chair	putting the coat on a chair
22–0	O	in bag	pointing to a bag
	O	diaper out	taking the diaper out
	O	napkin out	taking the napkin out
	O	Mommy/skirt on	pointing
	O	Mommy/blouse on	pointing and reaching
	—	out truck	pushing a toy
	—	out school truck	pushing a toy
	O	pull cow in ———	(none relevant)
	O	help cow in table	(none relevant)
	O	cow out	removing pig
	O	sit down right here next truck	sitting down

TABLE 10.2
Postpositions in Izanami's Speech at MLU = 1.75

Position in Utterance	Orientation	Example	
Medial	R	kotchi ga ii	(the other one (I) want)
	R	papa ga ii	(papa (I) want)
	R	bāchan ga ii	(grandma (I) want)
	R	bata wa koko tsukete	(butter here (I) put; this should be "koko e bata o tsukete")
	O	gakko no sensei ga ii yo	(a school's teacher (I) want to be)
	R	fūsen ga ii	(a balloon (I) want)
	R	kore ga ii	(this (I) want)
	R	kotchi ga ii	(the other one (l) want)
	R	sensei ga kō itta	(a teacher this said)
	R	hon ga ii	(a book (I) want)
	R	densha ga ii	(the streetcar (I) want)
	R	kotchi ni aru da?	(on the other (page) is it?)
	R	——keiki ga iya	(cake (I) hate)
	R	chinpun ga iina	(a spoon (I) like better)
	R	boku ga shite a——	(I did——)
	R	atashi wa iya	(I don't like)
	R	kore a shite	(this do; should be "kore o shite")
	R	kiiro wa kore	(yellow this)
Final	R	kore wa? (X 26)	(this?)
	R	meme koko wa	(eyes here)
	R	bō wa (X 2)	(stick)
	R	mama wa (X 2)	(mommy)
	R	ningyō wa?	(a doll?)
	R	bāchan wa?	(grandma?)
	R	torakku wa?	(a truck?)
	O	machan no	(Masumi's)
	R	kore o	(this (marked as the patient))
	R	koko wa	(here)

with the relatum of the relation together with an object particle *ga* that marks the relation itself. (This particle has several different uses in Japanese.) The orientation is receptive. One of the expressions in Table 10.2, *kore wa?* accounts for half of all the postpositional uses. This expression is used for requesting the names of things, and *kore* performs a deictic function in this usage. The logical formula appears to be *name-of* (A, B), where B is the deictic referring word and A is the name of the thing to which B refers. The same formula corresponds to the English *what is this?* In the Japanese version, the orientation is receptive because the word order places the relatum B in the initial position. (In the English version, therefore, the orientation is operative.) The postposition *wa,* which follows a topic or subject, thus indicates a receptive relationship here.

The only operative orientations in Table 10.2 are both legitimate Japanese uses. They involve the genitive postposition (*gakko no sensei ga ii yo; machan no*) and are operative according to the formula *possesses* (A, B).

The meaning domains covered by Izanami's postposition utterances overlap those of her OV utterances. For example, *papa ga ii* (papa (I) want) and *kore a shite* (this (I) do) also involve the patient relation. If we confine our attention to the 37 final utterance positions for postpositions, there is no overlap with the OV domain. None of Allison's preposition examples involve a meaning that overlaps VO (with the possible exceptions of *out truck* and *out school truck*). Limiting our attention to such nonoverlapping domains, then, we can claim to have shown that there are largely operative (in English speech) and largely receptive (in Japanese speech) orientations in two separate places in each child's early multiword speech. This generalization of orientation suggests that each child has discovered how her language is oriented in general. Having made this discovery, many other structures can be worked into this overall scheme (Greenberg, 1963).

What could inform children, so early in development, of the overall orientation of their language? Adults might do this somewhat accidentally when they use simplified syntactic structures in their speech to young children (Snow, 1972). Adults' motivation for simplifying their speech to children probably has to do with a non-selective attempt to maintain a low level of complexity. But as a consequence, orientation-changing syntactic devices are avoided as well, which introduces a bias into the adults' speech toward the orientation of the language. In the case of Lois Bloom speaking to Allison, although there are many ways in which she might have introduced receptive orientations, speech to the child was in fact almost uniformly operative. The adults who spoke to Izanami were just as uniform in presenting receptive orientations, even though they could have introduced operative orientations in many ways at the expense of syntactic complexity. Thus, an important insight into the effects of speech modification (so-called "motherese") practiced by adults in talking to young children is that it leads adults to a single orientation, which would be the basic orientation of the language, and this would seem to be a great advantage for the child.

ACQUISITION OF SYNTACTIC DEVICES

Syntactic devices create symbolic signs that have specific meanings established through conventions. The ontogenesis of these signs often seems to depend on the child's reaching a stage of cognitive development where the corresponding meaning becomes conceptually possible. The emergence of the syntactic device can be explained in terms of the semiotic extension to this new conceptual function that is achieved through the symbolic sign. We can think of the symbol as being specialized for the particular conception that triggers it. The acquisition of the syntactic device therefore might be predictable from the child's stage of cognitive development (Slobin, 1973).

The sections that follow present examples of three syntactic devices of English that are acquired relatively late in ontogenesis: (1) the passive (Potts, Carlson, Cocking, & Copple, in press); (2) expression of timeless events (Cromer, 1968); and (3) violation of the Minimum Distance Principle (C. Chomsky, 1969).

The Passive

Potts et al. (in press) tested the ability of 3-, 4-, and 5-year-old children to produce passive sentence structures by having the subjects complete fragments of sentences. The fragments were presented by the experimenter in a context that unambiguously called for a passive construction.

Two main types of response occurred in this situation. A passive form was given by 36% of the 3-year-olds, increased to 63% of the 4-year-olds, and reached 88% of the 5-year-olds (*be* and *get* passives combined). (The figures were 48%, 49%, and 92%, respectively, for a second test sentence.) At the same time there was a decline in responses that consist of uninflected verbs, for example, *those pictures hafta—finish.* This kind of response was given by 43% of the 3-year-olds, 25% of the 4-year-olds, and 6% of the 5-year-olds (43%, 28%, and 5%, respectively, for the second test sentence). These reciprocal developmental trends suggest that the passive construction was replacing this particular type of nonpassive. In this nonpassive sentence the orientation was operative, assuming the NP (*pictures*) was treated by the child as the performer and patient of an intransitive action. The logical relations would be *performs* (Pictures, Finish) and *patients* (Finish, Pictures) in this case. The passive is receptive, however, with only the logical relation of *patients* (Finish, Pictures). Thus, one specific cognitive step to which development of the passive can be related is differentiation of the *patients* and *performs* relations or, more generally, differentiation of effects from causes. Piaget (1969) describes taking place during this same period the growth of "objectification"—the child's realization that what comes from himself or others is distinct from what comes from external reality—and this developing insight would seem to carry with it the distinction between the relations mentioned above on which the emergence of the passive depends. For the child who does not clearly distinguish a sphere of objective reality, there is no rational basis for seeing a difference in meaning between *those pictures have to finish* and *those pictures have to be finished,* and thus no conceptual foundation for the passive structure as a symbolic sign.

During the development of the passive construction, there was generally an absence of responses consisting of partially constructed passives, such as *those pictures hafta—be finish.* These never occurred as responses to the first test sentence and occurred in only 1–6% of the responses to the second. That these responses occur so rarely is evidence that the children were developing the sign vehicle of the passive as a whole.

"Timeless" Events

This type of utterance provides a particularly clear instance of a symbolic sign with a specific function, and it has a sharp developmental threshold (at 4 years). "Timeless" (the term used by Cromer, 1968) can be viewed as the semiotic extension of an Event (a change of state at a moment T) to a new concept of an Event that occurs without regard to the deictic reference of T to the speech situation (there is suspended motion or indeterminate repetition). Adult examples of "timeless" are the following:

he goes to the beach
I take one every day

In the first example, the event of going to the beach is lifted out of any change of state occurring at a certain moment. In the second, the event of taking something occurs over and over. In both of these examples, there is retained the idea of an Event but it is "timeless," i.e., it has had removed from it the idea of anchoring T in a particular moment of time.

"Timeless" consists of the ordinary idea of an Event extended to a certain other kind of Event. The present tense verb (*goes, take,* etc.) is used as the sign vehicle of this sign. This mode of reference with present tense appears to be symbolic, because the meaning of the tense is altered according to a conventional interpretation.

Cromer traced the emergence of "timeless" events in the speech development of Adam and Sarah, two children described in detail by Brown (1973). The first instances of "timeless" occurred at age 4–0 with Adam, and at 3–10 (flourishing at 4–2) with Sarah. A few examples from Adam and Sarah at different ages are the following:

Adam 4–0	always run sometimes, huh?
	I lock them up at night
	I never have one
Adam 5–2	I have good times at school
	I give him two each day
	it gets bigger and bigger when you do that
Adam 5–9	I think of different kinds of things
	I feel warm when I play that
Sarah 4–2	it goes in the blanket sometimes
	I get some candy and everything (re Halloween)
	he doesn't bite

Sarah 5–2   sometimes I watch Bozo
             he flies
             he scribbles, huh?
Sarah 5–5   it writes on boards

In all of these cases the symbol is used correctly, i.e., a present tense verb occurs with the meaning of a "timeless" event.

In contrast are the following in which the reference includes a deictic indication of the moment of speech:

Adam 3–6   I want
             see any garage?
             it's all finished
Sarah 3–6   I want the yellow one
             where's the button?
             it's... it's your turn

As Cromer notes, "timeless" sentences "...appear so very simple that it is difficult to believe that they are not being used prior to age 4;0, yet no examples... occur in the data before that time..." [p. 132]. What cognitive function could the advent of the new symbolic use of present tense for "timeless" events be due? Again turning to Piaget (e.g., Piaget & Inhelder, 1969), we find many descriptions of the decreasing contextualization of children's thought at this stage of mental development. The phenomenon of conservation, for example, presupposes such decontextualization. At first, the child is not able to abstract his or her ideas of quantity from the visible shapes of substances. In the use of "timeless" event sentences a connection with the context of speech has to be given up (in fact, this is the chief thing in these sentences). This new symbolic use of present tense verbs can be related to the perceptual decontextualization that introduces the cognitive stage of operational thought.

Violations of the Minimum Distance Principle

C. Chomsky (1969) studied children's understanding of several kinds of contrasting sentences, such as the following:

this doll is easy/hard to see

Bozo tells Donald to jump
Bozo promises Donald to jump

tell Laura what to put in the box
ask Laura what to put in the box

In the first, third, and last of these sentences, the subject of the complement verb is not next to the complement itself. These sentences violate what

Rosenbaum (1967) called the MDP (Minimum Distance Principle)—the principle that the subject of a complement clause is the NP minimally distant from it. This principle itself can be understood as a type of iconic sign, but the violation of the MDP in different contexts appears to involve several symbolic signs in which the performer of the action denoted by the complement is conventionally represented to be some other figure (possibly one not even denoted by the sentence). Chomsky tested the ability of children between 5 and 10 years to correctly interpret the subjects of complements in sentences of this kind, both violating and obeying the MDP, and found a gradual acquisition curve. The cognitive abilities for which violating the MDP is a linguistic means appear to relate to a general distinction between language and referent. If a child conceives of language as having a less than perfect correspondence with real-world events, conventions for departing from the (presumably iconic) MDP would become meaningful. This sophisticated conception of language would not appear suddenly. The gradual discovery of violations of the MDP can be related to this development over a period of several years of metalinguistic awareness.

To correctly understand the sentence, *this doll is easy/hard to see,* the listener must recognize that the performer of the action of seeing is the speaker and/or listener. It is not the NP mentioned in the sentence. That is, the role of the performer in this sentence is an event role, not a speech role, and these two are not the same here. In contrast, in *is this doll able to see?* the performer is both an event and speech role. Chomsky obtained responses such as the following, for example (from a child of 5–2):

Is this doll [which is blindfolded] easy to see or hard to see?
    Hard to see.
Will you make her easy to see?
    OK (removes the blindfold).
Will you explain what you did?
    Took off this (pointing to blindfold).
And why did that make her easier to see?
    So she can see.

Clearly, then, this child does not recognize an event performer apart from the speech role that is defined within the sentence itself.

Responses such as this were given by children who ranged in age from 5–0 to 8–10. Children who successfully sorted out the performer in the *easy/hard to see* sentence ranged in age from 5–2 to 10–0. The two age distributions overlap extensively, and there is no point in the 4-year span at which a "threshold" can be said to exist for the onset of the correct (violate the MDP) interpretation of this sentence.

The situation with *promise* depends on the same distinction between event and speech roles. The MDP applies to the sentence with *tell,* in which the event and speech roles coincide. With *promise*, however, the event role (the one who jumps) is given to the other NP in the sentence rather than to the nearest NP to the complement. The age range of children incorrectly applying the MDP with *promise* was 5-0 to 8-10, and that of children correctly violating it was 5-10 to 10-0. Again the overlap is extensive, and there is no evidence of a threshold for violating the MDP.

The third violation of the MDP, *ask* in the sense of *question* (not *request*), like *easy/hard to see,* requires understanding that the event role of putting something in the box is filled by the one who asks the question rather than by the one referred to by the NP closest to the complement. Children's mistakes with *ask* confuse the performer with this NP (e.g., *Laura, what are you gonna put in the box?* and *Laura, put in the apple,* where the child does not ask but tells Laura what to do). Errors in response to *ask* occurred between ages 5-2 and 10-0. Correct responses occurred between 5-10 and 9-9. Here is complete overlap, therefore, and no threshold for acquisition of violation of the MDP. In contrast to passive and "timeless" event, violation of the MDP includes a metalinguistic function, and the gradualness of the change shown in Chomsky's experiments could be due to the pervasiveness of this function.

In general, syntactic devices are acquired by children in order to perform specific functions, and these functions often correlate with new mental operations during ontogenesis. A sequence of developmental steps is generated in this way with devices that specialize in more advanced mental operations being acquired at later points.

SUMMARY

The evidence surveyed in this chapter supports several findings regarding ontogenesis that can be related to the theoretical arguments we have discussed. These findings show the three types of sign—indexical, iconic, and symbolic—emerging separately in development. First of all, semiotic extension is present in children's speech production from the earliest stages of multiword speech. These extensions are, in English and Japanese, due to iconic signs based on the discovery, possibly due to a bias in adult speech, of the overall orientation of the language. Thus English-speaking and Japanese-speaking children show opposite patterns from the beginning at several points. Secondly, this semiotic extension rests on a base of sensory-motor content that thoroughly permeates early speech, both multiple- and single-word. Thirdly, symbolic signs (produced by syntactic devices) often initially serve specific functions and in some languages—e.g., Turkish—may serve functions that lead children to acquire some symbolic signs at a very young age.

11 Gestures

The AB model of the syntagma (Chapter 4) predicts that gestures should be correlated with syntagmata in time and form. Syntagmata are said to arise when the motor control hierarchies of speech articulation (B) and sensory-motor representations (A) fuse. The A hierarchy is thought to derive ultimately from coordinations of actions directed toward objects and persons in the world (Piaget, 1954). Even though sensory-motor schemata are interiorized, the motoric hierarchies of A are still intact; they are in fact involved in the integration of nonspeech motor actions (Bernstein, 1967). Thus it is possible, during the organization of utterances on the basis of AB, that movements based on A can also occur. These movements form a type of gesture. Such gestures are actions without objects. Such gestures should be correlated with syntagmata in time because they depend on the same action schemata as speech output does, and they should agree with syntagmata in form because they are produced from the same A schemata. (What is meant by the term "form" will become clear from the examples to follow.)

Fig. 11.1 represents this hypothetical relationship between speech and gesture. The figure clarifies what we should expect when we examine speech and gesticulation. Gestures ought to coincide in time with sensory-motor segments in speech stream, and they should be re-enactments of movements (possibly quite reduced) that could be based on the same sensory-motor representations. The gesture should be a visible external trace of the A part of the AB speech program in the same sense that movements of the speech articulators are external traces of the B part. Such gestures are not pictures of objects, therefore, but pictures of action schemata. It is worth noting that, according to Fig. 11.1, gestures do not correspond to speech output directly but only indirectly by way of scheme A.

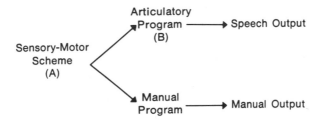

FIG. 11.1   Correlation of gestures and speech via sensory-motor representations.

PREVIOUS RESEARCH ON GESTURES

Not all hand movements that are communicative are gestures of the type I have described. The subset of gestures that might be synchronized and homologous with sensory-motor representations in the way predicted by Fig. 11.1 can be identified by reference to the classification schemes that have been devised by others for describing distinctions among gestures. The modern study of spontaneous speech-accompanied gesturing begins with Efron (1941), whose classificatory categories have been the basis of most recent studies (e.g., Ekman & Friesen, 1969). Efron compared the speech-accompanied gestures of "traditional eastern Jews" and "traditional southern Italians" who were immigrants living at the time in New York City. Efron's basic categories distinguish between gestures that emphasize the concept of the spoken message (Type A), and gestures that have a significance independent of speech (Type B).

The first type is further subdivided as follows:

—*baton-like* movements, in which the gesturer beats time for "successive stages of referential activity."

—*ideographic* movements, in which the gesturer traces or sketches "paths" or "directions" of thought patterns. These gestures are thought to express the internal mental processes of the speaker, rather than external objects.

The second type of gesture is also subdivided as follows:

—*deictic* movements, in which an existing object or event is pointed out.

—*physiographic* movements, in which the gesture depicts the form of a visual object or a spatial arrangement.

—*emblematic* movements, which represent visual or logical objects in a standardized form. Examples are the "OK" sign used by speakers of American English and other emblems less polite.

Efron's categories are often difficult to distinguish in practice, but they state a distinction between internally and externally focused gestures that appears to be sound in principle. It seems that Type A, the ideographic and baton-like gestures that emphasize the content of speech, are the ones most plausibly generated by the processes suggested in Fig. 11.1. Such Type A gestures are inwardly focused around the speaker's organization of ideas and might therefore coincide with sensory-motor representations.

Efron's classification scheme is based on presumed correlations with internal mental representations. Gestures can also be classified in terms of correlations with phonological patterning. Kendon (1972) found that the timing of gestures is synchronized with different types of phonological segment. Both the gestures and the phonological segments apparently are arranged hierarchically, larger phonological segments being associated with more extensive but less precisely synchronized postural adjustments of the whole body. The level of movement at which Efron's Type A gestures occur (i.e., fingers, hands, and arms in motion but not necessarily the entire trunk or the legs) appears at levels of phonological organization that Kendon terms the levels of the prosodic phrase and the locution. These phonological segments are of approximately the same magnitude as grammatical phrases and sentences, respectively. It is possible to extend Kendon's observations by making use of the semantic characterization of utterances in terms of sensory-motor structures. Kendon also noticed a tendency for the form of gestures to match the lexical content of the speech (e.g., the hand moving away from the self as the speaker says "you"), and for the fullest extent of the gesture to co-occur with the phonologically most prominent syllable in the phrase or locution. I have confirmed these observations and have found that the form of the gesture, in cases where this can be identified, corresponds to the content of syntagmata, and that the fullest extent of gestures tends to be timed to occur at the moment when the focal point of the strong component underlying the syntagma is reached.

To summarize this introduction, I intend to examine the relation between the sensory-motor content of speech and the synchronization and form of gestures. The gestures in question can be delimited in two ways, one in terms of the presumed correlations with mental processes, and the other in terms of correlations with phonological patterns. The intended set of gestures are, in the first case, approximately Efron's Type A speech-emphasizing gestures, and in the second case, Kendon's gesture type that occurs at the middle levels of the movement and phonological hierarchies.[1] Gestures that are described in these terms show evidence of being generated from the sensory-motor content of syntagmata, as suggested by Fig. 11.1. (Other types of gesture may or may not be generated in this way and I have not examined them.) The

---

[1]Only the movement hierarchy is considered in the study in this chapter.

gestures discussed below are restricted to those which co-occur with speech; this follows from the definition of Kendon's phonological criteria. Excluded are gestures that are completed before speech begins and those that occur without speech. Thus, we are asking about the form and synchronization of gestures that accompany speech, not of all gestures that speakers produce.

EMPIRICAL STUDY OF GESTURES

The examples of data described below are based on a videotaped technical conversation between two professional mathematicians (Professors Michael Anderson and Robert Morris, speakers L and R respectively, who were members of the Institute for Advanced Study at the time). I have chosen a conversation with a highly abstract subject matter in part to minimize the likelihood of Efron's Type B (externally focused) gestures, even though this abstractness imposes a limited range of content. (Only 2% of the gestures in this corpus are judged to be pictographic.) My impression on hearing the conversation is that the speech of L and R possessed a normal degree of fluency for these speakers. Speaker R by pre-arrangement did most of the talking and also produced most of the gestures, but data from both L and R are included in the corpus. This corpus consists of the first 500 gestures meeting the requirements given above (i.e., the gestures appeared to be Type A, were concurrent with speech, and were at the middle levels of the movement scale).

Technical difficulties in dealing with gesture material and the relation of gestures to speech are undeniably great. It is nearly impossible to detect synchronization of gestures and speech in real time. Speech events occur too swiftly, and there are perceptual illusions that rob one's immediate impressions of validity. It is necessary to film or videorecord the gestures and record the speech and to examine this record at reduced speed. The method of correlation used in the present case was to move the videotape by hand to find the exact moment in the gesture to which the speech was to be correlated, then start the playback and note whatever speech was audible. It is necessary to compensate for the slight delay during which the speech playback is not intelligible when the videotape starts to move. The accuracy of the correlation achieved by this method is estimated to be within one syllable (ca. 200 msec).

Three points in each gesture are distinguished and correlated with the concurrent speech:

1. *Gesture onset,* defined as the first detectable movement of the hands, fingers, etc., leading into the gesture.

2. *Gesture peak,* defined as the maximum extent of the movement of the hands, fingers, etc., in the execution of the gesture. It corresponds to the end of the "stroke" of the gesture, as defined by Kendon (1972). Kendon also

distinguishes between a preparatory phase of the gesture and the onset of the stroke, but this distinction has not been observed here.

3. *Gesture end,* defined as the first movement of the hands, fingers, etc., made in leaving the gesture for either a new gesture or for one of the characteristic rest positions of the speaker (the lap, chair arm, face, etc.). Note that the gesture end corresponds to the beginning of this movement, i.e., occurs before the hands, fingers, etc., have actually reached their rest positions. If the gesture had a sustained phase after reaching the peak, the gesture end is the first movement out of this sustained position toward the rest position or a new gesture.

These definitions have been adopted as the most likely to show a correlation with speech programming on the basis of syntagmata. It is not necessary to describe or name the gesture with these definitions, which focus only on locating boundaries.

An Example.   The hand movements of speaker R that accompanied the following utterance, [there's a complete] [[tensor product] [in the category]],[2] illustrate several characteristic properties of gestures (see Fig. 11.2). This utterance was accompanied by two principal gestures, the second of which was divided by a brief finger flexion. The first gesture coincided with *there's a complete* and consisted of a ring formed out of the thumb and index finger of the right hand, and simultaneously of an extension of the fingers of the left hand. These postures were taken immediately with the onset of *there's.* The right hand, holding the shape of a ring, dropped toward the left. The fullest extent of this movement was reached at the moment of producing the stressed syllable in *complete.* The gesture ended with the emergence of a new gesture coinciding with the start of *tensor.* The conceptual structure of *there's a complete* is (Entity (Existence) *indicates* (Entity (Property))). The missing noun phrase *tensor product* does not affect the second Entity. This Entity is still a concept containing the idea of a Property in the conceptual structure, and the overall structure is thus a strong component. The onset of the movements of the two hands coincided with the commencement of speech based on this strong component, therefore, and the fullest extent of the movement of the right hand coincided with the expression of the stressed syllable in the focal point (the focal point, as determined from a graph structure representation, is the second Entity).

The second gesture, interrupting the first, commenced immediately with the word *tensor* and continued through the rest of the utterance, *tensor product in the category.* The onset of this gesture thus also coincided with the beginning of a new conceptual segment, namely, an Entity, *tensor product* (an

---

[2]Brackets in this chapter indicate gesture onsets and ends.

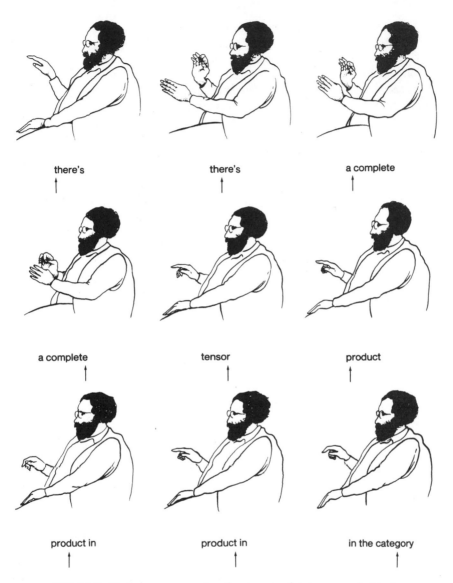

FIG. 11.2   Gestures accompanying *there's a complete tensor product in the category*. Arrows indicate the position of each illustration in relation to the speech stream as determined from stopped video images.

Entity within the larger Entity, *complete tensor product*). Apparently speaker R shifted the level to which his gestures corresponded, dropping to a lower level for this second gesture. On the lower level of the second gesture, the conceptual segments are (Entity (Tensor Product)), and (Location (Location) *is-located-in* (Entity (Category))). Although these are part of the same Level 3 conceptual structure at a higher level, there is no direct connection between this Entity and the Location on the lower level of the gesture (the Location is connected directly to the larger Entity, *complete tensor product*). Thus, at this level, we can consider each concept, Entity and Location, to be a strong component by itself.

The second gesture consisted of an extended index finger on the right hand. (The left hand returned to a rest position.) The peak of this gesture was reached immediately with the stressed syllable at the beginning of *tensor,* and this is appropriate (although uninformative), as the focal point of this strong component is the Entity, *tensor product.* This posture continued throughout the concept of Location as well, but the transition from Entity to Location coincided with a baton-like retraction and re-extension of the finger. Possibly this movement was triggered by the impending concept of Location. The retraction took place over the second syllable of *product* (illustrating once again that a gesture end may not occur at the end of a conceptual segment), but the re-extension coincided with the beginning of the Location strong component. The peak of this re-extension was immediate, and this also may be appropriate, as there is no single unique focal point within the phrase *in the category* when this segment is considered in isolation, although it occurred before the stressed syllable in this case.

To summarize the example, the onsets of the two gestures that accompanied the utterance of *there's a complete tensor product in the category* coincided with the vocal expression of strong components. The peak of the first gesture coincided with the stressed syllable in the expression of the focal point of its strong component. The onset of the second gesture interrupted the first, allowing the onset of the second gesture to coincide with the beginning of a new conceptual segment on a lower level in the conceptual structure. At this lower level, there is not a direct connection between strong components, and the transition between these components was in fact marked by a baton-like movement timed to coincide with the onset of the second conceptual segment. The peaks of these gestures also coincided with focal points in the utterance. In this way, we can interpret many of the details of the speech-accompanied gestures of R in terms of the conceptual structure of his corresponding speech.

If we view these movements as traces of the speech programming process, we can say that there is evidence of three syntagmata. The shifts between these syntagmata take place within a single conceptual structure in which all the parts are interrelated at Level 3 of connectedness. We cannot say why R shifted from a higher syntagma to two lower ones, although we can specify where such changes in the ecphoria process can take place. It is important to realize, however, that in a Level 3 structure the speaker has information about later parts of the utterance as he produces earlier parts; the effects of such information can be seen in the formation of speaker R's gestures. For example, the first gesture immediately takes the form of a ring, presumably under the influence of the idea of *complete.* The second gesture takes the form of a deictic pointing movement, and this may be related to the idea of Location, which is expressed only in the last syntagma. More delicately, the retraction of the index finger over the second syllable of *product* clearly anticipates the re-extension, which was timed to coincide with the beginning of the idea of a Location. This anticipation depends entirely on the Level 3 connectedness of the whole phrase, *complete tensor product in the category.* Ecphoria picks a particular output program, in other words, but it is not a filter that excludes other related parts of the conceptual structure that are not directly within the output program. The connectedness of the larger conceptual structure is not changed by choosing one or another syntagma (cf. the discussion of this property of connectedness in Chapter 6).

Conceptual Basis of Gesture Onsets

Each gesture was tallied according to whether its initial movement fell into one of the nine categories described below. The end of the gesture is relevant to the extent that the gesture was required to continue through all the elements described in a given category. However, gestures sometimes end prematurely from the point of view of a category. This effect is illustrated at two places in Fig. 11.2. Such reduced precision of gesture ends was disregarded in the classification of gestures that follows, because the gesture end rarely occurred more than one syllable before the end of the category.

   1. *Whole concepts* (C). In this category the onset of the gesture coincides with the beginning of a speech segment that is the vocalization of one whole concept. Whole concepts range from a single concept upwards through complex structures containing several other concepts. Nonetheless, the whole concept is a single point (strong component) in the conceptual structure, regardless of the internal complexity, and all relations are inside this concept. Examples of whole concepts (internal concepts underscored) are the following:

   [ideal]

   [it's an inverse limit]

   [that it's pro-] Artinian

   [there's a complete] [tensor product]

   2. *Relation-concept* (rC). In this category the gesture commences with a relation and continues through a concept to which it is related. The concept, again, may have internal structure, as in this example:

   [of Artinian rings]

3. *Concept relation* (Cr). In this category the gesture commences with a concept and is sustained through the encoding of a following relation related to the concept. Some constructions encode two such relations in a row, e.g., the verb *be* and an article (treated as a relation in Chapter 8). Because these are distinct branches from a common concept, a gesture terminating in either the first or second relation is considered to be in the Cr category. For example,

[that's the]	Cr-r
[if it's] the	Cr
[have a basis of]	Cr

(The problem of successive relations does not arise with the rC category in this sample.)

4. *Relation-concept-relation* (rCr). In this category the gesture both commences with and continues through relations related to the same concept (which may be internally complex). The same rule for successive (terminal) relations is observed here. An example of rCr is:

[and has a]

5. *Single relation* (r). In this category a single encoded relation is accompanied by its own gesture, separated from the gestures (if any) accompanying the concepts to which it is related. Two examples are the following:

[a] basis

[and uh] have

6. *Two or more relations* (rr). In this category two or more encoded relations that happen to be successive are produced with a gesture that accompanies them alone but not with any concept(s) to which they are related. The following is an example:

[and the] exactness

7. *Partial concept* (¢). In this category a gesture accompanies only a partial vocalization of a concept, starting some place other than the boundary between two concepts. For example,

com[plete formalism]

8. *Two or more unrelated concepts* (C | C). In this category the gesture coincides with the boundary of a concept at its start but continues to other concepts that are not related. The C | C category includes examples in which the gesture begins and/or ends with an encoded relation, such as the following:

sub-[co-algebras the duals will be]

you have [there's this gives] complete duality

[it's not a (unintelligible) so] it's not

9. Two relations not related (r | r). In this category are structural breakdowns, as in this example,

a [a of] it turns out

It should be noted that the segmentations of speech in these examples are according to the onsets of gestures. In many cases speech itself is produced continuously (possibly with a terminal contour at the gesture boundary). (Gestures are related to dysfluencies in various ways, and these are described in later sections.)

Of the 9 categories of gesture, any gesture that falls in one of the first 4 categories (i.e., C, rC, Cr, or rCr) is considered to be an explained case. Such gestures coincide with the encoding of a single point and one or two connected lines in the conceptual structure. Gestures in categories 5 or 6 (r or rr) are questionable cases. Some may be consistent with a theory that gestures arise from meaning (especially in the r category), but as others may not so arise, the support of this theory is less strong than with the first 4 categories. The last 3 categories (₵, C | C, and r | r) are clearly inconsistent with the theory that gestures arise from the conceptual basis of speech.

It is true, nonetheless, that very few gestures fall into these last 3 categories. More gestures, but still a relatively small number, fall into the questionable categories. Most gestures are in the categories considered to be consistent with the theory. Table 11.1 gives the results leading to these conclusions.

That is, if we proceed from the idea that gestures reflect speech encoding based on concepts, only between 6 and 14% of all gestures (depending on how the questionable cases are counted) are a residual class requiring some other explanation. As will be seen, a coding of the same gestures in terms of grammatical categories produces a much larger such residue.

Grammatical Basis of Gestures

Each gesture was tallied according to two categories, whether "grammatical" or "antigrammatical." The former comprises gestures coinciding with any

TABLE 11.1
Classification of Gestures According to Concepts

	Consistent Cases				Questionable Cases		Inconsistent Cases		
	C	rC	Cr	rCr	r	rr	Č	C|C	r|r
Frequency	243	94	62	33	34	7	9	15	3
Percentage	48	19	12	7	7	1	2	3	1
Percentage for the case		86			8		6		
						14			

surface grammatical constituent, ranging in size from single words to entire clauses. The latter comprises, in all cases, gestures coinciding with incompletely encoded grammatical constituents. Some examples of each type (the conceptual classification will be referred to later) are the following:

Grammatical:
  [module]   C
  [is finite]   rC
  [to be finite with respect to some module | rC
Antigrammatical:
  [and it looks]   rC
  [An ideal has]   rC
  [have a basis of]   Cr
  [that means that]   C
  [and has a]   rCr

The antigrammatical specimens, which illustrate all the major types, are not explainable at either an underlying or surface grammatical level. In these cases the speaker treats as a single gestural unit any of the following: (1) a subject plus a transitive or complement verb without the verb phrase or complement (*an ideal has, and it looks*); (2) a noun or other antecedent plus a preposition without the following noun phrase (*have a basis of*); (3) a transitive verb and adjective or a transitive verb and article without the noun phrase (*if it has finite, and has a*); or (4) a complement verb and complementizer without the complement clause itself (*that means that*). In most of these cases the utterance continued without dysfluency to include the verb phrase, propositional phrase, noun phrase, or complement clause.

Classifying gestures according to grammatical and antigrammatical categories, we obtain Table 11.2. To put the best possible interpretation on

TABLE 11.2
Classification of Gestures According to Grammatical Constituent Structure

	Grammatical		Antigrammatical
	Single words	Phrases, clauses	
Frequency	103	219	178
Percentage	20.6	43.8	35.6

these results, by combining single words and grammatical constructions as "grammatical," the correspondence of gestures with grammatical constituents is 64%. In other words, 36% of the gestures in the sample consist of counterexamples, a result to be compared to the 6–14% of the gestures that are counterexamples in the case of the conceptual classification.

The examples of grammatical and antigrammatical gestures previously mentioned show the conceptual classification, and we see that the two types are equivalent in terms of conceptual organization. As in the case of dysfluencies (cf. Chapter 9), so with gestures—speech output seems less well organized from he point of view of grammar than it does from the point of view of conceptual structure.

Selected Constructions.   Several construction types show segmentations other than grammatical and are of particular interest—transitive or complementizing verbs grouped with their subjects and not with the rest of their verb phrases, articles grouped with their antecedents and not with their nouns, and prepositions grouped with their antecedents and not with their following noun phrases are such constructions with substantial numbers of examples.

For transitive and/or complementizing verbs, of which there are 154 occurrences, the result is in Table 11.3. This table shows that the antigrammatical subject-transitive or -complement verb combination is the most common type (40.3%). It is more common even than full surface clauses, and twice as common as a grammatically consistent truncation to a verb or complement phrase. If the speaker does not make a full clause into a production unit, therefore, there is no guarantee that he or she will choose the next smaller grammatical constituent. This result with gestures is essentially

TABLE 11.3
Gestures Related to Verbs

	Frequency	Percentage
Subject-Verb$_{tr/comp}$	62	40.3
Full VP	30	19.4
Full Subject-VP	50	32.5
Single V$_{tr/comp}$	12	7.1

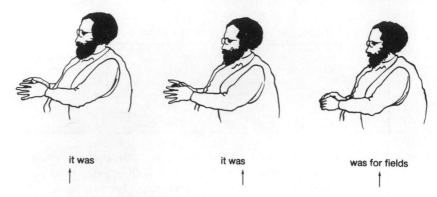

FIG. 11.3   Gesture accompanying *it was.*

the same as that shown in Chapter 9 with dysfluencies for the same constructions.

Fig. 11.3 shows a gesture associated with a subject and verb that excludes a grammatically required complement. The complement was also uttered, but it was not accompanied by a gesture. The full utterance was *but originally* [*it was*] *for fields,* with a gesture coinciding with the bracketed portion in which both hands reach out, fingers extended. The gesture peak and gesture end coincided, in this case, and occurred at the end of *was.*

Gestures made with articles show that the programming unit that produces the gesture may not always encompass the following noun, although in many cases the gesture that includes the article is produced with the preceding verb, preposition, or adverb. Moreover, there is an interaction with the definiteness–indefiniteness of the article, which further bolsters the conclusion that gestures arise from the meaning structure. It develops that the indefinite article shows an equal tendency to be produced with the preceding word and with the following noun or noun phrase. Definite articles, on the other hand, strongly go with the following noun or noun phrase. This difference obviously reflects the distinction in meaning between definite and indefinite articles.[3]

In the sample, there are 130 occurrences of articles accompanied by gestures, 89 of *the* and 41 of *a(n).* The percentage of these occurring with other elements accompanied by the same gesture is given in Table 11.4.

The sequence shown in Fig. 11.4 illustrates the production of *a* with a preceding verb that excludes the following noun phrase. The verb and article form a single gesture programming unit. The utterance was [*and has a* ϕ] *a*

---

[3]There is a corresponding difference in the distribution of speech disturbances (hesitations and errors) before or after articles of the two kinds in the sample. Disturbances are equally likely before and after *the* (7% and 5%, respectively, of all occurrences of *the*) but four times as likely after as compared to before *a(n)* (19% and 5% respectively).

TABLE 11.4
Gestures Related to Articles

	article-N	X-article[a]	article alone	X-article-N[a]
the	54%	9%	12%	24%
a (n)	27%	24%	12%	36%

[a]X represents some other speech element, often a verb.

basis of neighborhoods, with the gesture consisting of the right hand held motionless in the air and pointing. This is an rCr type of gesture. The example also illustrates the occurrence of a speech disturbance after the indefinite article, and also, in an outburst of comprehensiveness, the occurrence of *a* with the following noun phrase. (The speech sound before the hesitation was [æ] rather than [e], and therefore was presumably the indefinite article, not a filled pause.)

A third construction type which will be related to gestures is the prepositional phrase (excluding *for/to* complements). About one-third of the prepositions that accompanied gestures incorporated both the antecedent of

and has a   and has a ϕ
↑   ↑

a ϕ a   ϕ a basis
↑   ↑

FIG. 11.4   Gesture accompanying *and has a basis.*

TABLE 11.5
Gestures Related to Prepositions

	X-preposition	preposition-NP	X-preposition-NP	preposition alone
Frequency	28	24	33	9
Percentage	30	26	35	10

the preposition and the following noun phrase in a single gesture. A quarter of the gestures incorporated only the prepositional phrase. However, nearly a third incorporated the antecedent of the preposition but not the following noun phrase. The dysfluencies reported in Chapter 9 showed a similar result. Examples of each of these types are [*module* over *such* a *ring*], [*of finite co-length*], and [*consisting* of]. Ninety-four prepositions accompanied gestures and were distributed as shown in Table 11.5.

Figure 11.5 shows a gesture that includes the antecedent of a preposition and the preposition but not the following noun phrase. The utterance was [*inverse limit φ of*] [*Artinian*], the first bracketed portion consisting of a gesture in which the right hand touches the palm of the left hand, the fingers of which are extended, and both hands are motionless. The second bracketed portion, which begins with the noun phrase, is accompanied by a baton-like gesture made by the left and right hands moving up and down together (lining up with the bookshelf in the background).

GESTURES ACCOMPANYING SPEECH DYSFLUENCIES

Several forms of a relationship between gestures and speech dysfluencies exist. All of them can be seen to be consistent with a theoretical joint relation of speech disturbances and gestures to the construction of syntagmata.

inverse limit   limit φ of   of Artinian

FIG. 11.5   Gesture accompanying *inverse limit of.*

TABLE 11.6
Relation of Gestures to Accompanying Speech Dysfluencies

		Gesture Sustained	Gesture Cont'd	New Gesture	Unique Gesture	Relax- ation
Filled	Freq.	7	3	3	1	0
Pause	%	50	21	21	7	0
Unfilled	Freq.	5		5	9	1
Pause	%	25		25	45	5
Break-	Freq.	5	5	18	3	3
down	%	15	15	53	9	9
Build-	Freq.	16	7	14	3	3
up	%	7	16	33	7	7

(Gestures counted more than once in the case of multiple speech disturbances.)

Table 11.6 shows the result of tallying the speech dysfluencies accompanying gestures in the sample. This table has two dimensions: (1) the type of dysfluency involved, using the categories of Chapter 9; and (2) the "fate" of the gesture. Of the latter there are five kinds:

a. *Gesture sustained* means that the gesture commences before the disturbance and is held in place without significant movement through it. For example,

```
| the same | as um  |
|  points   sustained |
```

b. *Gesture continued* mcans that a gesture commences before the disturbance and continues to cvolve through it. This is a dynamic version of sustension. For example,

```
|  so      uh    |
|  hand↑  ↑more  |
```

c. *New gesture* means that a gesture commences with the disturbance, either replacing an old gesture or emerging out of stasis, and continues beyond the disturbance. An example is:

```
Suppose you have | suppose you look at |
                 |  hand ↑ and back    |
```

in which a new gesture appears in the breakdown, *you have suppose you look at.*

d. *Unique gesture* also means that a new gesture occurs, but it occurs only during the disturbance. In contrast to the category of new gestures, therefore, unique gestures do not extend beyond the disturbance. For example,

means that 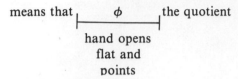 the quotient

e. *Relaxation* means that an already commenced gesture ceases, the hand falling to a rest position (to the lap, the arm of the chair, back to the chin, etc.).

Several findings are of interest in Table 11.6. First, nearly half of all gestures associated with unfilled pauses are unique. Conceivably some of these are associated with word finding problems, and the specificity of this function could explain the uniqueness.

Second, half the filled pause gestures are sustained. In other words, vocalization continues, despite a momentary lack of articulation, along with the sustaining of the gesture, possibly because both the gesture and the vocalization reflect control by the same speech program that is ongoing. Filled pauses are a strong cue in conversation, indicating that the speaker wishes to retain his speaking turn (Duncan & Fiske, 1977). The validity of this cue is explained if it relates to the continued control of speech programs.

Third, half the breakdown gestures are new. This is compared to only a seventh that are sustained. On the other hand, a third of the buildup gestures are sustained and another third are new. A breakdown involves changing concepts; hence there is a tendency for new gestures to appear (and there is a corresponding lack of any tendency to sustain old gestures). A buildup, in contrast, involves the addition of new concepts to old concepts that are maintained; hence there is a nearly equal tendency for gestures to be new or sustained.

The congruence of speech disturbances and the "fate" of the gestures that accompany them reinforces the claims of the model in Fig. 11.1. Even though the ecphoria process falters in the case of a dysfluency, the underlying structure of the syntagma and what is happening to it is reflected in the form of the gesture.

GESTURE PEAK

Figs. 11.6 through 11.9 show the relationship of the gesture peak of four gestures to concurrent speech. These can be added to Fig. 11.2, in which the gesture peak coincides with the focal point (the idea of an Entity) in *there's a*

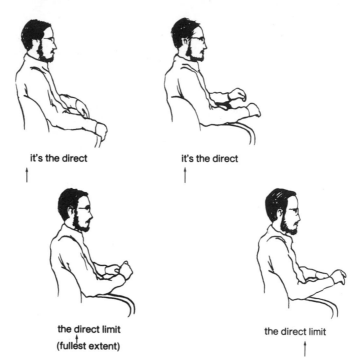

it's the direct

it's the direct

the direct limit
(fullest extent)

the direct limit

FIG. 11.6 Gesture accompanying *it's the direct limit.*

any complete

any complete

any complete
(fullest extent)

complete Noetherian

complete Noetherian

FIG. 11.7 Gesture accompanying *any complete Noetherian ring.*

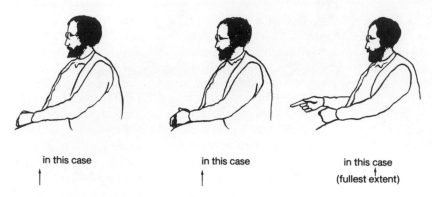

FIG. 11.8   Gesture accompanying *in this case.*

complete. The utterances in Figs. 11.6 and 11.7 (*it's the direct limit* and *any complete Noetherian ring,* respectively) have similar conceptual structures, and the gesture peak is at corresponding places in these examples. The conceptual structure consists of an Entity that contains the idea of Existence (*it, any*) related unidirectionally to a second Entity. The second Entity is further analyzed into the specific ideas of *direct limit* or *complete Noetherian ring.* (This is the same general structure as *there's a complete tensor product,* in Fig. 11.2.) The focal point of such a conceptual structure is the second Entity, and Fig. 11.6 shows the gesture peak occurring appropriately at the onset of the word *direct.* Similarly, in Fig. 11.7 it occurs at the onset of the word *complete.* (The definite article of *the direct limit* would not be the target of the gesture peak if the hand movement was timed to coincide with the stressed syllable of the focal point.) The pattern in Figs. 11.6 and 11.7 is thus comparable to that in the first half of Fig. 11.2.

The utterances in Figs. 11.8 and 11.9 (*in this case* and *over this topological ring,* respectively) have conceptual structures based on the idea of Location.

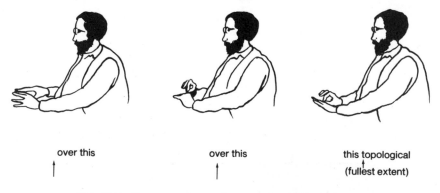

FIG. 11.9   Gesture accompanying *over this topological ring.*

In both, there is the idea of a Location that contains another idea of a Location related bidirectionally to the idea of an Entity. This Entity can in turn be analyzed into the idea of Existence (*this*) unidirectionally related to another Entity. The latter contains the specific idea of *case* or *topological ring*. (The Entity that contains *this* is thus comparable to the entire Entity involved in Figs. 11.2, 11.6, and 11.7.) The focal point of these utterances is just this larger Entity, *this case* and *this topological ring.* The gesture peak, however, does not coincide with the first word of this Entity (*this*), but with the principally stressed syllable within the conceptual focal point, namely *cáse* and *tópological.* Kendon (1972) also noted that the gesture peak tended to be synchronized with the point of the principal stress in prosodic phrases.

Table 11.7 contains data showing the extent of correspondence between gesture peaks and focal points. Gesture peaks were classified according to whether they occurred at, before, or after the vocalization of the conceptual focal point. The number of gestures is less than 500 for two reasons. Gestures that accompanied single words and gestures in which a gesture peak could not be recognized (e.g., the hand never ceased moving), have not been included. (A peak falling "at" the focal point means falling anywhere within the vocal expression of the focal point, but usually at the principally stressed syllable, insofar as this could be determined.)

Table 11.7 shows a strong tendency (70%) for the gesture peak to coincide with the focal point of the utterance. The situations represented in Figs. 11.2 and 11.6 through 11.9 are typical of the gestures in the sample. However, there is at the same time a substantial minority of cases (22%) where the gesture peak is reached before the focal point. (As the table shows, there are relatively few cases where it is reached after this point.) The gestures classified as "before" the focal point reach their peaks before any part of the vocal expression of the focal point has occurred. Insofar as the focal point may have been selected by the speaker in advance in programming the utterance, with the rest of the structure being constructed around this concept, some of these premature cases might reflect the real-time organization of the syntagma. For example, speaker R said at one point, "because they are already finite as modules," and performed a gesture in which the two fingers of the right hand were dropped into the supinated palm of the left hand, a gesture typically

TABLE 11.7
Gesture Peak and Focal Point

	Location of Gesture Peak		
	Before Focal Point	*At Focal Point*	*After Focal Point*
Frequency	36	114	14
Percentage	22	70	8

associated by R with the concept of a module. This gesture was initiated with the onset of *because* and peaked with the pronoun *they*. The focal point of the utterance, however, is the State, *finite as modules,* (the entire utterance is also a State), and this idea evidently affected the form of the gesture. In the context of the conversation, it is possible that this focal state had been organized by the speaker before articulating it, as the entire utterance is an s_1 produced after its s_2, and the gesture peak may have coincided with the moment of this organization. If we look at the context of all the gestures that peak in advance of the focal point, we find that half of the instances involve ideas of State, Existence, or Equation, which could plausibly have been organized in advance of articulation.

The general picture of the gesture peak is that gestures reach their fullest extent at the same moment that the conceptual focus of the utterance is articulated. This can be understood in terms of the model in Fig. 11.1. Due to semiotic extension, the focal point is represented within the syntagma, and can influence the motor programming of both output channels from a single source in the speech program (leading to stressed articulation and gesture peak). Thus, not only are the boundaries of syntagmata apparently represented by the synchronization of gestures, but at least one aspect of the internal syntagma structure seems to be represented as well.

FORM OF GESTURES

There are other, more subtle aspects of gestures that also appear to be related to the information structure of syntagmata. Some gestures are "iconic," in that the movements of the hands seem to depict the meaning of the corresponding words; an example was shown in Fig. 11.2 and another is the rotation of the hand in a stirring motion while saying "consisting," shown in Fig. 11.10. About 16% of the mathematicians' gestures are recognizably

consisting of

consisting of

FIG. 11.10   Gesture accompanying *consisting of.*

TABLE 11.8
Form of Gestures Associated with Certain Sensory-Motor Ideas

Sensory-Motor Representations	Pointing before Characterizing	Characterizing before Pointing	Probability
action	6	0	.016
state	0	5	.031
event	1	0	———

iconic in this way. (With highly technical material, of course, some iconic gestures may not have been recognized.) The model in Fig. 11.1, however, predicts a different level of form that can be related to meaning. Gestures, if they are pictures of action schemata, might re-enact this schema. This level of form is not a specific, lexically based iconic gesture such as depicted in Fig. 11.10. Instead, form at this level is based on the sensory-motor content of the syntagma. The two types of form, of course, lexical and sensory-motor-based, can co-occur in the same gesture, and other meaningful influences on the morphology of gestures can be anticipated as well. However, here it is the influence of the sensory-motor content that I wish to stress.

To search for gestures that could agree in form with sensory-motor content specifically, I have relied on what is admittedly a crude and limited index of form. It is, nonetheless, a gesture for which the argument can be made that it relates, in different ways, to different sensory-motor representations. This is the gesture of the hand or index finger in pointing as it combines with other gestures that characterize the sensory-motor content and that are made sequentially with it.

In the case of Events, a natural sequence for an English speaker seems to be for the pointing gesture to precede the characterizing gesture. This matches the direction of the Event schema, from the initial state to the new state. For example, if an event is closing a door, a natural sequence is to first point to the open door, then to simulate closing it. If the idea is that of State, on the other hand, a natural sequence seems to be for the characterizing gesture to come before the pointing gesture, probably because this blocks, reverses, or negates the direction of change. If a state is that a door is closed, a natural sequence is to first simulate something that is closed, then to point to the door.

Table 11.8 shows the distribution of the gestures of R and L that involved pointing and that were combined sequentially with other movements (presumed to be characterizing). With the critical ideas of Action and State (the idea of an Event is accompanied by a pointing movement only once), the form of the gesture corresponds to the sensory-motor content in the sense described above. The probabilities in the table are from the binomial expansion (for p = .5) and relate to the departure of the observed difference from a 50–50 split within each sensory-motor type between the two orders.

Considering the opposed pairs (Action–State), χ^2 gives a probability of p < .001.

COMPLEXITY

A hypothesis about the cause of gesturing holds that gestures tend to occur more often when the speech processing load becomes greater. This hypothesis is plausible at first glance, and may be correct for the sample of gestures described here if we index processing load by the internal complexity of sensory-motor segments. Table 11.9 shows the distribution of gestures that accompanied sensory-motor segments of different degrees of complexity, and also the frequency distribution of sensory-motor concepts not accompanied by gestures. To estimate this latter distribution, I have made a count of an additional sample of sensory-motor segments in the speech of speaker R where the speech was gesture-free. The processing load hypothesis can be tested by comparing this gesture-free distribution to the distribution with gestures. If increasing processing load stimulates gesturing, internally complex concepts should be relatively more frequent in the "with gesture" distribution than in the gesture-free distribution. At intermediate levels of complexity gestures are relatively more frequent (3.9%). The direction of the difference reverses and then vanishes at the highest levels, but the number of observations is relatively small.

SUMMARY

The AB model predicts that gestures correlate with syntagmata in time and form. In turn, this correlation suggests that gestures can be regarded as externalized traces of the internal speech programming process (ecphoria).

TABLE 11.9
Frequency Distribution of Internal Complexity of Sensory-Motor Concepts

	Number of Internal Concepts						
	1	2	3	4	5	6	*Total*
With Gestures							
Frequency	159	126	76	35	11	9	416
Percentage	38.2	30.3	18.3	8.4	2.6	2.2	
Not with Gestures							
Frequency	52	45	21	6	5	3	132
Percentage	39.4	34.1	15.9	4.5	3.8	2.2	
% (G) – % (Not G)	–1.2	–2.8	2.4	3.9	–1.2	0	

Entries based on only speaker R.

Analysis of the gestures that accompanied the utterances of two participants in a conversation showed the following:

1. The onset of gestures tends to coincide with the boundaries of sensory-motor segments in the concurrent speech. Gesture ends correlate less closely with these segments.

2. The peaks of gesture movement tend to coincide with the conceptual focal point of the corresponding strong component.

3. The morphology of gestures tends to be different corresponding to aspects of the meaning of the concurrent sensory-motor segments.

4. The internal complexity of the corresponding sensory-motor segments correlates with the probability that gestures occur, supporting the hypothesis that processing load is a stimulus to gesturing.

These results (especially the first 3) are taken as evidence for the AB model and for its extension to the generation of gestures.

IV

CONCLUSION

12 Processes, Goals, and Grammatical Systems

In this final chapter I want to introduce and briefly discuss two relationships that go beyond the account of the conceptual basis of language developed thus far. These are the relationships of sign processes to (1) the use of utterances and (2) grammatical systems. In a future publication I hope to treat these relationships at greater length.

PROCESS AND USE

An explanation of when and how utterances occur requires that we consider two main elements: the process by which utterances are constructed and the uses to which they are put. Knowing these elements, we can explain to some degree both how utterances come into being and the reasons for their doing so. The account of speech production developed in this book has emphasized the processes involved in the construction of utterances. I have applied the concept of sign structure and have attempted to describe, however roughly, the process of speech production as the formation of a network of interlocking signs. This account is incomplete in innumerable details but it is incomplete in the deeper sense that no aspect of the conceptual structure can be linked (as yet) to the speaker's ongoing mental life, especially his or her purposes and goals. No explanation is therefore yet possible for the occurrence of any particular conceptual structure, although once given a conceptual structure we can trace a path (schematically) that leads to the organization of speech output.

In terms of the theory of this book, if a speaker says, for example, *he is an Englishman; he is, therefore, brave,* (Grice, 1975, p. 44), an explanation can be proposed that describes the processes involved in terms of sensory-motor speech programs combined with the extension of these concepts to the rest of the conceptual content. To explain, in addition, why this utterance was said at all we should consider the speaker's purposes—for example, self-congratulation. The same vocalization could have been produced for a totally different purpose by another speaker (for example, one who wanted to be ironic).

It seems that, in general, a complementary relationship exists between the processes of speech and the speaker's goals and purposes. Rather than two distinct processes, a single process that is more autonomous at one end and more goal-oriented at the other should be proposed. A way of thinking about this relationship is to regard the utterance as a tool or instrument for reaching the speaker's goals.

In a recently translated work, Vygotsky (1978) describes tools as examples of indirect activities. An indirect activity is directed toward a goal but the activity is carried out not on the goal itself but on an intermediary. The intermediary then carries the activity onto the goal. The activity is indirect because it employs a tool to achieve some other goal. The use of a tool presupposes that it is integrable in some way into the goal-directed activity. For example, a simple manual tool such as a screwdriver is integrable into the same activity of rotating the screw as would be carried out, not using the tool, with the hands alone (except for the greater mechanical advantage of the screwdriver). The network of signs built up during speech production also is integrable into goal-directed nonspeech activity, and this integration is what we must try to understand in order to account for the interaction of speech processes with the speaker's goals. The integration of simple manual tools is often based on *continuity* between the direct and indirect activities. One performs roughly the same rotation of the hand with a screwdriver as one would perform without one. The same is true of many other uses of tools. The use of utterances to achieve the speaker's goals relies on a kind of continuity also, although it is a continuity at the level of concepts rather than of movements.

Two processes can be said to converge to produce conceptual structures. One is semiotic extension as already described, which provides the sign structure whereby the speaker can control his own articulation. The other is the form of representation in terms of which the speaker's thought processes take place. I suppose that these mental representations may take a variety of specific forms (such as images), but I will consider only one particularly powerful form discussed by Vygotsky (1962), namely, inner speech. By this term I do not mean talking to oneself. Inner speech is thinking which is carried out with verbally based categories of meaning. If the thinker also retrieves words or phrases from his mental dictionary corresponding to these categories of thought, there will be words or phrases carried along with the process of thinking, but this step is not an essential part of inner speech.

Inner speech provides the concepts and relations that enter into the conceptual structure of utterances. These concepts must be supplemented and related to sensory-motor content through semiotic extension. For example, a person may conceive in inner speech of a verbal concept such as Location. This nucleus becomes the basis around which the rest of the conceptual structure forms. It is the focal idea of the conceptual structure (corresponding to what Vygotsky, 1962, called the psychological predicate). The process of building up the rest of the conceptual structure around this idea may, in turn, demand further representations in terms of verbal categories from thought as the utterance takes form. An interaction often seems to develop between the processes of thought and speech. The convergence of inner speech (or other type of representation) and semiotic extension to form the conceptual structure of utterances is the basis of the continuity between goal-directed thought (which conceives of the goal) and goal-directed speech (the indirect or tool-mediated activity). In this way, a single process can be proposed that is more goal-directed at one end and more autonomous at the other.

Having established that the use of utterances as tools in indirect activities can be based on continuity through the conceptual structure of utterances, we can consider two situations in which utterances are not tools in this sense. In both these situations there is no tool use and utterances, rather than tools in indirect activities, are themselves the direct activities. These situations, however, are in other respects quite different. It is in fact curious that the minimally extended utterances of very young children, on the one hand, and utterances which contain explicit performative verbs (Austin, 1962), on the other hand, should both be direct activities. It is possible that culturally significant activities are given their own performative verbs in order to be performed directly rather than indirectly with speech, avoiding the use of speech as a tool in these cases. In very young children, utterances (e.g., *up*) are parts of ongoing nonspeech actions (e.g., climbing); such utterances appear to have the same goals as if they were nonspeech actions. Utterances are not (at this stage) necessarily the means to any other ends but are parts of the direct activities the child performs for their own sakes. In explicit performative utterances with performative verbs (e.g., *I promise you x*) speech is the primary activity in question. The goal of speaking is to produce the particular speech form and this performance *is* the intended activity. Saying the utterance (under the appropriate conditions for performing the activity) is nothing less than carrying out the activity (e.g., making a promise) directly. No semiotic extension occurs with explicit performative verbs because the goal (e.g., to bind oneself to some future action), represented as a verbal category in thought, is already identified with the meaning of an Action. The speaker can control his speech output straight away from his intention to perform this action. Activities in these cases require no instruments. The inseparability of action from speech in explicit performatives is explained by this analysis as well as the restriction of explicit performatives to the first person subjects.

Indirect speech acts, on the other hand, such as the performance of requests by asking questions (*may I ask you to move?*), are indirect activities and should be analyzed as arising from the same type of interaction between goals and speech processes (analogous to tools) as discussed above for nonperformative utterances. Davison (1975) describes a number of examples of the use of utterances to perform illocutionary acts indirectly. These uses are regulated in various ways to effect the continuity described above of the tool with the goal-directed activity. It is this regulation (in part) that makes indirect speech acts stand out as a class of utterances. For example, sentence adverbials such as *unfortunately* can occur in indirect statements which are phrased like questions, although they are banned from real questions (two of Davisons' examples are: *may I tell you that, unfortunately, our spy got caught?* and **do the anarchists, unfortunately, have any organization?*). This use of adverbials clearly indicates the continuity between the goal-directed activity of making a statement and the tool (in this case) of the question form. The question form in this use has a conceptual organization normally associated with statements. This treatment of indirect speech acts as indirect activities contrasts with the assumptions of abstract performative grammar (Ross, 1970), according to which every utterance includes a performative meaning and where the distinction between direct and indirect activity seems to be impossible to draw.

PROCESSES AND GRAMMATICAL SYSTEMS

In this section I intend to argue for a strong separation between what has been called competence and performance. I do not believe that it is possible to subsume grammatical descriptions under process descriptions or vice versa, or to put both under some third type of description. This cannot be done because process and grammatical descriptions have different purposes and different empirical domains. The relationships between them are less direct than has been supposed. Contrary to a current trend in linguistics and psycholinguistics, therefore, which is to incorporate linguistic descriptions somehow into cognitive psychology (e.g., Pylyshyn, 1973), I am led in the opposite direction. The two realms are to be kept apart. Confusion results when they are combined (and examples of such confusion are easy to find, some of which are described below).

The differences between production processes and grammatical systems can be best appreciated by comparing parallel analyses of the same sentence structures. There is no reason to doubt the validity of either analysis and it becomes clear that they relate to quite distinct empirical domains. Any direct connection we attempt to establish between them is artificial. When we add to the picture speech forms which cannot be analyzed in parallel ways, the impression of divergence is unavoidable. My plan of exposition is to consider, first, several areas where parallel analyses can be given in terms of processes and grammatical structure; then some forms where parallel analyses are not possible; and finally what can and cannot be said about the relationship of processes to grammatical systems.

Parallel Analyses

In Chapter 4 the principle of Kozhevnikov and Chistovich's was given according to which there can be only one sense indication of a given type in a single sense unit, or syntagma. A syntagma presupposes simultaneous instructions and so cannot have two identical instructions with different meanings. If two or more sense indications of a given type occur, different semiotic extensions of the same sensory-motor idea would have to take place, and these would be incompatible within the same speech program. A number of grammatical constraints can be viewed as having the function of avoiding this kind of problem for the speaker. In particular, the constraints discovered by Ross (1967) and called by him *the complex NP constraint, the coordinate structure constraint,* and *the left-branch constraint* appear to have this function. An analysis of the examples given by Ross to demonstrate these constraints in terms of grammatical form can be compared to the explanation of the same examples in terms of the effects they have on conceptual structures; and this comparison will provide the parallel analyses we need.

   The Complex NP Constraint.   This constraint permits generation of such sentences as *the hat which I believed that Otto was wearing is red,* the relative clause of which derives from *I believed that Otto was wearing this hat,* but blocks *the hat which I believed the claim that Otto was wearing is red,* the relative clause of which derives from *I believed the claim that Otto was wearing this hat.* The complex NP constraint (Ross, 1967, p. 70) states that nothing from an underlying sentence (S-node) that is dominated by a NP that has a lexical head N (e.g., *the claim* is the lexical head N of the NP dominating the S *Otto was wearing this hat*), can be removed from the NP (in the embedding of the relative clause, *this hat* is removed and placed at the front of the clause).

   From a conceptual point of view, *the claim that S* is a single concept, Entity. The complex NP constraint states that it cannot be disturbed if the transformation in question moves another occurrence of the same concept. Such a movement would violate the Kozhevnikov and Chistovich rule, because the same sense indication (Entity) would have to receive two expansions within a single speech program—Entity would have to be both *the claim that S* and *the hat which S* in this example. When there is not a lexical head noun, however, as in *I believed that S,* it so happens that only one expansion of Entity ever occurs—*the hat which S* in the example. The complex NP constraint therefore guarantees that Kozhevnikov and Chistovich's rule will not be violated during the formation of relative clauses. It permits using a single speech program. Its performance of this function explains the occurrence of the constraint.

Ross points out that if instead of a lexical head N there is the pronoun *it,* the complex NP constraint does not apply. Thus we can have *this is a hat which I'm going to see to it that my wife buys,* where the relative clause has derived from *I'm going to see to it that my wife buys this hat* by moving a part (*this hat*). To account for this exception, Ross incorporates into the complex NP constraint a specification (ad hoc) of the head noun that it must be lexical [+ lex]. The reason for this exception is easy to see in terms of conceptual function. The pronoun *it* in this situation is deictic, not anaphoric. There is, therefore, only a single Entity involved, *a hat which S.* Clearly, *it that S* is not an Entity or any other concept (unlike *the claim that S* in the earlier example). Moving the NP therefore does not violate the Kozhevnikov and Chistovich rule.

The complex NP constraint is expressed in terms of grammatical forms and the modifications that can be made of these forms. It states the properties of grammatical derivations that must be met. It does not express the functional reasons that can be given for the constraint such as those suggested above. This statement of the complex NP constraint in terms of grammatical form relates to one of the basic goals of linguistic analysis, namely to make explicit the sources of sentences within a grammatical framework. For example, given the complex NP constraint, it is possible to include among the sources of the sentence, *the hat which I believed that Otto was wearing is red,* the other sentence, *I believed that Otto was wearing this hat.* The performance processes of producing the relative clause, on the other hand, include expanding sense indications (sensory-motor segments) while at the same time avoiding, as required by the Kozhevnikov and Chistovich rule, nonsensical double expansions. Aiming for such conceptual coherence creates conditions within the grammatical system of English with complex NPs that are described by the complex NP constraint.

The Coordinate Structure Constraint.   This constraint prevents such odd constructions as **what table will he put the chair between and some sofa* from being formed out of *he will put the chair between the table and the sofa.* In this example an entire conjuct, *the table,* was moved forward to the front of the sentence following the rules of question formation. The coordinate structure constraint states that in a coordinate structure no conjunct or part of a conjunct may be moved from the position of the conjunct (Ross, 1967, p. 89).

A construction in whch just part of a conjunct is moved is *what does Henry play and sings madrigals,* which is formed out of *Henry plays the lute and sings madrigals* by moving the NP forward out of the conjunct *plays NP.* The same sense indications would have to have two different meanings in both these transformed sentences. The coordinate structure constraint, like the complex NP constraint, thus avoids a violation of the Kozhevnikov and Chistovich rule. In the first example, Entity would be expanded as both *what table* and as *some sofa,* whereas in the untransformed source there is a single Entity formed of the conjunction, *the table and the sofa.* In the second example, Entity would be expanded twice as *what does Henry play* and *madrigals,* whereas in the untransformed source sentence these Entities are contained in a single Event, *Henry plays the lute and sings madrigals.*

Ross discusses exceptions to the coordinate structure constraint, but these involve sentences where disregarding the constraint happens not to entail a single sense indication having two meanings. The following example uses *and* to convey the idea of a purpose: *here's the whiskey which I went to the store and bought.* This sentence derives from *I went to the store and bought some whiskey,* apparently violating the coordinate structure constraint. However, *and* in the source sentence does not conjoin like concepts. *I went to the store* is an Event at a Location, whereas *bought some whiskey* is the purpose of the Event and an Action; the purpose of the Event was to carry out this Action. A second sentence with the same purpose meaning brings out the Action content explicitly—*I went to the store to buy some whiskey.* Thus, the relative clause transformation in this situation does not require one sense indication to have two meanings and it could appear in a single speech program. In contrast, where the second conjunct is another Event, the coordinate structure constraint does apply, blocking *here's the whiskey which I went to the store and Mike bought* from being formed out of *I went to the store and Mike bought the whiskey.* Activities denoted with complex verbs such as *gone and ruined* and *try and find* are single sense indications of Action and can be moved around transformationally without requiring the same sense indication to have more than one meaning. Thus, there can be questions such as *which dress has she gone and ruined?* and *which book have you got to try and find?*

A third type of exception to the coordinate structure constraint is different from the others. These are sentences such as *Sally might be, and Sheila definitely is, pregnant,* which derives from *Sally might be pregnant and Sheila definitely is pregnant.* In this case, two identical sense indications (State) do in fact appear, and one is moved transformationally. The Kozhevnikov and Chistovich rule predicts that such an operation could not be performed within one speech program, and I believe this prediction is quite correct. The possible intonation patterns for this type of sentence suggest that multiple syntagmata are involved—for example, *Sally might be| and Sheila definitely is | pregnant #.* The Kozhevnikov and Chistovich rule explains why such an intonation pattern appears.

The coordinate structure constraint, like the complex NP constraint, can be seen to have the function of preventing constructions in which the same sense indication would have two or more expansions within a single syntagma. Where two expansions do occur, as in the last example, they need not be simultaneous because different syntagmata are involved.

The Left Branch Constraint.   This is one of several constraints which refer to the positions of constituents on the branches of structural trees. The left branch constraint states that when a NP is leftmost in a larger NP, it cannot be moved from this larger NP (Ross, 1967, p. 114). Because of this constraint the larger NP itself has to be moved. The left branch constraint, for example, blocks forming *which boy's did we elect guardian's employer president?* from *we elected the boy's guardian's employer president.* Such a derivation attempts to remove one NP (*the boy's*) from the larger NP of which it is the leftmost branch (*the boy's guardian's employer*). In a right branching tree, on the other hand, it is possible to form questions which move subordinate NPs. For example, from *we elected the employer of the guardian of the boy president,* one can derive *which boy did we elect the employer of the guardian of president?* and *which guardian of the boy did we elect the employer of president?* by respectively moving *the boy* and *the guardian of the boy.*

To explain the left branch constraint in terms of the Kozhevnikov and Chistovich rule, we can note the following difference between left and right branching structures. In the left branching sentence (*the boy's guardian's employer*), each higher constituent is like the constituent it contains. Thus $NP_1 = NP_2$ (*the boy's guardian's*) + N (*employer*); and $NP_2 = NP_3$ (*the boy's*) + N (*guardian's*). In the right branching structure, however, each higher constituent is different from the one that it contains; thus $NP_1 = NP$ (*the employer*) + NP_2; $NP_2 = P$ (*of*) + NP_3; $NP_3 = NP$ (*the guardian*) + NP_4; $NP_4 = P$ (*of*) + NP_5; and $NP_5 = $ *the boy.* If we assume that sense indications differ where constituents are different,[1] the Kozhevnikov and Chistovich rule would allow speech programs to include different simultaneous indications for *the boy* and for *the employer of the guardian of* to produce *which boy did we elect the employer of the guardian of president?* However, it would block simultaneous sense indications corresponding to the same symbol in *the boy's guardian's employer* and prevent deriving *which boy's did we elect guardian's employer president?*

---

[1]One such difference is the following: NP by itself corresponds to Person in these examples, whereas NP + P corresponds to Person *possessed-by.* The motor programs controlled by these sense indications are plausibly different, because in the latter sense indication the relation must be lexicalized as well as the concept. Thus Person *possessed-by* could be expanded simultaneously with Person.

The left branch constraint can be understood as guaranteeing that the Kozhevnikov and Chistovich rule will be met in sentences which have chains of NPs. It permits producing such chains with single speech programs. It is comparable to the complex NP and coordinate structure constraints in terms of function. Avoiding nonsensical multiple expansions of the same sense indication produces structures involving NP chains which obey the left branch constraint.

Grammatical and Performance Analyses.   In the three cases of parallel analyses that I have presented, the Ross grammatical constraints refer to situations in which there is a potential for the same sense indication to have more than one meaning. The grammar determines these places. The Kozhevnikov and Chistovich rule, in turn, forbids the same sense indication from having more than one meaning; it does so for a reason that has nothing to do with the grammar of the language. It is not surprising that the grammatical forms of a language should be systematically organized toward meeting the Kozhevnikov and Chistovich rule. However, it would be a mistake to conclude from this relationship that the Ross constraints are nothing but the Kozhevnikov and Chistovich rule in a different guise. The Ross constraints and the Kozhevnikov and Chistovich rule refer to different empirical domains—one a framework in which sentences are interrelated and derived from source sentences, and the other a conceptual structure in which coherence must be maintained during speech programming. It is for this reason that the same processing rule has quite different effects on the grammatical structure, depending on the other parts of the framework that are involved. Each of the Ross constraints describes one specific effect within a different region of the grammatical structure of avoiding conceptual incoherence.

Nonparallel Analyses

A number of examples were given in Chapters 9 and 11 in which the predominant segmentation in the speech output conflicted with a grammatical segmentation of the same sentences. In such examples it cannot be said that there is, as has been supposed in nearly all psycholinguistics and linguistics, a strong equivalence between the grammatical description and the processing steps. There is, at most, a weak equivalence. Strong equivalence requires that the structures defined by the grammatical description for a given string of words and the structures produced in the speech process should be the same, whereas weak equivalence requires only that the strings of words themselves should be the same. In all of these cases some words are produced with grammatical constituents of which they are not directly a part. Prepositions are produced with the preceding nonprepositional phrase more often than with the NP of the prepositional phrase itself; articles are more often produced with the preceding non-NP than with the following N; transitive verbs are more often produced with the preceding subject than with the following object NP; *that* and *to* in complements are more often produced with the preceding main clause than with the following sentence of which they are a part. When these patterns occur it is probably because the speaker momentarily is unable to find a lexical item. A production process evidently then exists by which the speaker can combine elements that are not parts of the same constituents according to a grammatical description.

As an example of this discrepancy I will take the production of transitive verbs. When a speaker cannot immediately recover the word for the direct object or for some other reason does not organize a constituent after the verb, he still can program the verb with the NP subject and separately produce the NP object of the VP. This pattern radically disrupts the sentence constituent structure. In Fig 12.1, I have prepared two simple grammars (expressed in arbitrary notation), one of which, G_1, corresponds to the (S) (VO) structure of English sentences with transitive verbs. The other, G_2, directly generates structures of the (SV) (O) type that are observed so frequently. However, G_2 is incorrect for English, as is clear from many conflicts between it and other grammatical structures. For example, if the structure of a sentence is (*Bill ate*) (*seven oysters*), the passive formed out of this should be *(*seven oysters*) *were* (*Bill eaten*); the *to*-complement should be *it was decided for* (*Bill eats*) *to* (*seven oysters*), and so forth. A reformulation of the constitutent structure

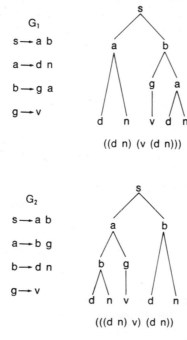

FIG. 12.1   Alternative grammars producing the same strings of symbols but different grammatical structures.

along the lines of G_2, although generating (SV) (O) directly, conflicts with the rest of the grammatical structure of English.

Moreover, such a reformulation would miss the point, for grammatical descriptions are not concerned with the processes of speakers' generating sentences. Grammars focus on the interrelation of sentences, particularly the derivation of sentences from source sentences. The best framework for this, as judged in terms of economy of rules, generality, and esthetic criteria, is by definition the grammatical structure of language. The speaker's production processes are not part of this description.

The Place of Grammar in a Theory of Performance

The separation of process descriptions and grammatical descriptions for which I have been arguing can be carried only so far. Now we must be concerned to find relationships between the two insofar as this is possible. I will begin, however, with what I think cannot be said of these relationships.

The view that has been prevalent in linguistics and psycholinguistics for 15 years or so I will call the Miller–Chomsky requirement, after its first authors (Miller & Chomsky, 1963). This view holds that a strong equivalence should exist between grammatical descriptions and performance descriptions of the same sentences. That is, the processes of sentence comprehension and production should produce the same structural descriptions (trees and transformational structures) as the grammar assigns to the same sentences. They write,

> We require...that M [a finite performance device] assign a structural description $F_i(x)$ to x only if the generative grammar G stored in the memory of M assigns $F_i(x)$ to x as a possible structural description [p. 466].

As we have seen, the requirement of strong equivalence is too strong for many utterances, and these utterances cannot be explained if we hold to the Miller–Chomsky requirement. At best, in these cases, there is a weak equivalence.

Nonetheless, the Miller–Chomsky requirement of a strong equivalence has been widely accepted as the standard for psycholinguistic theorizing and experimentation.[2] The same view is stated, for example, by Fodor, Bever and Garrett (1974) in the following passage:

> There are thus intimate logical relations between an optimal grammar and a model of an ideal sentence recognizer for the language the grammar describes.

---

[2]In an earlier paper on this subject (McNeill, 1975b) I mistakenly attributed acceptance of the Miller–Chomsky requirement to Watt (1970). He has kindly pointed out my error and I am happy to correct it now.

Since the latter device assigns each utterance one of the structural descriptions
that the former device generates, the output of the optimal grammar constrains
the output of the ideal sentence recognizer [p. 277].

Despite extensive changes in theoretical models over the years, the
Miller–Chomsky requirement has not been abandoned. For example, in the
early kernelization hypothesis (Miller, 1962), transformed sentences are said
to be understood by reducing them to their non–transformed sources
(kernels). In the later clausal hypothesis (Fodor, et al., 1974), sentences are
said to be understood by relating them to the internal clauses that are the
sources of sentences according to the later version of transformational
grammar assumed by Fodor, et al. The same requirement has guided
experimental investigations that do not proceed from a basis in transformational grammar. Clark and Chase (1972), for example, assume that during
comprehension negative sentences are reduced to their positive counterparts
with the predicate False attached.

The working assumption has been that, at some level of processing, the
interrelationships shown in a grammatical description of sentences (syntactic,
semantic, logical, and so forth) also appear as the steps of the processes of
producing or comprehending the sentences. If one is understanding or saying
a passive sentence, for example, then at some level the corresponding active
sentence must also appear, even though it is not the sentence being
understood or said (according to one type of grammatical description).
Similarly, underlying clauses are assumed to be the end–points of speech
understanding. This hypothetical level of the source sentence exists for no
other reason than to meet the Miller–Chomsky requirement of strong
equivalence. The grammar is concerned with the interrelationships of
sentences. According to the Miller–Chomsky requirement, so is the
psychological model.

In recent writings on the topic of competence and performance, this
requirement has appeared in an expanded and still more ambitious role. It has
become a rationale for regarding language as a window onto the mind.
Pylyshyn (1973), for example, writes,

...the development of a more general theory of cognition should proceed by
attempting to account for the structure which is the output of a competence
theory, together with other kinds of psychological evidence, rather than to
incorporate the competence theory as formulated [pp. 45–46].

Miller (1975), quoting this same passage, adds with his usual clarity, "My own
version of this insight was that a linguistic theory of competence is not a
component of but an *abstraction from* the cognitive theory that I wanted [p.
204]." According to Miller's and Pylyshyn's view, one can gain a picture of

cognitive functioning from the structures which are shown in grammatical descriptions. However, when one examines actual examples, as we did in the parallel analyses of the Ross constraints, there are no such psychological connections to be seen. The grammatical and process descriptions are indeed parallel and on lines that do not meet. Nothing is gained if one somehow tries to make one incorporate the other.

If we want to avoid the restrictiveness of the Miller–Chomsky requirement of strong equivalence, we can try stating the relationship between grammatical and process descriptions in the following way, which seems to express the relationship between the Ross constraints and the Kozhevnikov and Chistovich rule:

> The grammatical interrelationships of sentences can take any form that does not impose nonsensical conceptual combinations.

The grammatical framework within which sentences are interrelated is the outcome of historical, institutional, social, psychological and other factors. The organization of this framework will create different responses at various places to the same psychological function. The response of English to the Kozhevnikov and Chistovich rule takes at least the three different forms described in the Ross constraints. Speakers, however, operating in a completely different sphere, are only trying to achieve mental coherence as they program speech output. Nothing in the speech process corresponds directly to the Ross constraints. These constraints emerge only when we consider the grammar as a whole.

I wish to maintain a realist position regarding grammatical descriptions, even though I reject the view that grammars are idealizations of psychological processes. Grammars can be regarded as more than mere formal arrangements of linguistic intuitions (cf. Bever, 1970). They refer to real structures, although not to psychologically real structures in a processing sense. (A recent paper by Sober, n.d., contains a useful definition of psychological reality in this sense as a mental representation which both expresses grammatical rules and plays a causative role in determining the behavior and cognitive activity of the language user.) Along with many others (Sapir, 1949), I will suggest that a grammar is a description of our *knowledge of a social institution*—the language—and because of this basis in social or institutional reality, rather than in cognitive functioning, grammars and psychological processes have no more than the loose relationships they appear, in fact, to have. The role of grammar during speech programming is analogous to the role of other social institutions during individual behavior. This role is to define and evaluate the behavior of individuals. It is not to cause the behavior. Analogies with other kinds of individual behavior cannot be pressed far, because the behaviors in question are totally different, but in common with knowledge of language, knowledge of the economic system, of driving practices, of family roles, and so forth supply the values and intuitions by which individual practices are judged. This fact helps explain the principal method by which grammars are in fact discovered in linguistic analyses: They are constructed on the basis of intuitions to codify the knowledge (values) by which speech practices (such as sentences) are judged. The resulting grammar describes a social institution, or language. It does not describe (however ideally or abstractly) the cognitive functioning of individual language users.

References

Abrams, K. & Bever, T. Syntactic structure modifies attention during speech perception and recognition. *Quarterly Journal of Experimental Psychology,* 1969, *21,* 280–290.

Anderson, J. R. & Bower, G. H. *Human associative memory.* Washington, D. C.: Hemisphere, 1973.

Austin, J. L. *How to do things with words.* Oxford: Oxford University Press, 1962.

Baars, B. J. & Motley, M. T. Spoonerisms as sequencer conflicts: Evidence from artificially elicited errors. *American Journal of Psychology,* 1976, *89,* 467–484.

Bennett, D. C. Some observations concerning the locative-directional distinction. *Semiotica,* 1972, *5,* 58–88.

Bernstein, N. A. *The co-ordination and regulation of movements.* Oxford: Pergamon, 1967.

Bever, T. G., Lackner, J. R. & Kirk, R. The underlying structures of sentences are the primary units of immediate speech perception. *Perception and Psychophysics,* 1969, *5,* 225–234.

Bever, T. G. The cognitive basis for linguistic structures. In J. R. Hayes (Ed.), *Cognition and the Development of language.* New York: John Wiley & Sons, 1970.

Bloom, L. *One word at a time.* The Hague: Mouton, 1973.

Bloom, L., Lightbown, P. & Hood, L. Structure and variation in child language. *Monographs of the Society for Research in Child Development,* 1975, *40*(2), serial no. 160.

Bolinger, D. Accent is predictable (if you're a mind reader). *Language, 48,* 1972, 633–644.

Boomer, D. S. Review of F. Goldman-Eisler *Psycholinguistics: Experiments in spontaneous speech. Lingua,* 1970, *25,* 152–164.

Brown, R. *A first language: the early stages.* Cambridge, Mass.: Harvard University Press, 1973.

Chapin, G., Smith, T. S. & Abrahamson, A. A. Two factors in perceptual segmentation of speech. *Journal of Verbal Learning and Verbal Behavior,* 1972, *11,* 164–173.

Chomsky, C. *The acquisition of syntax in children from 5 to 10.* Cambridge, Mass.: The M.I.T. Press, 1969.

Chomsky, N. *Syntactic structures.* The Hague: Mouton, 1957.

Chomsky, N. *Aspects of the theory of syntax.* Cambridge, Mass. The M.I.T. Press, 1965.

Chomsky, N. & Halle, M. *The sound pattern of English.* New York: Harper & Row, 1968.

Clark, H. H. & Chase, W. W. On the process of comparing sentences against pictures. *Cognitive Psychology,* 1972, *3,* 472–517.

295

Cohen, J. A. A coefficient of agreement for nominal scales. *Education and Psychological Measurement*, 1960, *20*, 37–46.

Cromer, R. *The development of temporal references during the acquisition of language.* Unpublished doctoral dissertation, Harvard University, 1968.

Cruttenden, A. A phonetic study of babbling. *British Journal of Disorders of Communication*, 1970, *5*, 110–117.

Curme, G. *Syntax.* New York: D. C. Heath, 1931.

Danks, J. H. Producing ideas and sentences. In S. Rosenberg (Ed.), *Sentence production: Development in research and theory.* Hillsdale, N.J.: Lawrence Erlbaum Associates, 1977.

Davison, A. Indirect speech acts and what to do with them. In P. Cole and J. L. Morgan (Eds.), *Syntax and semantics, Vol. 3: Speech acts.* New York: Seminar Press, 1975.

Duncan, S., Jr. & Fiske, D. W. *Face to face interaction: Research, methods and theory.* Hillsdale, N.J.: Lawrence Erlbaum Associates, 1977.

Efron, D. *Gesture and environment; A tentative study of some of the spatio-temporal and "linguistic" aspects of the gestural behavior of eastern Jews and southern Italians in New York City, living under similar as well as differnt environmental conditions.* New York: King's Crown Press, 1941.

Ehlich, K. Anaphor and deixis: parallelity–identity–difference? Paper given at a conference on Deixis and speech production, Nijmegen, The Netherlands, 1978.

Ekman, P. & Friesen, W. The repertoire of nonverbal behavior categories. Origins, usage, and coding. *Semiotica*, 1969, *1*, 49–98.

Faile, N. F., Jr. *Correspondence of behavior planning segments, conceptual chunks and phonological phrases in spontaneous speech.* Unpublished doctoral dissertation, Pennsylvania State University, 1972,

Fillmore, C. J. The case for case. In E. Bach & R. T. Harms (Eds.), *Universals of linguistic theory.* New York: Holt, Rinehart & Winston, 1968.

Fodor, J. A. & Bever, T. G. The psychological reality of linguistic segments. *Journal of Verbal Learning and Verbal Behavior*, 1965, *4*, 414–420.

Fodor, J. A., Bever, T. G. & Garrett, M. F. *The psychology of language: an introduction to psycholinguistics and generative grammar.* New York: McGraw-Hill, 1974.

Fromkin, V. A. The non-anomalous nature of anomalous utterances. *Language*, 1971, *47*, 27–52.

Garrett, M. F. The analysis of sentence production. In G. Brown (Ed.), *Psychology of learning and motivation Vol. 9.* New York: Academic Press, 1975.

Garrett, M. F. Syntactic processes in sentence production. In R. J. Wales & E. Walker (Eds.), *New approaches to language mechanisms.* Amsterdam: North-Holland, 1976.

Goldin-Meadow, S. *The representation of semantic relations in a manual language created by deaf children of hearing parents: A language you can't dismiss out of hand.* Unpublished doctoral dissertation, Univesity of Pennsylvania, 1975.

Goldman-Eisler, F. *Psycholinguistics: Experiments in spontaneous speech.* New York: Academic Press, 1968.

Gough, P. B. The verification of sentences: The effects of delay of evidence and sentence length. *Journal of Verbal Learning and Verbal Behavior*, 1966, *5*, 492–496.

Greenberg, J. H. Some universals of grammar with particular reference to the order of meaningful elements. In J. H. Greenberg (Ed.), *Universals of language.* Cambridge, Mass.: The M.I.T. Press, 1963.

Greene, J. Syntactic form and semantic function. *Quarterly Journal of Exprimental Psychology*, 1970, *22*, 14–27.

Greene, J. *Psycholinguistics: Chomsky and psychology.* Baltimore: Penguin, 1972.

Greene, P. Problems of organization of motor systems. In R. Rosen & F. M. Snell (Eds.), *Progress in theoretical biology Vol. II.* New York: Academic Press, 1972.

Greene, P. *Coordination of effectors and transfer of adaptation. (Memo No. 15).* Chicago, Institute for Task Analysis, 1973.

Greenfield, P. M. & Smith, J. H. *The structure of communication in early language development.* New York: Academic Press, 1976.

Grice, H. P. William James Lectures, Harvard University, 1967. Published in part as "Logic and conversation." In P. Cole & J. L. Morgan (Eds.), *Syntax and semantics Vol. III: Speech acts.* New York: Seminar Press, 1975.

Halliday, M. A. K. Notes on transitivity and theme in English: I. *Journal of Linguistics,* 1967, 3, 37-81. (a)

Halliday, M. A. K. Notes on transitivity and theme in English: II. *Journal of Linguistics,* 1967, 3, 199-244. (b)

Harary, F., Norman, R. Z., & Cartwright, D. *Structural models: An introduction to the theory of directed graphs.* New York: John Wiley & Sons, 1965.

Harris, J. *Levels of speech processing and order of information.* Unpublished doctoral dissertation, University of Chicago, 1978.

Harrison, B. *Meaning and structure.* New York: Harper & Row, 1972.

Henderson, A., Goldman-Eisler, F. & Skarbeck, A. Sequential temporal patterns in spontaneous speech. *Language and Speech,* 1966, *9,* 207-216.

Hornby, P. A. The psychological subject and predicate. *Cognitive Psychology,* 1972, *3,* 632-642.

Ingram, D. Fronting in child phonology. *Journal of Child Language,* 1974, *1,* 233-241.

Jaffe, J. & Feldstein, S. *Rhythms of dialogue.* New York: Academic Press, 1970.

Jakobson, R. *Child language, aphasia and phonological universals.* The Hague: Mouton, 1968.

James, W. *The principles of psychology.* New York: H. Holt and Co., 1890.

Jarvella, R. J. Syntactic processing of connected speech. *Journal of Verbal Learning and Verbal Behavior,* 1971, *10,* 409-416.

Jarvella, R. J. & Herman, S. J. Clause structure and speech processing. *Perception and Psychophysics,* 1972, *11,* 381-384.

Johnson, S. C. Hierarchical clustering schemes. *Psychometrika,* 1967, *32,* 241-254.

Kempen, G. On conceptualizing and formulating in sentence production. In S. Rosenberg (Ed.), *Sentence production: Development in research and theory.* Hillsdale, N.J.: Lawrence Erlbaum Associates, 1977.

Kendon, A. Some relationships between body motion and speech. An analysis of an example. In A. Siegman & B. Pope (Eds.), *Studies in dyadic communication.* New York: Pergamon, 1972.

Kintsch, W. Notes on the structure of semantic memory. In E. Tulving & W. Donaldson (Eds.), *Organization of memory.* New York: Academic Press, 1972.

Kozhevnikov, V. A. & Chistovich, L. A. *Speech: articulation, and perception.* Washington, D. C.: U. S. Department of Commerce, Joint Publication Research Service, 1965.

Lackner, J. R. & Tuller, B. The influence of syntactic segmentation on perceived stress. *Cognition,* 1976, *4,* 303-307.

Lakoff, G. Linguistic gestalt. *Papers from the 13th Regional Meeting of the Chicago Linguistic Society,* 1977.

Lakoff, R. Passive resistance. *Papers from the 7th Regional meeting of the Chicago Linguistic Society,* 1971.

Lashley, K. S. The problem of serial order in behavior. In L. A. Jeffress (Ed.), *Cerebral mechanisms in behavior.* New York: John Wiley & Sons, 1951.

Leech, G. *Towards a semantic description of English.* London: Langman, 1969.

Lehiste, I. *Suprasegmentals.* Cambridge, Mass.: The M.I.T. Press, 1970.

Lenneberg, E. H. *Biological foundations of language.* New York: John Wiley & Sons, 1967.

Levelt, W. J. M. Hierarchical clustering alogrithm in the psychology of grammar. In G. B. Flores d'Arcais & W. J. M. Levelt (Eds.), *Advances in psycholinguistics.* Amsterdam: North-Holland, 1970. (a)

Levelt, W. J. M. Hierarchical clustering in sentence processing. *Perception and Psychophysics,* 1970, *8,* 99-102. (b)

Levelt, W. J. M. *Formal grammars in linguistics and psycholinguistics: Psycholinguistics applications Vol. III.* The Hague: Mouton, 1974.

Lewis, M. M. *Infant speech: A study of the beginnings of language.* New York: Harcourt, Brace, 1936. Reprint: Arno Press, 1975.

Lieberman, P. *Intonation, perception, and language.* Cambridge, Mass.: The M.I.T. Press, 1967.

Lindig, K. D. *Contextual factors in shadowing connected discourse.* Unpublished doctoral dissertation, University of Chicago, 1976.

Lindsley, J. R. Producing simple utterances: How far ahead do we plan? *Cognitive Psychology,* 1975, *7,* 1–19.

Lindsley, J. R. Producing simple utterances: Details of the planning process. *Journal of Psycholinguistic Research,* 1976, *5,* 331–354.

Lyons, J. *Introduction to theoretical linguistics.* Cambridge: Cambridge University Press, 1968.

MacKay, D. G. Spoonerisms: The structure of errors in the serial order of speech. *Neuropsychologia,* 1970, *8,* 323–350.

MacNeilage, P. *Linguistic units and speech production.* Presented at the 85th Meeting of the Acoustical Society of America, Boston, Mass., April 13, 1973.

Marslen-Wilson, W. Linguistic structure and speech shadowing at very short latencies. *Nature,* 1973, *244,* 522–523.

Marslen-Wilson, W. Sentence perception as an interactive parrallel process. *Science,* 1975, *189,* 226–227.

Marslen-Wilson, W. & Teuber, H. L. Memory for remote events in anterograde amnesia: recognition of public figures from newsphotographs. *Neuropsychologia,* 1975, *13,* 353–364.

Marslen-Wilson, W., Tyler, L., & Seidenberg, M. Sentence processing at the clause boundary. In W. J. M. Levelt & G. Flores D'Arcais (Eds.), *Studies in the perception of language.* London: John Wiley & Sons, in press.

Martin, E. Toward an analysis of subjective phrase structure. *Psychological Bulletin,* 1970, *74,* 153–166.

McMahon, L. *Grammatical analysis as part of understanding a sentence.* Unpublished doctoral dissertation, Harvard University, 1963.

McNeill, D. Semiotic extension. In R. Solso (Ed.), *Information processing and cognition-The Loyola Symposium.* Hillsdale, N.J.: Lawrence Erlbaum Associates, 1975. (a)

McNeill, D. The place of grammar in a theory of performance. In D. Aaronson & R. Rieber (Eds.), *Developmental psycholinguistics and communication disorders.* New York: New York Academy of Sciences, 1975. (b)

Mehler, J. Some effects of grammatical transformations on the recall of English sentences. *Journal of Verbal Learning and Verbal Behavior,* 1963, *2,* 346–351.

Menn, L. On the origin and growth of phonological and syntactic rules. *Papers from the 9th Regional Meeting of the Chicago Linguistic Society,* 1973, 378–385.

Miller, G. A. Some psychological studies of grammar. *American Psychologist,* 1962, *17,* 748–762.

Miller, G. A. A psychological method to investigate verbal concepts. *Journal of Mathematical Psychology,* 1969, *6,* 169–191.

Miller, G. A. Some comments on competence. In D. Aaronson & R. Rieber (Eds). *Developmental psycholinguistics and communication disorders.* New York: New York Academy of Sciences, 1975.

Miller, G. A. & Chomsky, N. Finitary models of language users. In R. D. Luce, R. R. Bush, & E. Galanter (Eds.), *Handbook of mathematical psychology Vol. II.* New York: John Wiley & Sons, 1963.

Miller, G. A. & Johnson-Laird, P. *Language and perception.* Cambridge, Mass.: Harvard University Press, 1976.

Miller, G. A. & McKean, K. E. A chronometric study of some relations between sentences. *Quarterly Journal of Experimental Psychology,* 1964, *16,* 297–308.

Ohala, J. *Aspects of the control and production of speech.* Unpublished doctoral dissertation, University of California at Los Angeles, 1970.

Peirce, C. S. *The collected works of Charles Sanders Peirce.* (C. Hartshorne & P. Weiss, Eds.), Cambridge, Mass.: Harvard University Press, 1931–1958.

Peters, S. & Bach, E. Pseudo-cleft sentences. In *On the theory of transformational grammar.* Report to National Science Foundation. Austin, Texas: University of Texas, 1971.

Piaget, J. *The origins of intelligence in children.* New York: International Universities Press, 1952.

Piaget, J. *The construction of reality in the child.* New York: Basic Books, 1954.

Piaget, J. *The child's conception of the world.* Totowa, N.J. Littlefield, Adams, 1960.

Piaget, J. *Play, dreams, and imitation in childhood.* New York: Basic Books, 1962.

Piaget, J. *The child's conception of physical causality.* Totowa, N. J.: Littlefield-Adams, 1969.

Piaget, J. & Inhelder, B. *The psychology of the child.* New York: Basic Books, 1969.

Potts, M., Carlson, P., Cocking, R., & Copple, C. *Language production in preschool children.* Ithaca, New York: Cornell University Press, in press.

Premack, D. *Intelligence in ape and man.* Hillsdale, N.J.: Lawrence Erlbaum Associates, 1976.

Price, H. H. *Thinking and experience.* London: Hutchinson University Library, 1953.

Pylyshyn, Z. W. What the mind's eye tells the mind's brain: A critique of mental imagery. *Psychological Bulletin,* 1973, *80,* 1–24.

Reichenbach, H. *Elements of symbolic logic.* New York: Macmillan, 1947.

Rochester, S. R. The significance of pauses in spontaneous speech. *Journal of psychological Research,* 1973, *2,* 51–81.

Rodgon, M. M. *Single-word usage, cognitive development and the beginning of combinatorial speech.* Cambridge: Cambridge University Press, 1976.

Rodgon, M. M., Jankowski, W., & Alenskas, L. A multi-functional approach to single-word usage. *Journal of Child Language,* 1977, *4,* 23–43.

Rosenbaum, P. S. *The grammar of English predicate complement constructions.* Cambridge, Mass.: The M.I.T. Press, 1967.

Ross, J. R. *Constraints on variables in syntax.* Unpublished doctoral dissertation, M.I.T., 1967.

Ross, J. R. On declarative sentences. In R. A. Jacobs & P. S. Rosenbaum (Eds.), *Readings in English transformational grammar.* Waltham, Mass.: Ginn, 1970.

Rummelhart, D. E., Lindsley, P. H., & Norman, D. A. A process model for long-term memory. In E. Tulving & W. Donaldson (Eds.), *Organization of memory.* New York: Academic Press, 1972.

Sankoff, G. & Brown, D. *On the origins of syntax in discourse: A case study of Tok Pisin relatives.* Unpublished paper, Université de Montréal, 1976.

Sapir, E. *Language, an introduction to the study of speech.* New York: Hartcourt, Brace and World, 1949.

Savin, H. & Perchonock, E. Grammatical structure and the immediate recall of English sentences. *Journal of Verbal Learning and Verbal Behavior,* 1965, *4,* 343–353.

Schank, R. C. Cognitive dependency: A theory of natural language understanding. *Cognitive Psychology,* 1972, *11,* 296–309.

Scoville, W. B. & Milner, B. Loss of recent memory after bilateral hippocampal lesions. *Journal of Neurological Psychiatry,* 1957, *20,* 11–21.

Silverstein, M. Shifters, linguistic categories, and cultural description. In H. Basso & H. H. Selby (Eds.), *Meaning in anthropology.* Albuquerque, N.M.: University of New Mexico Press, 1976.

Sinclair-deZwart, H. *Acquisition du langage et développement de la pensée.* Paris: Dunod, 1967.

Sinclair-deZwart, H. Language acquisition and cognitive development. In T. E. Moore (Ed.), *Cognitive development and the acquisition of language.* New York: Academic Press, 1973.

Slobin, D. I. Grammatical transformations and sentence comprehension in childhood and adulthood. *Journal of Verbal Learning and Verbal Behavior,* 1966, *5,* 219–227.

Slobin, D. I. Cognitive prerequisties for the development of grammar. In D. I. Slobin & C. A. Ferguson (Eds.), *Studies in child language development.* New York: Holt, Rinehart & Winston, 1973.

Slobin, D. I. *Universal and particular in the acquisition of language.* Unpublished paper, The Department of Psychology , University of California, Berkeley, 1978.

Snow, C. E. Mother's speech to children learning language. *Child Development,* 1972, *43,* 549–565.

Sober, E. The psychological reality of grammar. Unpublished paper. Department of Philosophy, University of Wisconsin, Madison.

Taylor, I. Content and structure in sentence production. *Journal of Verbal Learning and Verbal Behavior,* 1969, *8,* 170–175.

Terbeek. D., Fenwick, K. & Grossman, R. *Hierarchical clustering of sentence relationships.* Unpublished paper, University of Chicago, in preparation.

Terkel, L. *Hard times: An oral history of the great depression (by Studs Terkel).* New York: Pantheon Books, 1970.

Trager, G. L. & Smith, H. L. *Outline of English structure.* Norman, Ok.: Battenburg Press, 1951.

Turvey, M. T. Preliminaries to a theory of action with references to vision. In *Status Report on Speech Research (Jan.–March, 1975).* New Haven, Conn.: Haskins Laboratory, SR–41, 1975.

Tyler, L. K. *Aspects of the structure of sentence processing.* Unpublished doctoral dissertation, University of Chicago, 1977.

von Wright, G. H. *Norm and action.* New York: Humanities Press, 1963.

von Wright, G. H. And next. *Acta Philosophica Fennica,* Fasc. *18,* 1965, 293–304.

Vygotsky, L. S. *Thought and language.* Cambridge, Mass.: The M.I.T. Press, 1962.

Vygotsky, L. S. *Mind and society: The development of higher psychological processes.* Cambridge, Mass.: Harvard University Press, 1978.

Wason, P. C. The contexts of plausible denial. *Journal of Verbal Learning and Verbal Behavior,* 1965, *4,* 7–11.

Wason, P. C. & Johnson-Laird, P. *Psychology of reasoning.* Cambridge, Mass.: Harvard University press, 1972.

Watt, W. On two hypotheses concerning psycholinguistics. In J. R. Hayes (Ed.), *Cognition and the development of language.* New York: John Wiley & Sons, 1970.

Weir, R. H. Questions on the learning of phonology. In F. Smith & G. A. Miller (Eds.), *The genesis of language: A psycholinguistic approach.* Cambridge, Mass.: The M.I.T. Press, 1966.

Werner, H. & Kaplan, B. *Symbol formation: An orgnismic-developmental approach to language and the expression of thought.* New York: John Wiley & Sons, 1963.

Winston, P. H. *Learning structural descriptions from examples.* Unpublished doctoral dissertation, M.I.T., 1970, (AITR-231).

Woods, W. A. Transition network grammars for natural language analysis. *Communications of the A.C.M.* 1970, *13,* 591–606.

Yngve, V. A model and an hypothesis for language structure. *Proceedings of the American Philosophical Society,* 1960, *104,* 444–466.

Author Index

Numbers in *italic* indicate the page on which the complete reference appears.

A

Abrahamson, A. A., 18, 19, 20, *295*
Abrams, K., 21, *295*
Alenskas, L., 66, *299*
Anderson, J. R., 95, *295*
Austin, J. L., 283, *295*

B

Baars, B. J., 31, *295*
Bach, E., 158, *299*
Bennett, D. C., 172, *295*
Bernstein, N. A., 6, 57, 254, *295*
Bever, T. G., 15, 16, 17, 18, 21, 291, 292, 293, *295, 296*
Bloom, L., 8, 66, 240, 241, 245, 246, *295*
Bolinger, D., 103, *295*
Boomer, D. S., 29, *295*
Bower, G. H., 95, *295*
Brown, D., 146, *299*
Brown, R., 8, 66, 69, 241, 250, *295*

C

Carlson, P., 249, *299*
Cartwright, D., 104, 113, 117, 129, 162, *297*

Chapin

Chapin, G., 18, 19, 20, *295*
Chase, W. W., 292, *295*
Chistovich, L. A., 6, 55, 56, 57, 58, 181, *297*
Chomsky, C., 249, 251, *295*
Chomsky, N., 12, 103, 151, 291, *295, 298*
Clark, H. H., 292, *295*
Cocking, R., 249, *299*
Cohen, J. A., 179, *296*
Copple, C., 249, *299*
Cromer, R., 249, 250, *296*
Cruttenden, A., 71, *296*
Curme, G., 136, *296*

D

Danks, J. H., 28, *296*
Davison, A., 284, *296*
Duncan, S., Jr., 27, 215, 270, *296*

E

Efron, D., 255, *296*
Ehlich, K., 145, 154, *296*
Ekman, P., 255, *296*

Subject Index